For the Love of Music

For the Love of Music
Invitations to Listening

MICHAEL STEINBERG
and
LARRY ROTHE

OXFORD
UNIVERSITY PRESS
2006

OXFORD

UNIVERSITY PRESS

Oxford University Press, Inc., publishes works that
further Oxford University's objective of excellence
in research, scholarship, and education.

Oxford New York
Auckland   Cape Town   Dar es Salaam   Hong Kong   Karachi
Kuala Lumpur   Madrid   Melbourne   Mexico City   Nairobi
New Delhi   Shanghai   Taipei   Toronto

With offices in
Argentina   Austria   Brazil   Chile   Czech Republic   France   Greece
Guatemala   Hungary   Italy   Japan   Poland   Portugal   Singapore

Published by Oxford University Press, Inc.
198 Madison Avenue, New York, NY 10016
www.oup.com

Oxford is a registered trademark of Oxford University Press

Library of Congress Cataloging-in-Publication Data
Steinberg, Michael, 1928–
For the love of music : invitations to listening /
Michael Steinberg, Larry Rothe.
p. cm.
ISBN-13: 978-0-19-516216-5
ISBN-10: 0-19-516216-1
1. Music—History and criticism. 2. Music appreciation.
I. Rothe, Larry. II. Title.
ML160.S84 2006
780—dc22
2005026128

9 8 7 6 5 4 3 2 1
Printed in the United States of America
on acid-free paper

An excerpt from this book, "The Sounds We Make," appeared in *Symphony* magazine in November 2005.

Grateful acknowledgment is made for permission to use passages from the following:

In "Sibelius and Mahler: What More Could There Be?": From Robert Layton's translation of Erik Tawaststjerna's *Sibelius*, Volume II, 1904–1914 © 1986. Reprinted with permission, The Regents of the University of California.

In "On the Trail of W. A. Mozart": From *A Mozart Pilgrimage: The Travel Diaries of Vincent & Mary Novello in the Year 1829*, edited by Nerina Medici and Rosemary Hughes, © 1955 Novello & Co. Ltd. Efforts to contact the copyright owners have been unsuccessful. Should those claiming legitimate copyright ownership identify themselves, the author and Oxford University Press will be pleased to add appropriate acknowledgment in future printings.

In "A Short Life of J. S. Bach": From *The New Bach Reader: A Life of Johann Sebastian Bach in Letters and Documents* by Hans T. David and Arthur Mendel, eds., rev. by Christoph Wolff. Copyright © 1998 by Christoph Wolff. Copyright © 1966, 1945 by W.W. Norton & Company, Inc. Copyright © 1972 by Mrs. Hans T. David and Arthur Mendel. Used by permission of W.W. Norton & Company, Inc.

In "B. H. Haggin the Contrarian": From *Music Observed* by B. H. Haggin, © 1964 by B. H. Haggin, Oxford University Press (1964), and from *The Listener's Musical Companion*, New Edition, by B. H. Haggin, compiled and edited by Thomas Hathaway, © the estate of B. H. Haggin, Oxford University Press (1991). Used by permission of Oxford University Press.

From M.S. to Ayla, Julian, and Rae

From L.R. to Karen and Tom

*And from both of us
to Katherine Cummins
and to Bill Bennett, whose idea it was*

Contents

Introduction

With a few exceptions, these pieces all appeared originally (some in slightly different and others in very different form) in the program book of the San Francisco Symphony, an organization with which we have been affiliated for many years, L.R. since 1984, M.S. since 1979.

Among the program books of American orchestras, the San Francisco Symphony's is singular in that, each month, a section is devoted to a feature article of fairly substantial length, in which writers can take on virtually any musical subject they wish to address. These pieces are aimed at a general audience of educated readers, not at those with specifically musical backgrounds. Our intent is to inform and even to proselytize, our aim to be popular in the sense that we wish everyone knew and loved the music we know and love. Over the years, we have written many of these pieces ourselves, enough of them to move the San Francisco Symphony's Principal Oboist, William Bennett, to suggest that we collect them into a book. Bill is a fine artist and also very smart and very funny, a good guy, someone you take seriously, and we were happy to pursue his flattering suggestion.

We're grateful to the San Francisco Symphony for giving us the opportunity to write these pieces. The idea of such a forum was that of Peter Pastreich, the Symphony's Executive Director from 1979 until 1999. Peter loves music and words. He offered stimulus through an inspired fusion of encouragement and prodding, friendly motivation, and periodic nagging. Peter was both good cop and bad. We have tried to realize his belief that an audience deserves to know as much as possible about the music, and deserves that information in a form that offers readers not simply facts, but respect. In Peter's successor as Executive Director, Brent Assink, we have been fortunate to find someone equally committed. At a time when symphony program books are becoming a species endangered by castration, by what is now with brutal frankness called dumbing down, we have been particularly grateful to work for an orchestra where the assumption is that our audience is intelligent, inquisitive, and either imbued with a deep love of music or deeply interested in discovering what that kind of love can mean.

We thank Brent Assink especially for his excitement about this collection and the graciousness and readiness with which he granted permission to reissue material originally written for the SFS. The San Francisco Symphony has also been extraordinarily fortunate in its music directors of the past three decades—Edo de Waart (1977–1985), Herbert Blomstedt (1985–95), and Michael Tilson Thomas (since 1995). Each of these men, while keenly aware that it is the music itself that must finally tell, is equally aware of how words can help an audience find a way into the music. We thank them for their involvement and encouragement no less than for the performances through which they continue to explore music's beautiful and perilous landscapes.

Some of the pieces that follow were written in connection with San Francisco Symphony performances or events, and in preparing them for this book we have revised and in some cases updated them. So as not to tie our words to a particular time and place, we have usually removed topical references, though what remains may have been suggested by the occasional nature of these pieces. For example, the article on the sacred and profane in music, written originally in connection with a 1997 festival, includes references to works performed during that festival, but those references are not intended to suggest that concepts such as "sacred" and "profane" can be illustrated only by those works; just as the piece "Three American Composers in Pursuit of the White Whale" focuses on a trio (Charles Ives, John Corigliano, and John Adams) whose music was spotlighted at San Francisco Symphony concerts during November 1991, when that article appeared originally. Because these pieces were written at widely scattered times, a few stories and a few observations appear more than once. When we did not eliminate these very few repetitions, it was not because of carelessness but because we felt that each served well in its place.

Because of their origin, most of these pieces have to do with Western orchestral music. Even within the boundaries of European and American orchestral works, we are less than broad in the subjects we address. You will find a concentration on music of the nineteenth and early twentieth centuries. Our subject, though, is broader than the specifics suggest. The subject is music, and how it nourishes our lives. Unabashedly, our enthusiasms have colored our judgment. We have organized these pieces in thematic groups. Authorship is identified through the initials at the end of each piece.

We have already mentioned a handful of those who helped bring this book into being. We want also to thank our respective wives, Jorja Fleezanis and Karen Borst-Rothe, for the tough love with which they read so many of these pieces, again and again giving new life to the old truth that no writing is ever really finished. Throughout our years at the San Francisco Symphony we have been fortunate—*blessed* is the better word—to work with Katherine Cummins. Katherine is the program book's managing editor, but if we left the description at that we would have said nothing about her merciless intelligence, nor would we have hinted at the friendship, affection, and completeness with which she has improved the quality not just of our work, but also of our lives. Others whose support and help we happily acknowledge are Karen Ames, Styra Avins,

Kathy Brown, KC Congedo, Robert Guter, Margo Hackett, Renée Harcourt, Caitlin Hartney, Barbara Heyman, Linda Joy Kattwinkel, Ralph Locke, Garrick Ohlsson, Thaddeus Spae, Patricia Spaeth, Luna Steiner, Markus Stenz, Jan Swafford, and James Utz. It has been wonderful to have and enjoy the support and encouragement of Sheldon Meyer, our editor at Oxford University Press. And, also at Oxford University Press, our warm thanks for their help and support go as well to Joellyn Ausanka, Betsy DeJesu, Norman Hirschy, Patterson Lamb, and Kim Robinson. Our gratitude goes to all of these, and we extend apologies to any we should have named but haven't. The roster of those who have had a part in this project reminds us again of how nothing like this is achieved in isolation, yet we acknowledge also that responsibility for shortcomings in what follows is ours alone.

Michael Steinberg, Minneapolis, Minnesota
Larry Rothe, Berkeley, California
June 2005

I.
BEGINNINGS

How I Fell in Love with Music

I fell in love with music in a murky alley when I was eleven. Sometimes I ask friends when and where and how it happened to them, and they recount childhood memories of hearing a beautiful cousin play a Chopin étude, of being stunned by a broadcast of the *Saint Matthew Passion*, or sent into reveries lying under the family piano while Mother practiced *Songs without Words*. My own fall was less romantic.

More precisely, I was seduced and then proceeded to fall in love. It was *Fantasia*, the original 1940 version, that did me in. I saw it just once, at the Cosmopolitan, a dingy movie house in Cambridge, England, and although this was more than sixty-five years ago, I remember it more vividly than most of the movies I've seen in the last sixty-five weeks. I saw it just once because as a schoolboy on threepence a week in pocket money—even in 1940 that bought hardly anything, and surely not more than half a movie ticket—I couldn't afford to go again. Besides, the guardians of Good Taste would not have encouraged, let alone subsidized, a return visit. But I also realized I did not need to see it again because the most important part was available for free. Behind the sweet little fleabag where *Fantasia* was playing, there was this alley where I could stand every day after school, stand undisturbed, and listen to the soundtrack of Leopold Stokowski and the Philadelphia Orchestra playing Bach, Beethoven, Schubert, and Stravinsky. On a recent visit to Cambridge I was happy to see there is still a movie theater on the same site, but it is now called the Arts Theatre and is a lot cleaner.

I should have been at my desk doing my homework, but these sneak auditions were one more escapade in my fairly consistently disreputable academic career. That afternoon music fix became a compulsion for as long as it was available. At least once at that time, *Fantasia* even entered my dreams. I saw the erupting volcanoes Walt Disney had set to the Dance of the Adolescents in *The Rite of Spring*, heard something like Stravinsky's so bafflingly irregular choom-choom-choom-choom-choom-choom-choom-choom-choom-choom-CHOOM-choom-CHOOM, and woke up to the real-life sounds of anti-aircraft fire.

Not that *Fantasia* was my first encounter with "classical" music. I had done the first phase of my growing up in Breslau in a cultivated, affluent, German Jewish household with a Bechstein grand and a good radio (but no record player, not an uncommon lack for the day). My mother and older brother played the piano, not brilliantly, but well enough to impress me, though I have no recollection of any particular item in their repertoires. I took lessons, but they were deadly finger lessons, not ear and music lessons, and so I was bored and didn't practice. The radio was rarely switched on, but I recall—I must have been eight or so—my homeroom teacher, Frau Garbell, telling us the story of *Lohengrin*, which was to be broadcast that evening. I found it fascinating and frightening, this business of the glamorous and wronged princess who was not allowed to ask her savior and husband his name, and that evening I lay on the floor next to the big brown Telefunken and waited for Lohengrin, index finger extended in warning, to tell Elsa, "*Nie sollst du mich befragen!*"—"Never may you ask me!" What Frau Garbell didn't say was how long it would take Wagner to get to the point, how much of tedious King Henry and his tiresome Herald I would have to put up with first, and I never made it to the great moment. I eventually caught up with *Lohengrin* when I was a college freshman. It was my first visit to the Met, with the aging and rather improvisatory Lauritz Melchior, Helen Traubel, Kerstin Thorborg, Herbert Janssen, and with Fritz Busch conducting his first performance in that house.

Going to concerts in Breslau was out because by the time I was old enough to be taken, public events of that sort were forbidden to Jews. Not knowing what I was missing, I was much more bothered by not being able to go ice-skating or to the zoo anymore. So, while there was a general sense at home that music was A Good Thing, and a few names and titles were familiar—Beethoven, Brahms, Furtwängler, Adolf Busch, *Eine kleine Nachtmusik,* and *Die Meistersinger* prominent among them and always pronounced with reverence—I had nearly nothing by way of actual musical sounds to tie to them. The exception was *The Threepenny Opera,* whose premiere had taken place not quite two months before I was born. I have been told that "Mack the Knife" and Mr. Peachum's song about the perpetual insufficiency of human endeavor, "*Der Mensch lebt durch den Kopf,*" both sung to me by my brother, were the first music I heard, and that "Mack the Knife" was also the first song I learned to sing myself.

At ten I went to England on a *Kindertransport*. There I spent most of the year in boarding school, the rest with the highly literate, politically aware, and quite unmusical English family that had taken me in. Even so, the *paterfamilias* maintained a surprising totemic reverence for two symphonies, Beethoven's Ninth and Elgar's Second, actually suspending his obsessive gardening when they showed up on the radio, which we still called "the wireless." Otherwise, indifference to music was complete. No, not quite: I remember *materfamilias* bristling indignantly at a broadcast of something from Verdi's *Otello*, dark comments being made about "foreigners" and "our English Shakespeare." There was an upright piano in the house, and on that I played tunes from the *Oxford Book of Carols* and a score of *The Mikado*. Oddly, I knew a few of the Sullivan songs, though with German words, because my mother had seen *The Mikado* in Breslau around the turn of the century. I also continued not to practice for a continuing series of unstimulating and unenlightening lessons. When I visited my old school, the Perse, a few years ago I was happy to see that they now have varied and flourishing musical activities, but during my time there music only meant bawling *Loch Lomond, Shenandoah,* and *The Campbells Are Coming* for an hour a week under the tutelage of the pompous Mr. Macfarlane-Grieve, and though I liked the songs themselves, that hardly stretched my musical experience. At my first schools in Germany, "music" also meant classroom singing, but at least there one of my teachers was Erich Werner, a real musician who went on to a distinguished career in musicology.

All of this meant that I had to find my way to music on my own. Or, rather, it found me. *Fantasia* came to the rescue at the right moment, and after that it was a question of learning how to still my growing hunger. I remember the happy distraction, or so it seemed at the time, of jazz and other nonclassical music. Someone at school must have had a record player; at any rate I remember delighting in Benny Goodman, then the most idolized musician in the world, and my excitement over Artie Shaw and the sizzling trumpet of Harry James (also my disappointment upon finding at the library at twelve or so what unreadable books he wrote when he called himself Henry). Jazz or classical: that was an either/or question in those days. You chose up sides and went for Beethoven or Louis Armstrong but not possibly for both. Part of my fun with this music was in the annoyance that my pleasure, and for that matter the music itself, caused the Elders of the People. I had made that fundamental discovery of childhood and adolescence—that if the grownups hate it, it can't be all bad. To avoid pleasing them too much, I went a little bit underground with my more "serious" musical passions, but it was becoming clear to me where my heart belonged.

I discovered record stores, which in those days had tiny listening rooms in which one could try those imposing, shiny, black, dangerously fragile disks. (When I revisited Cambridge for the first time more than twenty years later I wanted to go into Miller's to thank them for what, unwittingly and probably not happily, they had done for me on my journey toward music, but I am sorry to say I didn't actually do it.) I began by listening to the pieces I had come to know through *Fantasia*. My favorite at first was *The Dance of the Hours* played by what on English HMV labels was called the Boston Promenade Orchestra under Arthur Fiedler. Next came Schubert's *Ave Maria* because I had so loved that glorious Disney hokum when the sinister trees of *Night on Bald Mountain* magically turned into the Gothic arches of a sylvan cathedral. Trying different recordings of *Ave Maria* brought the amazing revelation that sung by Elisabeth Schumann it sounded different from the tarted-up Stokowski orchestration, or that the violin versions of Heifetz and Menuhin were astonishingly unlike even though the notes were the same. Miller's was a treasure trove, and I took pains to learn the schedules of the various salespeople so that no one of them would see me too often and I would not wear out my thinly based welcome. Even the *Goldberg Variations* came my way there, but I had not the slightest idea of what to make of Goldberg, variations, or harpsichord. I did, however, find the name Wanda Landowska, whom I assumed to be a man, captivatingly elegant.

After *Fantasia*'s brief stay at the dingy Cosmopolitan was over, Miller's was virtually my only source of music during the school year, a long desert of no radio, no records, no concerts, no sympathy. Piano lessons were as limited and unstimulating as they had been in Breslau. But there were a few memorable concert experiences. Once, my mother took me to a Mozart concert conducted by Herbert Menges, which brought me my first encounter with the G-minor Symphony and in which I loved most the high horns in the Trio of the Minuet.[1] On another occasion I managed, by virtue of looking pitiful but presentable, to get someone to take me into the Guildhall to hear Myra Hess play a couple of Mozart concertos with an orchestra from London. And on one of my only two dizzyingly exciting trips to London, I was taken to one of the lunchtime concerts she had started in the National Gallery, denuded for the time being of its greatest paintings. It was then that I heard my first string quartet, the Zorian, who played Schubert's *Death and the Maiden*. Hess was in the audience, and I watched her, as they say in England, "go behind" to thank the performers. That, too, was a good lesson.

What made more of an impact than any of these was a school concert—the only one we were ever taken to—at the Guildhall by the London Philharmonic conducted by Anatole Fistoulari, a name older record collectors will remember. I recall three things about that hour. One is that for most of the other kids it was *not* the most thrilling event of their lives thus far. Another was that Fistoulari conducted Weber's *Invitation to the Dance* and explained to us how the lively waltz is preceded by a tender cello solo in which we were to imagine a young

[1] I have more to say about that experience in the essay *Another Word for Mozart*.

man asking a lady for a dance, and that it is followed by a postlude, also quiet and with solo cello, which depicts his escorting her back to her chair and thanking her. Therefore, he said, we should not applaud when the waltz ends because the little scene of the postlude was yet to come. I need hardly say what actually happened. The third thing was that the program ended with the Hungarian March from Berlioz's *The Damnation of Faust,* and Fistoulari showed us the huge bass drum and had the player demonstrate that, amazingly, this instrument makes its most stunning effect when it is hit as softly as possible. Sixty-some years later, that still gives me goosebumps. That morning hooked me on orchestras, and it was a crucial step onto the road that led me to spending the happiest years of my professional life working for them.

And there was Mr. Hardacre. The Perse School was one of two in England that had a separate boarding house for Jewish boys. Its housemaster, Mr. Dagut, was a cultured and kind gentleman, but he was beyond being able to maintain order, and the task of keeping things running fell to the assistant housemaster. For the last year I was at Hillel House that position was occupied by Mr. Hardacre—Kenneth Hardacre, a young pipe-smoking teacher of English. I think this may have been his first job after university. He loved music, and he had a small radio, some books about music, and a few miniature scores. Every now and again—and this had to be managed with great discretion—when there was something on the radio he thought I should not miss, he would invite me into his tiny, smoke-filled room to listen to a Brahms symphony or a Mozart piano concerto. He offered a bit of instruction and some opinions, and he would also press the appropriate volume of Tovey's *Essays in Musical Analysis* into my hand in preparation for our clandestine listening sessions. The six slender blue volumes had a place of honor on his overcrowded shelves. In fact, I could hardly understand a word of Tovey's essays, but I was immensely flattered by those loans and loved carrying those books around. To this day I find it amazing, sometimes incredible, that my own books bear the same Oxford University Press imprint as Tovey's.

Later, when I was in college, equipped with some more background and more musical vocabulary, I looked for Tovey in the library and, one at a time, acquired his writings. Reading Tovey and having him before me as a never-to-be-equaled example had, I am sure, everything to do with my landing up as a writer of program notes in my fifties. Sooner or later I would of course have found Tovey anyway, but because it was Mr. Hardacre who got my unprepared self there first, I have always mentally thanked him for setting my foot on that path. We corresponded for a while after I left the school and left England, but eventually we lost touch. I mentioned the role he had played in my life in the introduction to my first book, *The Symphony: A Listener's Guide,* and a little later tried to locate him, only to learn that he was a widower completely lost in an Alzheimer fog.

Radio also made a huge difference when I was home for the holidays. The BBC was generous with music, live and recorded, and I discovered—an ominous sign surely—that like people in wartime getting outrageous pleasure from reading cookbooks full of recipes calling for the butter and eggs they hardly believe they will ever see again, I could generate shudders of delight simply by reading concert listings in the *Radio Times*. When I arrived at my next home, St. Louis, the radio was on in my brother's apartment—I still remember that it was Toscanini and the NBC Symphony, with Horszowski playing, of all things, the Martucci Piano Concerto.

I quickly got to know how and when to find Toscanini myself (Sunday late afternoon), and also the New York Philharmonic (Sunday early afternoon), the Boston Symphony (Saturday night), the Cleveland Orchestra (Friday night), and that astonishing world opened up by the Metropolitan Opera (Saturday afternoon). I could still reconstruct, stick by stick, the living room of our friends, the Arndts, where, bug-eyed, I heard Jan Peerce sing *Che gelida manina*. "*Talor dal mio forziere . . .* "—nothing had prepared me for being so swept away by a single phrase of music! Two stations tied to schools—WEW at St. Louis University and KFUO at Concordia Seminary—offered an hour or so of records a day; these were limited, repetitious, with titles and names mispronounced, record sides played in the wrong order (they never seemed to look whether a set was in manual or automatic sequence), and they ALWAYS stopped Brahms's Alto Rhapsody during the long silence before the final "Amen" cadence on "*sein Herz.*" That infuriated my mother every time, even more than Marian Anderson's version of German vowels, and she always supplied the missing two notes herself. Still, it added up to indispensable nourishment and pleasure.

All this was haphazard, determined by the taste of the time and what by today's standards were the exceedingly limited contents of record company catalogues. I am sure that by the time I went to college I had heard only one symphony each of Mahler and Bruckner, only the most famous Tchaikovsky and Dvořák, hardly any chamber music or songs, virtually nothing from our century (though someone at KFUO was very fond of Howard Hanson's *Lament for Beowulf*). I also remained ignorant of everything to do with music except how it sounded. I scarcely knew what harmony meant, certainly had no idea of what counterpoint was, and had only the vaguest sense of the history of music. By the time I was fifteen I had read only one book about music, *The Orchestra Speaks*, a still absorbing account by Bernard Shore, the BBC Symphony's witty and literate principal violist, of what it was like to work with the famous conductors of the day. Of course that made me want to be a conductor. All in all, I don't think my long-sustained ignorance did me any harm. No doubt it is best to learn what is so oddly misnamed "theory" at eleven or twelve, which is also a good age to learn languages, but it was all right at sixteen as well. As for history, I enjoyed it more for getting to it when I already had a sense of what some of the music sounded like, so that it was an entertaining and often even illuminating way of reexamining and ordering material to which, in some other and more important sense, I already had a key.

By no means did I just bliss out to every musical sound that came my way. For instance, brought up as I was in a thoroughly Austro-German orthodoxy, I was absolutely unequipped to deal with Debussy. I couldn't make head or tail of him, thought him a fraud, and still remember—and here too I can place myself exactly in the corner armchair in the living room at 1341 McCausland Avenue in St. Louis—being rattled into blind rage by *Nuages* and *Fêtes* (Stokowski's recording). Mahler seemed absurdly incoherent nonsense too, as did some of the weirder patches in Beethoven's late quartets like the scherzo in Opus 131 and the first movement of Opus 135. For that matter I quarreled for years with Wagner and particularly Brahms.

Occasional encounters with modern music were mostly dismaying. It bothered me that Stravinsky's Symphony in C did not sound like my beloved *Rite of Spring*. After a promising half-minute waltz at the beginning I didn't know what to make of the rest of Schoenberg's Piano Concerto on an NBC Symphony broadcast (Stokowski lost his job for insisting on programming it), and his *Ode to Napoleon Buonaparte*, whose premiere was broadcast by the New York Philharmonic, was equally baffling and the weirdly singsong declamation of Byron's text was inclined to make me giggle. Even a few years later, when I should have known better, Schoenberg's String Quartet No. 3 was unintelligible to me when I heard it at a Kolisch Quartet concert at Princeton, and so was Elliott Carter's Piano Sonata, which I stumbled onto not knowing what it was, having arrived late at a concert for which the program had been changed.

This list could now serve as the beginning of an inventory of pieces I especially love. The first classical album I ever bought was Debussy's Violin Sonata with Zino Francescatti and Robert Casadesus, one of the most challenging and joyous experiences of my musical life has been the opportunity to perform the *Ode to Napoleon* a number of times as well as the *Sprechstimme* parts in *Gurre-Lieder* and *A Survivor from Warsaw*, and Carter is for me one of the most exciting of living composers. Every one of my musical loves began with a strong reaction, with passion. I can think of plenty of examples of love at first hearing (also of the occasional crush I mistook for love), but I cannot forget that sometimes the first powerful response was one of rejection.

What have I learned? In the alley behind the Cosmo I learned—happily without realizing I was actually learning something—that I did not need Mickey Mouse or those bra-clad centaurettes or even the beautiful images of darting violin bows in the Bach Toccata and Fugue in D minor to make the music enjoyable. I learned that music repaid repeated listening. Most music anyway.

The *Dance of the Hours* did not get more interesting (though it continued to be fun), but the Bach and the *Pastoral* Symphony did, and *The Rite of Spring*, whose sounds I had adored from the beginning, started to reveal intelligible and remembered shapes and patterns. I learned to pay attention, because if I missed something it was gone, at least till the next afternoon. I learned that my focus changed from details to at least something like the whole, from the raisins to the cake. And I learned that there was a lot to hear in some of those pieces and that they did not cease to be full of surprises. I could of course not have articulated any of this then.

One *Fantasia* lesson I wish I had learned more quickly, but here I was slow on the uptake. At some point it was revealed to me that Stokowski, with his cuts and splices and re-orchestrations, had treated Beethoven, Schubert, Musorgsky, and Stravinsky pretty damn willfully, not to say brutally. I grew to be awfully sniffy about this sort of thing. It was years before it dawned on me that Stokowski had ultimately done no serious harm, that first meeting the *Pastoral* Symphony or *The Rite of Spring* in his versions did not keep me or need not keep anyone else from eventually discovering that what Beethoven and Stravinsky had written was even better than what Stokowski—or perhaps Stokowski and the Disney people—thought they ought to have written. Making a piece sound unintelligible or just plain boring is a worse sin.

What else did I eventually learn? To pay heed to my first reactions but also not to take them too seriously and certainly not to assume that they have permanent value. Not to think too much at the beginning and not to think at all about what I thought I was maybe supposed to be thinking. To be patient or—better—suspenseful, to wait and see how the piece or I might change (the former is of course an illusion), and to remember my fifteen-year-old self in righteous indignation over the Debussy *Nocturnes*. That in the end the only study of music is music, that good program notes and pre-concert talks are helpful ways of showing you the door in the wall and of turning on some extra lights, but that the only thing that really matters is what happens privately between you and the music. That, as with any other form of falling in love, no one can do it for you and no one can draw you a map. That listening to music is not like getting a haircut or a manicure, but that it is something for you to *do*. That music, like any worthwhile partner in love, is demanding, sometimes exasperatingly, exhaustingly demanding. That—and here I borrow a perfect formulation from Karen Armstrong's memoir, *The Spiral Staircase*—"you have to give it your full attention, wait patiently upon it, and make an empty space for it in your mind." That it is a demon that can pursue us as relentlessly as the Hound of Heaven. That its capacity to give is as near to infinite as anything in this world, and that what it offers us is always and inescapably in exact proportion to what we ourselves give.

—M.S.

Preliminary: The Professor's Legacy

When my father arrived in the United States from Germany in 1925, he was already almost thirty. He spoke no English and was a veteran of the Western Front who had fought on the losing side. He moved in with a distant cousin, Wilhelm Alvin, who lived in Chicago—where, in a red brick three-story building at the intersection of Lincoln, Diversey, and Racine avenues, he had founded the Lincoln Conservatory of Music. In Germany, Wilhelm Alvin had always been known as *der Alvin*, and in the neighborhood around the Lincoln Conservatory of Music, heavily populated with German immigrants, you might have expected he would be called the same. (*Alvin*: My father always used the German pronunciation, the accented *Al* matching the sound of the first syllable of *olive*, and the *vin* sounding like *veen*.) But this was America, and here Alvin was William A. His students and their parents called him Professor. His friends called him Bill. Or Big Bill. He had girth—the photos show that—and his bearing suggests power as well. He liked to drink, claimed to have cured himself of malaria by a steady intake of dark rum while serving in Cuba in the Spanish-American War, and despite Prohibition knew how to slake his thirst. His hospitality made him popular, right down to a drinking friendship with the beat cop. He must also have had a genuine streak of generosity, else he would not have sponsored my father's emigration.

My father suspected that Alvin's music background was more rudimentary than the title of Professor suggested. He did not recall ever hearing him play any instrument, though in the obituary Alvin would write for himself, published in the *Abendpost* when he died in 1931, he claimed to have sounded a trumpet flourish as the Stars and Stripes was raised at Morro Castle in 1898. At the Lincoln Conservatory of Music, Alvin employed a cadre of teachers, some of them musicians down on their luck; one, at least, was an alcoholic ex-member of Frederick Stock's Chicago Symphony Orchestra. By planting these men throughout his student ensemble, Alvin managed to give concerts that convinced parents that their children were learning the basics of a craft, if not an art. And by relying on the professional musicians in the group to take the lead, Alvin stood on the podium in front of an orchestra that essentially conducted itself while he waved his arms in a soulful way and pretended to cue entrances. Maestros more famous than Alvin have sinned more gravely, and since he was not famous, I think he deserves points for being resourceful. What I relate here about Alvin I know only from stories my father told me, thirty years after the fact. Though my father remembered Alvin with affection and humor, he must have thought this odd relative and his Conservatory of Music a parody of the world in which he himself had grown up.

That world was one that had been formed by nineteenth-century music. Indeed, my father was born in the nineteenth century, in 1897, in the old Kaiserstadt of Goslar, at the foot of the Harz Mountains. The household he was raised in was full of music, all the time. He was the third youngest of twelve children, six of each gender, one of those large Victorian families presided over by an all-but-absentee father. His father was all-but-absent because he was the town's overworked *Musikdirektor*, the one responsible for the music at municipal functions, and a respected teacher who, with a staff of lieutenants he employed, oversaw the musical apprenticeships of adolescent boys who also lodged with the family. At any given time during my father's childhood, a minimum of twenty students lived in the household. Goslar was also a community that supported a silver-mining industry, and the miners had their own band, a *Bergkapelle*, for which the Musikdirektor was responsible. Through my father I have inherited an ebony baton whose handle end is trimmed in finely wrought silver and engraved, in gratitude, to Musikdirektor Julius Rothe. So far as I can determine, my grandfather was the genuine article. Certainly he was a different article than *der Alvin*, or Big Bill, or whatever he might be called—the Professor and founder of the Lincoln Conservatory of Music.

Music in various forms, some more legitimate than others, was part of my father's family, but my father was not a musician himself. As the ninth of twelve children, he was hardly a novelty at home. The effort my grandfather gave to teaching, civic responsibilities, and his own studies of the violin, piano, and French horn must have diverted his attention from the cause-and-effect realities of human reproduction. Perhaps he was simply bewildered by his youngest children, but by the time child number nine appeared he was tired and had pretty much stopped teaching his own offspring. My father had, however, grown up hearing music and loving it, and by the time he was fourteen, when he was already far from home and a baker's apprentice, he saved his meager earnings so that now and then he could purchase a standing-room place at the opera in Braunschweig. From his apprenticeship he went to war, and after the war he returned to the Weimar Republic and the deprivations and wrecked economy of those hard years. When an older brother, Siegfried, declined Alvin's offer to come to America, my father eagerly took Siegfried's place.

My father's knowledge of music's expanse remained limited, yet he was always concerned that I be steered in a "proper" musical direction. During one of our regular pilgrimages—I must have been nine or ten—to Chicago's Lincoln Avenue shopping district, where every other store window still boasted a hand-painted sign proclaiming *Hier wird deutsch gesprochen*—German Spoken Here— my father steered me out the door of Kuhn's Delicatessen and, while my mother shopped for *Wurst und Schinken*, led me down the street into a record store. There he purchased a single black disc in a brown paper sleeve. It was Mozart's Overture to *Don Giovanni*, spread over both sides of a 78 RPM disc. Gray lettering on a blue Columbia label told me that the Royal Philharmonic Orchestra performed this music under the direction of Sir Thomas Beecham. Perhaps my father thought I should be impressed by this, but I was not. A friend of mine who is a great lover of music maintains that we do a disservice to children by trying to make them like works they cannot possibly understand. Such a concept, based on what is "age-appropriate," might not be true in all cases, but it was for me. Don't get me wrong. Even as a kid, I loved music; it was just that my father never thought my favorites were legitimate, ranging as they did from "Red River Valley" to "The Bunny Hop" to "Love Me Tender" and Elmer Bernstein's music for the soundtrack of *The Ten Commandments*.

My father did, to his credit, tolerate these musical tastes. Periodically he nagged me about not listening to the classical canon, and one Christmas he even gave me three installments of the fifteen- or twenty-volume Philharmonic Library of Classical Music, the sort of record collection that used to be sold at supermarkets, a new volume each week, like the Funk & Wagnalls Encyclopedia set we had accumulated over half a year's shopping at the neighborhood Jewel store. Mostly, though, he let me alone, and when I was sixteen I discovered classical music on my own.

Nothing, however, ever really happens on one's own, nor did my discovery of music. I'm sure a lot of pump-priming had gone on. Leonard Bernstein certainly had something to do with it. I spent some snowbound Sunday afternoons in front of my parents' Muntz TV, watching Bernstein's Young People's Concerts, and it was Bernstein who, more than any other figure, became associated in my mind with classical music. If someone as engaging as he could get excited about it, perhaps it bore examination. One evening I caught a glimpse of a very different kind of TV program that my father was watching. It was some cop or detective show, and to background music that struck me as sublime—slow and stately, deliberately paced and grandiose with fanfares— the scene unfolded in slow motion as two thugs, their fists cleaving the air in gestures as graceful as those of ballet, pummeled a man in a back alley. What was that music? My father said he thought it was from Beethoven's *Pastoral* Symphony. The next weekend, I was at the record bins at Polk Brothers, a store that sold appliances and furniture but also, for some reason, records, and the recording of the *Pastoral* Symphony I purchased was Leonard Bernstein's. Of all the recordings of the *Pastoral* Symphony I saw for sale that day, Bernstein's was the only one that came with a name I recognized. As it turned out, my father had been wrong, though not by much. I learned later that the music to which that slow-motion beating had been choreographed was the second movement of the Beethoven Fifth. The *Pastoral* had its own merits, though. And as far as music went, I was on my way.

That was in 1966. In the next eighteen years I gradually broadened my knowledge of basic concert repertory—through recordings, and through concerts. I was lucky to discover live music during the glory years of Georg Solti's Chicago Symphony Orchestra. In the early 1970s, gallery seats for Friday matinees cost students two dollars, a bargain even by that time's standards.

In early 1984, I had been living in the Bay Area for a year. I was newly married and making a scrappy living in the on-again, off-again world of freelance writing. My wife and I had started coming to San Francisco Symphony concerts the previous year (she was completing a doctorate at the University of California and was able to get her hands on a student subscription series, made even more affordable by splitting the series with a friend). My first encounter with the San Francisco Symphony was also my first encounter with the orchestra's program book. In my years of concertgoing, I had learned not to take program books seriously. I expected bad writing, incomprehensible with jargon, leeched of joy and passion and life and beauty. In other words, what was in program books had nothing, nothing at all, to do with the music. In every way, the program book I held in my hands that first evening at Davies Symphony Hall was different. The program notes were written by a man, Michael Steinberg, who had *the* credential that seems basic to every writer of music commentary but which I had never found before. He wrote with grace and wit and love of music. Not since my days in front of the TV set, listening to Leonard Bernstein talk, had I run into anything like this.

It was probably in February 1984 that I learned the San Francisco Symphony was seeking a new editor for its program book. Neither my academic nor my life credentials enabled me to call myself a musician or a musicologist. But with degrees in English and American literature, plus seven years of magazine work behind me, I thought I knew a little about publishing, so I made my case. It was a whim, inspired by one of those moments when you want something desperately, believe you are unworthy to have it, but imagine yourself convincing those with the power of granting the prize to confer it on you. I won. My job would be to edit Michael Steinberg. I was terrified.

I have calmed down over the years. Michael and I have continued to work together, and out of our work a friendship has grown. My writing about music is in many ways a correlative to the growth of this friendship. For it was through reading Michael and in editing and absorbing his work that I began to get a new appreciation for how love of music could be translated into words. I knew before I met Michael that music had important things to say about life, but he helped me understand how to consider these things, and his example emboldened me to write about them. In a way, my own lack of formal training makes me proof that the pleasures of music are open to all, and that the route to experiencing those pleasures begins in the gut. Though mine is only one perspective on a subject that can tolerate an infinity of perspectives, I have tried to reach music lovers with no more formal training than my own but who might, given suggestions and road signs, discover bigger thrills in listening. Music speaks to each of us, and while we will not always concur on the thrust of its messages, we can agree that it springs from a common well, as natural and unknowable as life.

In all this, I realize now, I am following in a family tradition. I like to think that I am continuing in the wake of my grandfather, the august Musikdirektor, but it's possible that I am more akin spiritually to Alvin and his Lincoln Conservatory of Music. Neither music nor musical matters, however, can be neatly compartmentalized, and one may not cancel the other. It comes down to this. I love music. To write about it as though I have anything special to share is presumptuous. Music, whether it comes from a hundred-piece orchestra, the smoky chambers of John Coltrane's sax, or a steel band in the subway, is god and goddess, holy spirit. Music can be broken down into constituent parts just as the human body can be analyzed chemically, yet, like the body, only the whole form says something about divinity. I am not music's servant. I am someone who wishes to be worthy of such servitude, and for me it seems that writing about music is the only way to approach that forever unattainable goal. For while it is never enough to say that, because the truth is unknowable we should not bother pursuing it, I believe that Alvin in his unlettered way was on to something. I am confident that someone is the happier today for having been led to music by the child of a child who sat on the edge of his seat, ready with his trombone, as Alvin gave the downbeat to start the *American Patrol March*. We use music to shape and reshape our responses to the world, just as the books we read and the films we see become part of us. In the end, music—the orchestra, Coltrane, the steel band—is what we make of it, and what we allow it to make us.

—L.R.

II.
CREATORS

Another Word for Mozart

In 1991, the year of the Mozart bicentennial, a friend in Germany wrote to me that even she, who had no contact with the world of classical music, had noticed it was "Mozarting like mad everywhere." She asked whether Mozart was born or died two hundred years ago, and I liked her own answer that "it makes no difference really." Of course the music historian in me wanted to get on his high horse and tell her not only that Mozart *died* in 1791, on 5 December, at 12:55 in the morning, but also to point out that if Mozart had been *born* that year, he'd be a contemporary, more or less, of Weber, Meyerbeer, Marschner, Loewe, Schubert, Donizetti, and such characters, and he would have written a very different sort of music. Which actually raises an interesting question. Assuming that he would have been just as gifted, would we love his music just as much? In other words, to what extent is his apparently permanent and indestructible popularity tied to the fact that he composed in that specific style we call Classical?

He was born in 1756, on 27 January, a day I bet a few ancient Germans still celebrate silently as the birthday of the last Kaiser. I remember 1956, the bicentenary of Mozart's birth, very well. We took notice of the anniversary with special concerts, opera productions, and tons of recordings. A new complete edition of Mozart's music was begun, and there was even a scattering of new pieces composed in his honor (not much of moment). I was in the army that year, stationed in Stuttgart, and I have a happy and grateful memory of a concert with Carl Schuricht conducting and the wonderful Clara Haskil as piano soloist in the beautiful baroque theater at Ludwigsburg, a visually rich and acoustically exquisite room of the kind that must have been very familiar to Mozart. Overall, though, 1956 was nothing like 1991. In thirty-five years, Mozart's popularity had soared. In trying to explain that phenomenon, I slide into an attempt to answer another question my friend put to me: *What is it about Mozart?*

He was a child prodigy. That's a species not held in much regard nowadays, but Mozart, immensely gifted, and shrewdly "managed" by his ambitious father, enjoyed a phenomenal career for a few years. He did not have an easy journey through adolescence into adulthood, partly because that is never easy, but not least because his father, himself a distinguished musician, did his best to imprison his son in childhood. (The "child" was thirty-one when the father died.) For that matter, when Mozart visited Paris in his twenties, he had cause to complain that the public there treated him as though he were still seven, his age at his first visit. And equating Mozart with innocence, presenting him as a child, a pre-Freudian child of course, is an idea that has never quite gone away.

But Mozart did become a grownup, impulsive, passionate, sexual, playful, moody, affectionate, not always clever about practical matters or politically adroit, and, let us not forget, incredibly hard-working. Just once he fell achingly in love, with the teenage soprano Aloysia Weber. She was cold and indifferent to him, and he later married her younger sister Constanze. It was a contented and companionable union, full of sex, but I don't know that he ever got over Aloysia. It is about the time he realized he was getting nowhere with her that a persistent strain of melancholy enters his music. At any rate, marrying the beloved's sister is probably not the best cure (as Antonín Dvořák would discover a century later). Aloysia herself entered a fairly unhappy marriage with Joseph Lange, an actor and painter who has given us the most sensitive as well as the most famous of all Mozart portraits.

At twenty-five, Mozart managed to get away from Salzburg, which, but for his posthumous glory, would still be as oppressively provincial today as it was in the 1770s. He took the plunge and established himself in Vienna as a freelance artist. He would have preferred the security of a well-paid position at court, but that never came along, at least not on an adequate scale. Nonetheless, in his first few years in Vienna he once again enjoyed stunning success as a composer, pianist, and teacher. Though local, it was a popularity so dizzying that it could not be sustained. The truly musical public stayed with Mozart, but some of his audience consisted of people who valued him less as an artist than as the currently fashionable sensation, and they lost interest.

In the second half of the 1780s he experienced a slump. He wrote only two piano concertos after 1786 and no symphonies after the summer of 1788. That is indicative, for then composers always wrote in response to demand. In 1791 he found a new audience with *The Magic Flute*, produced not at an elegant house in the city, but in a suburban musical comedy theater. Seven weeks later, ill, overworked, depressed, convinced at moments that he had been poisoned, struggling to compose a Requiem for which he had received a mysteriously anonymous commission during the summer, he took to his bed. He died a fortnight later. People still argue about the cause of his death, but even if you saw it at the movies or had read it in Pushkin long before that, he was *not* poisoned by his admired colleague Salieri.

That he died young is part of his fascination—"those whom the gods love" and all that. His early death is also part of the mechanism that seems to lock him into perpetual childhood. Because it invites us to feel superior to his contemporaries, we dearly love the story of his funeral in a snowstorm so terrible that everyone gave up and turned back before they reached the cemetery and his burial in an unmarked pauper's grave (I remember as a child being shown a picture of the hearse followed only by Mozart's little mutt). When in 1959(!) Nicolas Slonimsky looked up the weather report, it turned out that the day was mild, with just a trace of mist. If Mozart ended in an unmarked grave, so did nearly all Viennese who died in or soon after the reign of Joseph II, an idealist sorely lacking in common sense and who insisted that death and the disposal of bodies be treated as a purely practical problem without regard for human feeling.

A legend that is harder to dispel—and harder since Peter Shaffer and Milos Forman—is that of Mozart's name. Not once did he call himself Wolfgang Amadeus. His family called him Wolfgang and its various affectionate diminutives. The "Amadeus" part appears in the baptismal register and in his father's first accounts in its German and Greek forms as Gottlieb and Theophilus. Mozart himself liked the French and Italian forms *Amadé, Amadeo,* and *Amadè*. Once or twice when he is fooling around he signs as *Wolfgangus Amadeus Mozartus*; otherwise Amadeus is a posthumous solemnization of a very serious but blessedly unsolemn man.

The musical world in which he grew up and worked revolved around opera. That was Mozart's strong suit, or let us say the strongest suit of an artist who had nothing but strong suits. Wherever it is that they give out particular musical gifts, they don't do it even-handedly. There are opera composers who are musicians of the first order but who lack a sense of theater, of atmosphere and pace; then there are those who have the theatrical gift in abundance but who do not write first-rate music. Mozart is one of the very few who have it all.

He had an amazing knack for observing his fellow humans and of getting down onto paper just what he saw. His effervescent letters are full of uncannily vivid descriptions and characterizations of people he met as he traveled about; that same gift of seeing (in this case in his mind's eye) and expressing (in music rather than in words) goes into the creation of his operatic characters. Often the orchestra brings them to life even before they sing. Mozart was blessed with some very good librettos, but the music tells us far more about the individualities of Susanna and the Countess, of Fiordiligi and Dorabella and Despina, of the three women in *Don Giovanni*, than the elegantly and wittily fashioned texts.

This magical transmutation occurs because Mozart has so much feeling for the complexity, the ambiguity of human creatures and therefore of the situations into which they maneuver themselves. He can to perfection express pure grief, as in Pamina's "*Ach, ich fühl's*," or pure giddy joy, as when Papageno and Papagena plan their family, but he is most quintessentially and uniquely himself when smiles and tears come together as inconsiderately and perplexingly as they can in real life, when we sense the remembrance of joy even as the Countess Almaviva laments the fading of her marriage, or in those countless places where the shadow of a minor chord or of some strange harmonic coloration darkens the ground for a moment.

His dark side came as a surprise to me when I was a boy. The first Mozart pieces I remember hearing were *Eine kleine Nachtmusik* and the Overture to *The Abduction from the Seraglio*. The former is one of his few works with very little sense of shadow; in the latter, which was my special favorite, the jolliness of the quick music with the triangle must have been what got to me, for I have no recollection of the slower middle section in minor.

When I was twelve or so, I was taken to an all-Mozart concert that included the great G-minor Symphony, No. 40. I was completely unprepared for that turbulence. I remember being irresistibly drawn into the piece but also being confused and even annoyed because it didn't correspond to my exceedingly sketchy idea of who Mozart was. A while later, I had a chance to hear Myra Hess play a couple of the piano concertos, ever-present now but very little performed sixty years ago, and while I enjoyed that very much—and I damn well should have—I also remember being confused because Mozart couldn't seem to make up his mind whether he was writing happy or sad pieces. (I had just developed a taste for the Tchaikovsky *Pathétique*, partly no doubt because some grownup had warned me it was considered vulgar.)

But to get back to the operas. They not only offer us a portrait gallery unsurpassed in the theater for vividness and insight, but they also provide us with a sort of Rosetta Stone for the decoding of Mozart's instrumental music. His concertos, string quintets and quartets, symphonies—whatever—all turn out sooner or later to be transposed opera. The key to their gestures is in the operas, and the operas are the essential source of our understanding of his music.

Why does Mozart get to people so? Which indeed he does. From my friend David Cairns, the great Berlioz scholar, I heard the story of the little boy saying to his mother, "You mean to say Mozart was a man? I thought it was just another word for music." In composers Mozart has inspired awe and love and envy. Most performers will tell you that to play and sing Mozart is the most monumental challenge in their professional lives. The public has always taken pleasure in Mozart—or better, in many different Mozarts.

He is so complete. He touches us everywhere—mind, heart, and senses. We delight in the richness and generosity of his invention (which his contemporaries often found overwhelming and disturbing), that inexhaustible plenty of melodies, those recklessly rich harmonies, the amazing sense of instrumental color (my single most indelible impression when I first heard the G-minor Symphony was that of the high horns in the trio of the minuet, a place I especially look forward to every time). Simplicity and complexity come naturally to him, and in equal measure. He is funny, too, though it makes me sad that audiences today seem not to be trained to hear that or to respond to it. He knows pain, but he never feels sorry for himself, neither does he beg us to feel sorry for him.

And I suppose that is *the* special Mozart characteristic, the exquisite balancing act between the passion—the roiling emotional content—and the unshakably perfect manners. Almost unshakable, I should say. There are two or three places in Mozart where the surface cracks, where for a moment the harmonies and the rhythm reveal him to have been a potential master of excess. All Mozart-lovers know and cherish those places, and cherish them the more because they are so extremely rare. It is in that perfectly calculated tension between center and surface that we find the essence of Mozart.

Perhaps—and who, after all, can do more than speculate—the restraint and the nobility of spirit that this restraint implies are at the heart of Mozart's power over us. When I was first learning music, it was Beethoven, Beethoven, Beethoven. He was the ideal artist and our ideal voice. Yes, Schroeder in *Peanuts* spoke for millions of us. Peter Ustinov liked to tell the story of a general knowledge test when he was a schoolboy. Having to name the world's greatest composer he put down "Mozart." He failed. The correct answer was Beethoven. Then in the last quarter of the twentieth century we made Beethoven roll over to allow room for Mahler, thus adding heterogeneity, unrestrained pathos, actually uninhibited *everything*, and not least, extreme vulnerability. And now we have added Mozart—yes, always admired, always in the repertory, but never so fully as now.

We don't need to castrate him, to make him into the innocent child he was not. His songs are songs of experience. Perhaps it does after all make a difference that he was not *born* in 1791, that he lived and worked before Beethoven had made heroics and the heroic ambition part of the common musical language. It is wonderful at this messy moment in the world's history to find someone who can speak to us about everything: bathroom humor, a misplaced pin, the sadness of lost love, and the awesome and incalculable powers of eros, thanatos, and forgiveness. As the novelist Maeve Brennan said about the Andante of the Symphony No. 29, "It is *the voice you can say anything in.*" Wonderful, too, that he does all this without heroics, with delicious wit, and with an unruffled sense of beauty. It was wry hyperbole, but one knows just what Rossini had in mind when he said that while Beethoven was undoubtedly the greatest of composers, Mozart was the only one.

—M.S.

Thinking of Robert Schumann

Robert Schumann? Yes, of course. The name is one of the most reassuringly familiar on our musical landscape, yet we know Schumann the composer less than we sometimes assume. How many people reading these words have heard, let alone performed, *Das Paradies und die Peri* after Thomas Moore's *Lalla Rookh;* the opera *Genoveva,* the music for Byron's *Manfred* beyond its stupendous Overture; the Scenes from Goethe's *Faust;* the Requiem; the Overture, Scherzo, and Finale for Orchestra; the Romances for Oboe and Piano; the *Spanisches Liederspiel* for vocal quartet with piano; the Justinus Kerner songs; even the Piano Quartet?

While Schumann may in some ways be surprisingly elusive, many of us can quickly summon up a picture: a handsome, distinctly Germanic face, the good looks in middle age slightly compromised by a bit too much fat and one of the more unfortunate hairdos in the history of Western music. And lots of us must have cut our pianistic teeth on *The Happy Farmer* (in England, where I learned it, *The Merry Peasant*) or another of the many useful and enjoyable gems he composed for beginners—no one between Bach and Bartók wrote such fine keyboard music for teaching. And what an adventure it was, on first deciphering that cheery little piece, to wrestle down that for us right-handers so counter-intuitive distribution of playing the tune in the left hand and the accompaniment in the right!

Moreover, Schumann stories and images come flooding: the boy growing up in his father's bookstore, an easy and natural pianist, but imagining his grown-up self as a literary man, not a musician; the later and serious piano lessons with the esteemed and fearsome Friedrich Wieck; the amorous complications when the professor's miraculously gifted daughter Clara, just nine the first time Herr Schumann passed through the Wiecks' front door, had grown into her teens—she falling in love first, he being the inconstant one; Daddy's determination to put a stop to all that, willing even to take daughter and boyfriend to court to do so; the mechanical device with which Schumann sought to strengthen his fourth finger, but whose effect was to disable the hand completely; Robert's and Clara's marriage on the day before her twenty-first birthday when he was thirty; the union at first ecstatically happy, marked in its first years by a deluge of passionate songs, succeeding the fantastical piano pieces for Clara that had come during the years of courtship and secret engagement; the strain of sustaining a marriage with rather too many children arriving too frequently; the angst for Robert, a composer of "difficult" new music and not a dependable wage-earner, of sharing a life with an immensely loved virtuosa—a celebrity—and occasionally being asked backstage whether he was musical as well; the growing frequency of his bouts of melancholia, as it was then called; his failure as a conductor (natural shyness plus myopia plus too much vanity to wear glasses in public); the brief happiness of friendship with the very young Brahms (a friendship that in its loving and occasionally scratchy way would sustain Clara to the end of her days when she had outlived her husband by forty years); Robert's suicide attempt by jumping into the freezing Rhine one February morning; and the last wretched two and a half years in the asylum at Endenich outside Bonn, with Clara not allowed to visit him for fear her presence would excite him and speed his disintegration. He was forty-six when he died.[1]

We remember as well that Schumann wrote copiously *about* music, and, being a practical and energetic man as well as one of the great dreamers, he founded and edited his own journal, the *Neue Leipziger Zeitschrift für Musik* (*New Leipzig Musical Times*) as a vigorous alternative to the more conservative publications around. Sometimes he signed his articles with an initial standing for a poetic nom de plume—"F" for Florestan, representing Romantic exuberance and enthusiasm (only Berlioz could work up such a fever as a critic), or "E" for Eusebius, the voice of his contemplative, pianissimo, introverted self.[2] Does the Florestan/Eusebius split, as is sometimes asserted, portend the future schizophrenic? I think not: besides acknowledging what is to varying

[1] How strange I have found it to be driving or riding around Bonn and see road signs for Endenich, as though it were just any old suburb.

[2] We tend to forget about the occasional appearances of Doctor Raro, who was supposed to represent the sensible compromise between the F. and E. extremes. We lose nothing, though; he was a dull fellow. Schoenberg was right when he observed that the middle road is the only one that does not lead to Rome.

degrees true in all of us, it is an ingenious literary device that keeps Schumann from being locked into single, simple-minded critical positions and allows for interesting conversations between his Florestan and Eusebius selves. He and like-minded literary and musical friends and colleagues also founded the *Davidsbund,* or League of David, the sworn enemies of the Philistines.

I remember reading as a boy that Schumann's reputation as a critic was exaggerated because he had the good luck to open his career by hailing one of his most extraordinary contemporaries, Frédéric Chopin ("Hats off, gentlemen, a genius!"), and to close it when he welcomed another, Johannes Brahms ("This is the chosen one"). Those were indeed amazing and enviable opportunities for a writer, but we also need to remember that those two articles took perception, not just luck. You also cannot just dismiss the many other words that come between 1831 and 1853. People have pointed out that Schumann could get wildly carried away as a critic, overstating the case for Niels Gade, for example, or for the prodigiously gifted, tragically short-lived Christian Ludwig Schuncke. But they were excellent composers both, and are not our newspapers and professional journals filled with what will surely come to seem quite wacky encomia, in less vibrant prose, too, and with less love, which is the element that speaks most compellingly in Schumann's writings about music?

And Schumann's own music? Each of his works is part of a puzzle which, put together, creates a complete picture, but most of us overlook some of the key pieces. Music lovers are less likely to focus on composers (with a few exceptions—most prominently Mozart, Wagner, Mahler) than to be segregated as orchestra audiences, opera buffs, piano aficionados, lieder lovers, and the like. For instance the piano aficionado is likely to have recordings of Schumann's Concerto, *Carnaval, Kreisleriana, Davidsbündlertänze, Scenes from Childhood,* and the C-major Fantasy, maybe even in multiple versions, but perhaps none of the Violin Concerto or *Dichterliebe (Poet's Love).* And Schumann—obviously not unique in this respect—manifests in highly characteristic fashion in a lot of genres: symphonies and concertos, chamber music in many colors and flavors, piano music, solo and part songs, and large-scale vocal works such as operas and oratorios.

Not only is Schumann a composer rather too narrowly known to most of us—as is of course not less true of Bach, Handel, Haydn, Schubert, Tchaikovsky, and Dvořák, among others—but he is also one who has been misunderstood and misrepresented in much of the writing and talking about him. *Myth No. 1:* He could not orchestrate, and his orchestral works are basically clumsily scored piano pieces. I well remember, forty-odd years ago, hearing Leonard Bernstein demonstrate this to a New York Philharmonic audience by deliberately making the orchestra play with bad balances and raucous tone. In fact the orchestral works sound very well, though they need care from the conductor. Moreover, their sonority has a strongly personal flavor: Schumann is one of those composers you can recognize from a single chord in a blind tasting. *Myth No. 2:* He could not handle large forms and was successful only in miniatures and character pieces. The symphonies are utterly convincing big pieces, risky, personal, original, inspired, ever fresh and awaiting our delighted discovery and rediscovery. *Myth No. 3:* The late works are feeble and not worth our attention. But the late clarinet *Fantasiestücke* or the music for Byron's *Manfred* show no trace of a decrepit mind devoid of inspiration.[3]

Schumann wrote a number of what I think of as "good boy" pieces, ones in which law and order are of paramount importance and where one can sense Beethoven as an exceedingly commanding and dauntingly masculine presence (as we know he could be for Brahms as well). Such pieces can be strong. The popular Piano Quintet, full of energy and brio, is an example. But compare it to the Piano Quartet, no less vigorous and fiery, no less enjoyable to play, and you quickly sense that here is an utterance far more personal, more special. I have never left a concert hall because the Quintet was about to be played and have often with great pleasure listened to it at home, the 1927 recording with Ossip Gabrilowitsch and the Flonzaley Quartet still being my favorite. But I love more those pieces that show Schumann's quirky side—sudden and drastic changes of mood, rhythmic dislocations, events passing by at a startling speed and vanishing. That is the music that invites us into his innermost self.

We can also distinguish between Schumann's public and his private pieces— a distinction I believe first articulated by Charles Rosen.[4] In the public pieces Schumann addresses (and seeks to wow) an audience; in his private ones he muses to himself and, to cite the verse by Friedrich Schlegel he placed at the head of his C-major Fantasy, speaks "to him who furtively listens in." The Piano Quintet is public, the Piano Quartet is private. The Fantasy's middle movement is public, between two very private ones. Also on the public side: the symphonies and concertos (the Violin Concerto *perhaps* leaning toward the private), most of the big vocal works such as *Das Paradies und die Peri* and the opera *Genoveva,* the big piano sonatas, and *Carnaval.* Private: *Scenes from Goethe's Faust,* their large scale notwithstanding; the *Requiem for Mignon;* virtually all the lieder (with a song such as *Die beiden Grenadiere* to remind us that there can be exceptions); and among the piano works, *Davidsbündlertänze, Kreisleriana,* and *Scenes from Childhood.*

Yesterday I took a break from writing this essay and filled part of that hour with the magic of Etsko Tazaki's recording of *Davidsbündlertänze.* I could have picked *Kreisleriana* or *Scenes from Childhood,* even the more "public" statements of *Carnaval* or the C-major Fantasy, all of them musical wonders, but—and

---

[3] The late John Daverio's 1997 biography *Robert Schumann: Herald of a "New Poetic Age,"* a landmark in Schumann criticism, deals firmly with these mindlessly repeated canards.
[4] Rosen's highly personal 1995 survey *The Romantic Generation* is well worth knowing.

this is as subjective as the music itself—*Davidsbündlertänze* is of all of Schumann's piano sets the one I am most in love with, the one that most surely gets those "energies which animate our psychic life" going for me (a phrase I borrow from Roger Sessions), the one where the soul of Robert Schumann is enshrined.

Eighteen short pieces, amounting to about a half hour of music—six signed by Florestan, seven by Eusebius, four by both (including No. 1, which is based on a motif by Clara), one unsigned. How arresting the tempo and character directions are: along with "lively" and "simply" we read *Etwas hahnbüchen* (A bit outrageous), *Ungeduldig* (Impatient), *Sehr rasch und in sich hinein* (Very fast and turned into itself), *Wie aus der Ferne* (As though from a distance), and of course we find that most indispensable and untranslatable of German Romantic adjectives, *Innig* (Inward). Over the ninth piece, ardent edging on the desperate, Schumann writes: "And here Florestan stopped, and there was an agonized trembling about his lips." As for the "not fast," deeply *innig* closing waltz, Schumann tells us that "quite unnecessarily Eusebius added the following, the while great bliss shone in his eyes."[5]

In all its intimacy, here is music of extremes. No composer was more joyful and ebullient, the music swept along on irresistible physical energy. No composer was ever possessed by such deep sadness. Neither Mahler nor Elgar could follow him into those dark places; Schubert, yes, his beloved Schubert, whom he was one of the first to appreciate fully—but only Schubert, no one else. Schumann can also create a sense of music coming from very far away, in time as well as place—and not only when he marks a piece *"wie aus der Ferne."* His rhythms are all his own. He likes ambiguous, even deceptive beginnings—where is the downbeat? Besides the *Davidsbündlertänze*, the Fourth Symphony and his greatest orchestral piece, the *Manfred* Overture, offer prime examples. The ends of his piano pieces are sometimes strangely unfinal. Melodies float independent of beat. How mysterious, even uncanny, it is when in the seventeenth of the *Davidsbündlertänze* we suddenly find ourselves back in the midst of the haunting phrases of the second. Are we lost in time? Are we dreaming? Is he? And in that last waltz there is a mystery, a melodic phrase that sounds like something in quotation marks—it must have had some special significance for him and probably Clara as well—which he will bring back a year later in *Kreisleriana*, another glorious essay in joyous and dark and humorous Romantic music. (Something not to miss: George Balanchine's heart-breaking, poignant, profoundly Schumannesque choreographic setting of *Davidsbündlertänze*, of which you can get a New York City Ballet DVD.)

[5] Probably not without some pressure from the devoted Clara, ever bent on wanting her husband's music to be more "accessible"—fatal quest—Robert prepared a revised edition in which he eliminated the F. and E. signatures, neutralized the tempo and character indications, made the suggested explicit, and normalized—sometimes one might almost say "dumbed down"—some of his more idiosyncratic musical procedures.

Then there are Schumann's songs, about half of them, two hundred or so, written in the year of his marriage. Again, the range is tremendous. The poets include German masters such as Chamisso, Eichendorff, Goethe, Heine, Kerner, Mörike, Platen, Rückert, and Schiller, but also Hans Christian Andersen, Burns, and Byron, all in German translation. The emotional and expressive range in the lieder is formidable. Some are as straightforward as folk songs and hymns; others are of extraordinary and compacted musical richness. Schumann was quick to learn from Schubert what the piano might be and do in such music and to extend those discoveries boldly. In *Frauenliebe und -Leben (Woman's Love and Life)* and *Dichterliebe* the piano gets movements of its own, raised to exalted poetical heights, especially in *Dichterliebe*. It was there that Mahler found the possibility for the breath-stopping vanishings into silence in the *Kindertotenlieder* and *Das Lied von der Erde*.

I love the symphonies and the concertos (all of them), and I am forever grateful to Erich Leinsdorf for introducing me forty years ago to the marvel that is the *Scenes from Goethe's Faust*. How right he was, too, in pointing out that Schumann's setting of the sublime closing lines comes closer to Goethe than Mahler's more famous one in his *Symphony of a Thousand*. Still, the greatest Schumann, the essential Schumann, the music without which you cannot know who this man was, this man so gifted and at home in exhilaration, in melancholy, in mystery, in the uncanny, in the sometimes baffling play of time and space, that music is found in these works for solo piano and his songs. And there is a happy dividend. Hearing the familiar symphonies and concertos will be a richer experience when you revisit them from the perspective of the piano cycles and the songs.

If this is territory new to you, begin with *Carnaval* and *Dichterliebe*. Then, if they speak to you, go on to *Kreisleriana*, the *Davidsbündlertänze*, and the wonderful feast of spook, nostalgia, and joy, the Eichendorff *Liederkreis*, op. 39. By sheer chance, the first piece of Schumann's I ever heard (aside from my own clattering through *The Happy Farmer*) was *Bird as Prophet* from the rather late *Waldszenen* in a haunting recorded performance by Alfred Cortot. Except for Franz Liszt's gnomic utterances in the last years of his life, is there a stranger four minutes of music in all of the nineteenth century? I would wish for that to find a place in your musical treasury as well.

Strangely—as it now seems to me—among the great masters it was Schumann that it took me longest to get close to. I enjoyed hearing and playing him, but he was not one of my indispensables, one of my desert island companions until late middle age. I don't know for sure what changed. Perhaps it was just the passage of years. In part I know it was better understanding of his life that captured me. Mary Oliver has a beautiful, deeply understanding poem, *Robert Schumann*, which ends with a vision of the nineteen-year-old musician on a spring morning, having "just met a girl named Clara," running "up the dark staircase, humming." I am haunted by what he found at the top of those stairs and by what became of that happiness—in so few years. I am haunted even more by two earlier lines in the poem: "Everywhere in this world his music/explodes out of itself, as he/could not."

With no other composer—not even Beethoven and Mahler—is my hearing and love of the music so tied to my sense of the man who invented it. None other makes a statement so urgent, so person-to-person, so naked and vulnerable. How close his greatest, his most *innig* music comes to *literally* stopping breath and unsettling my heart. How deeply and dangerously human are the strangenesses in his music. How amazed, how humbled I am by the command that allowed him to translate his own vibrations into music, music that "explodes out of itself, as he could not." And how thankful I am that now I can say along with Mary Oliver, "Hardly a day passes I don't think of him . . . "

—M.S.

The Sacred, the Profane,
and the Gritty Affirmations of Music

The sacred and the profane: the concepts have been with us all our lives, from our earliest days, even before we were able to name them. Growing up even in the most politically correct environment, with elders committed to moral relativism, we still formed ideas about should and shouldn't, about what separated the nice kids from the others. Only later, as our sensibilities were formed with help from the Bible or Torah or Quran, John Milton, Herman Melville, Mozart, Bach, Beethoven, Lincoln, Gandhi, Hitler, Stalin, Superman, Darth Vader, Martin Luther King Jr., Mother Teresa, and an array of hands known only to each of us, and which continue to shape our personal clay—only later did we develop and refine notions of Good and Evil. Given the either/or methods in which most of us were raised, it is natural for us to think about Good and Evil and their counterparts, the Sacred and Profane—the lofty and the raunchy, spirit and gland—as though they were separate entities. But eventually we recognize what a volatile mixture of opposites we are. Those who can resign themselves to this fact take a step on the path to wisdom. Those who cannot, join the evangelical wing of the Republican Party. Great art—and music, especially—will help steer us toward the first of these alternatives.

In the spring of 1997, when the San Francisco Symphony presented Celebrations of the Sacred and Profane, a festival that examined "sacred" and "profane" as expressed in works by Bach, Mozart, Schubert, Berlioz, Alban

Berg, and Kurt Weill, the time was right to reflect on what those concepts can mean in music.

"Sacred" and "Profane" are intangibles, yet artists from the beginning have fashioned representations of these grand ideas, which encompass our lives. The representations—in sounds and words and images—reflect what is at the root of us all. Call it soul. Art is the graven image of God himself that Jehovah cautioned us from creating—cautioned us, perhaps because he understood how images of the unknowable are not just misleading but rob it of its mysterious grandeur. Yet if we understand that no such image can be definitive, if we understand that such attempts are just efforts to comprehend ourselves and where we are headed—for aren't we created in God's image?—the transgression is a virtue.

And what about God's image? In the Art History Museum in Vienna, I overheard a woman comment on Brueghel the Elder's *Battle between Carnival and Lent.* "It's so dirty," she said, and she was not speaking about the condition of the canvas. This is what she saw: a scene of bedlam, solemn processions of the religious winding through the marketplace, alive with carnival revelers. She saw swarming motion, as if the framed scene were a heap of compost, buzzing and maggoty. She said it best: it's dirty. That is one of its glories. Consider another painting, the *Hell* panel of *The Garden of Earthly Delights* by Hieronymous Bosch. "Bosch," says a commentator whose name is written in a notebook since lost in the compost heap of my desk, "showed that the traditions and achievements of painting which had been developed to represent reality most convincingly could be turned around, as it were, to give us an equally plausible picture of things no human eye had seen." In other words, using the most advanced methods of his craft, Bosch takes us to the far side of the soul, a place peopled by horrible creatures. Disturbing, repulsive—they have no name and yet are terrifyingly familiar. But from where do we know them? We have to be honest with ourselves if we want the answer. Great art is honest, and honest art always has room for dirt and grit.

One of the ironies of the cultural scene is that concert music is thought of as the province of the elite, as a super-sanitary adjunct of society's upper stratum, as the art form best suited to those who have little or no firsthand knowledge of what its critics think of as "real life." That notion keeps the many from experiencing the much. How to dispel it? Not by the sort of "crossover" that brings us Pavarotti singing "Strangers in the Night"—that's not so much a meeting of sacred and profane as it is a convergence of opportunity and smart business. Pavarotti's is a great voice, and "Strangers in the Night" is a great song, but put together, each detracts from the other, and the result is distracting. Let's face it: the result is ridiculous. But the greatest Western concert music aims at the bull's eye, and the bull's eye is a representation of life as real as it comes, maybe not in a picture you can recognize—any more than you recognize

Bosch's creatures—but of whose truth you're convinced. Created in sweat and hard labor—it's not by accident that we speak of a *work* of art, and not by accident that we speak of such a work as being *born*—it springs from inner need and is a response to necessity: the necessity to embrace the parts of ourselves that grow from the earth along with the parts rooted in heaven, the need to see things steadily, as Matthew Arnold said, and to see them whole. Let me speak in specifics by looking at the composers represented in Celebrations of the Sacred and Profane, and their attempts to discern the fine line between spiritual calamity and salvation.

Salvation became necessary when damnation became a fact of human existence. In words less loaded with theological baggage, we invented the sacred to save us from the profane, or vice versa. We are made of dust and spirit, and no one knew this better than Mozart. Here is a man who set both the sacred and the profane to music. His scatological canons seem the work of a trash-mouthed teenager, and you can almost feel Mozart revving himself up by talking dirty—dealing genteel manners an especially low blow by setting his obscenities to elegant music, the kind that anchors itself in the memory. Then you encounter the Requiem, which he was still writing on his deathbed, and you marvel that the ears that delighted in foul language set to engaging tunes could embrace the text of the Latin Mass for the dead and set those grand and serious words into the musical equivalent of a baroque church: saints' images haloed with stars, radiant gold-leafed sunbursts framing pastel frescoes, all resplendent in white light.

Schubert, like Mozart, was one of those composers whose accomplishment and early death (he lived to be just thirty-one, while Mozart was a month shy of thirty-six) make them a source of wonder and speculation (what *might* they still have accomplished!). And, like Mozart, he was a man who had a good sense of life's underside. He had an advanced acquaintance with tobacco, alcohol, and prostitutes, and the delights his flesh took in these pleasures contributed to its corruption. Those offended by such facts might ask where justice was when such a man was given the insight that pulses in every bar of his *Unfinished* Symphony, music of vision that penetrates like an auger through the dimensions of this world into something beyond.

But to create great music, composers are not obligated to talk dirty, drink heavily, or die early. Johann Sebastian Bach was among the soberest and hardest working of men. Forced to hold a steady job to support his large family, he struggled throughout his career with bureaucrats whose imaginations appeared to shut down once they had hired him—and this was especially true in his last post, as Cantor at Saint Thomas's Church in Leipzig, where the town council seemed not to notice how his genius was actually stoked by the drudgery of churning out music for weekly services. Thwarted again and again ("No, Herr Cantor, an extra soprano is *not* in our budget." "Herr Cantor, what gave you the idea that you could take a two-day leave without approval from this council?"), he still managed to rise above circumstances and stay focused on the sublime. For Bach, the profane was launch pad for the sacred.

Closer to our own time, Alban Berg and Kurt Weill were both methodical workers who, like Bach, remind us that genius often blooms out of diligent application. Berg, combing through his experience for material that would make a fitting memorial to Manon Gropius, who had died at eighteen, uncovered elements both sacred and profane. This is especially telling, for the enchanting Manon—"an angel," Berg called her—was the daughter of Alma Mahler. Alma had been married to the composer Berg revered above all others, and Berg thought of her and Manon as links to this great figure who had done so much to father his own artistic consciousness. (This music adds another dimension to the complex interplay of profane and sacred, for its character is also determined by those who had helped form Berg's human consciousness: he makes coded reference to Hanna Fuchs-Robettin, with whom he had been carrying on a long-standing extramarital affair, and to Marie Scheuchl, his first love and mother of his own daughter Albine.) Gustav Mahler—perhaps more than anyone, including Charles Ives—managed to fuse in his music the coarsest elements with the most heavenly. ("The symphony must be like the world," Mahler is reputed to have said. "It must be all-embracing.") In his Violin Concerto, one of the greatest concertos of the last hundred years, Berg, like Mahler, pulled everything together: quotations from a Bach cantata, injections of Viennese waltz and Austrian folk song, even elements of jazz. As for Weill, his *Seven Deadly Sins* is in itself a work of mixed media, combining music, theater, and dance in ironic social commentary, based on a concept, the deadly sins, that has been with us since the Middle Ages and that provided subject matter to many artists of the early Renaissance, among them Hieronymous Bosch.

Bosch's images bring us full circle, to music of Berlioz. His *Symphonie fantastique*, the story of a romantic obsession, ends in a nightmare of a witches' sabbath that unfolds against a Boschian landscape. In the sequel to all this, *Lélio*, which Berlioz subtitled *The Return to Life*, the hero of the *Fantastique* has come to terms with a miserable past and comes to some kind of reconciliation with a love life that went wrong.

Episodes of real life are not always granted sequels, and mistakes made in a profane world do not always find forgiveness, or resolution, in heaven. But as much as anything, art can show us something about life's ebb and flow, it can help us understand the formulas of our spiritual chemistry, the DNA prints of heartbreak and emotional breakthrough. We need these formulas, these maps, because life passes so quickly. Sometimes the places we have come from seem so far behind us we can barely remember them. Music offers us a way of touching not only our collective roots but our personal past. Listen to Schubert's *Unfinished* Symphony. When did you first hear this music? Recall that time.

Recall it, and all that has come between that moment and this one, when you are hearing it again. Consider how your view of the work and your experience of it have changed. Time and change, those are the givens of life, along with birth and death, which are our personal borders of time and change. Time and change, beginnings and endings. Those are also the borders of music.

Music is an art we experience by hearing it as it is produced by mechanical means—instruments. But music is properly a physical art, a function of the body. It arises from song—from the throat and the gut. We translate feelings of joy and sadness and dejection and triumph into song, into music. What we hear in the concert hall is a translation into sound of another being's heartbeat and breathing pattern. When Mozart or Schubert, Berg or Berlioz are played, their sound-patterns are recreated and part of their physical presence is resurrected. This is what we mean when we say that music affirms life. It affirms the genuine physical thing itself: sacred, profane, full of sunlight and earth (from which we came, to which we will return), and, in the most real and utterly nonreligious sense, everlasting.

—L.R.

Franz Schubert, "A Rich Possession"

Franz Schubert's first biographer was a Viennese jurist and civil servant by name of Heinrich Kreissle von Hellborn. In 1861, he published what he modestly and accurately called a biographical sketch; at the end of 1864, he came out with his full-length book. It appeared in English in 1869 as *The Life of Franz Schubert*, translated by Arthur Duke Coleridge. Kreissle, who loved what he had heard of Schubert's music, was motivated to begin his work by his awareness that those who had known Schubert were growing old, that their fairly imminent departure from this life was something to be reckoned with, and that, once they were gone, the construction of a biography would become incalculably more difficult. He therefore set about tracking down those whom he called "the witnesses to Schubert's external existence," as well as whatever he was able to pull together by way of scattered documents relevant to Schubert's life.

It was Kreissle who laid the ground floor for Schubert studies, and everything that has been achieved in that field since his time rests on what he began. He was not, however, trained as a scholar, and critically sifting the material he collected was not his strength. Speaking and corresponding with the survivors of the Schubert circle, Kreissle gathered much that was valuable, vivid, and often deeply touching. But we also need to remember that he was dealing with aging men and women (mostly men) who were reminiscing about someone who had been dead for more than thirty years. Some of them misremembered plain and simple. Some misremembered by design, so as to augment and glamorize the parts they themselves had played in Schubert's life. Some, although they were writing or speaking in the past tense, were—unconsciously—writing or speaking not about the friend with whom they had talked, made music, partied, played cards, drunk, smoked, and hiked, but about the Franz Schubert who had meanwhile come to be ranked as a very important composer.

Something that made the situation when Kreissle was at work peculiar was that so many Schubert pieces—important, impressive ones—had only come into public view posthumously, among them the great Masses in A-flat and E-flat (published 1875 and 1865, respectively), the *Unfinished* Symphony (first played in 1865), the String Quintet (published 1853), along with many smaller works. It sometimes seemed as though Schubert were still alive and composing; indeed, one French critic was moved to remark that he seemed, more than thirty years after his death, to be both one of the most prolific as well as most interesting of contemporary composers.

One result of all this remembering—and "remembering"—was the formation during the second half of the nineteenth century of a highly *sympathisch* image of Schubert. Its essential points were that Schubert died very young (which always holds a certain prurient appeal) and that during his brief lifetime his genius was recognized only by a small and select group of discerning friends. The secondary features of this Schubert portrait were that he composed effortlessly, with uncanny ease and speed, and that he was a dear little man—"*Schwammerl,*" little mushroom, they called him—even if personal hygiene was not a high priority with him and even though he sometimes drank a few more glasses of wine than were good for him. It all fit well with the comfy Biedermeier spirit of mid-century Austria. It also helped create the impression, not yet completely erased, that Schubert was something of an amateur, although an inspired one. There are still those who see him as the most seductive of charmers but deny him the greatness that would place him on the same level as Haydn, Mozart, and Beethoven.

Obviously, some truth lies curled up inside all this mythology. Schubert was born on 31 January 1797, and when he died, at three o'clock in the afternoon on 19 November 1828, he was about ten weeks shy of turning thirty-two. No other great composer died so young—not Mozart, not even Purcell. The playwright Franz Grillparzer wrote the famous epitaph for Schubert's monument, erected in the Währing Cemetery in 1830: "Here the art of music buried a rich possession, but even fairer hopes." (In 1888, both Schubert and Beethoven, his neighbor just three graves away, were moved to Vienna's Central Cemetery. The Währing Cemetery was later deconsecrated and is now the Schubert Park.) Later, Grillparzer was criticized for underrating Schubert's actual achievement, but I would say two things in his defense. First, given that in 1830 some of Schubert's most extraordinary works were still unpublished and unperformed, Grillparzer's perspective is not that badly askew. Second, if we consider Schubert's achievements in his last year—including the three final piano sonatas along with some remarkable shorter pieces, the String Quintet, the Mass in E flat, the F-minor Fantasy for Piano Duet, and the songs later published as *Schwanengesang* (*Swan Song*)—and if we also keep in mind that he was only thirty-one, it is understandable that one might fantasize about a transcendent future of "even fairer hopes."

We still tend to cherish the picture of Schubert as Neglected Genius. Yes, his reputation was local, and even in Vienna, compared to Beethoven and Rossini, the two composers who most captivated that city during his lifetime (Rossini more than Beethoven, to the latter's fury), Schubert was obscure. But he was far from invisible, even though it did happen that mail from a German publisher addressed to "Franz Schubert, Esq., Composer, Vienna" was delivered to a musician named Josef Schubert. And a certain Franz Schubert in Dresden was indignant when a "piece of hackwork" by his Viennese namesake was mistakenly attributed to him, the "*Machwerk*" in question being the setting of Goethe's *Erlkönig*.

But Franz Schubert's music—our Franz Schubert's—was performed, quite often under the auspices of the Society of the Friends of Music, a high-prestige organization to whose directorate Schubert was elected in 1826. Admired virtuosi took him up. And Johann Michael Vogl, principal baritone at the Court Opera (he was the first Pizarro in the final version of Beethoven's *Fidelio*) and a most compelling artist, became a powerful advocate for his songs. When Vogl sang *Erlkönig* at a charity concert in March 1821, Schubert's obscurity in Vienna was over. The firm of Cappi & Diabelli published *Erlkönig* a month later: a hundred copies were sold at a single soirée when its availability was announced, and another three hundred were turned around in little more than a year.

Important publishers became interested in Schubert's music, although, to his annoyance and frustration, they were inclined to be exceedingly cautious, willing to take his songs and small piano pieces but turning down large instrumental works such as string quartets and symphonies. Still, for someone who was not a virtuoso performer and who, through general forgetfulness and negligence, tended to derail his friends' efforts to get him publicity and arrange useful contacts, Schubert managed to be quite a conspicuous figure in Vienna's musical life. In March 1828, his friends helped arrange the first concert entirely of his music. It was a huge success, and when Schubert died, plans were in the making for another such event. What turned out to be his last year, 1828, had shown every promise of being a great and positive turning point in his career.

Schubert obviously had the qualities that brought him a group of extraordinarily devoted friends, some of them musicians, more of them literary people and artists. He was not an easy friend, though. He could be fine company, charming, delightful, and good for serious conversation, but he could also be self-absorbed, peremptory, and rude, and his forgetfulness and negligence could be wounding. As you read the evidence collected in Otto Erich Deutsch's *Schubert: A Documentary Biography,* a wonderfully engaging book, and as you learn to decode his friends' tactful and protective language, it becomes clear that Schubert drank recklessly (today he would be considered an alcoholic), also that he smoked far too much and smelled like an ashtray. The ups and downs of his productivity suggest that he suffered from cyclothymia, severe and clinical mood swings. In his later years, he tended each spring to fall into severe depression that paralyzed his ability to compose.

Most of all, Schubert distressed his friends by the recklessness with which he stilled his gigantic sexual appetite. Here again, we are dealing with veiled language, but what emerges is that Schubert contracted syphilis toward the end of 1822, that by 1828 the disease had entered its tertiary stage, and that, his system catastrophically weakened by alcohol and nicotine, he died from the effects of that disease, aggravated by some form of typhoid fever. His suffering in the primary stage of syphilis in the winter of 1822–1823, a condition probably worsened by the then-favored mercury cure, may have been the reason he was unable to continue work on the great B-minor *Unfinished* Symphony.

Not surprisingly, Schubert's music is no less complex than the man, and often no less dark. He composed a lot of what we might call social music, light-hearted songs, vocal ensembles, marches for piano duet, and reams of dances that must be just like the ones he improvised at parties. (He was always happier at the piano than out on the dance floor.) Most of this music you will never hear in concert, but it is cherished by those of us who play it for our own pleasure, especially the piano music. If you go through a set of Schubert's landler or waltzes, polonaises, or marches, you will discover that he was hardly more capable than Mozart of composing three minutes of music across which some strange and disturbing shadow does not pass, even if just for a single beat. We also cannot forget that, hardly out of his adolescence, Schubert could capture the sinister world of *Erlkönig,* the ballad of the spectral king who seduces a sick boy out from his father's arms into the land of death. Nor that even earlier, on a numinous October day in 1814, he had, in *Gretchen am Spinnrade,* drawn a picture of a desperate young woman, and had done it with a depth of understanding that ought not to be within the reach of a boy of seventeen.

1820, the year of the Mass in A flat, the unfinished cantata *Lazarus,* and the *Quartettsatz* in C minor, is a turning point, Schubert's entry into maturity. Another such critical moment is the one when his music loses its innocence for good. That happens toward the end of 1822. He had turned twenty-five in January, and it was the year in which his health was ruined and the one whose labors culminated in the two movements of the B-minor *Unfinished,* a work one praises inadequately by declaring that it is the greatest symphony between Beethoven and Brahms.

"At last I can pour out my whole heart to someone again," Schubert wrote in 1824 to Leopold Kupelwieser, the most serious of his friends, an artist who had moved to Rome to prepare himself for a career as a painter of ecclesiastical subjects: "You are so good and so faithful, you are sure to forgive me things that others will only take very much amiss. To be brief, I feel myself to be the unhappiest, the most wretched man in the world. Picture a man whose health will never be sound again and who, out of sheer despair over that, constantly does everything he can to make matters worse instead of better. Picture, I tell you, a man whose brightest hopes have come to nothing, to whom love and friendship at best offer nothing but pain, someone whose response (whose creative response, at least) to everything that is beautiful threatens to vanish, and then ask yourself if this is not a wretched, unhappy man. 'My peace is gone, my heart is heavy. Never, but never, shall I find peace again.' That [lament of Gretchen's] could now be my daily song, because each night when I go to sleep, I hope never to wake again, and each morning brings yesterday's grief back to me."

Those whom Kreissle von Hellborn called the witnesses to Schubert's external existence noticed that when he sat at the piano to accompany Vogl, even when he himself sang his songs in his composer's falsetto, something transformed him beyond their recognition. He could invent music that frightened and dismayed them, never more so than in the death-possessed songs of *Winterreise*, which they rejected even though he insisted it was the best thing he had done. In the work of Schubert's last years, we find music that is madly driving and obsessed, strange and fantastical, deeply melancholic, and as violent as anything in Beethoven. (Try the slow movement of his A-major Piano Sonata from 1828.) "What I produce comes about through my understanding of music and through my pain," Schubert wrote in his diary, "and what is produced by pain alone seems to please the world least." He had warned his friends that *Winterreise*, those songs that chronicle a young man's despairing journey through a bleak winter landscape, would make them shudder. Paradoxically, their rejection was a form of understanding and love, because in rejecting the songs they were rejecting Schubert's knowledge of death, his own death, then just a year away. John Harbison's assertion that Schubert "got closer to full metaphysical revelation than any other composer" is a challenge to take seriously.

Schubert's self-awareness comprised a keen sense of his own worth, of his artistic goals and possibilities. He grew up in the shadow of Beethoven, who himself had overcome that most daunting challenge of following Haydn and Mozart, yet bit by bit he came to understand that he *was* qualified to step forward as Beethoven's heir. And contrary to the legend, Schubert could work hard, like Beethoven. The works in which he declares himself to be of Beethoven's lineage—from the Octet, the A-minor and *Death and the Maiden* quartets, and the Grand Duo for piano, all of 1824, to the compositions of the last year—all these involved sketches and erasures, and intense concentration. Schubert's final musical wish, fulfilled in his sickroom five days before he died, was to hear Beethoven's Quartet in C-sharp minor, op. 131. "The King of Harmony had sent the King of Song a friendly bidding to the crossing," said Karl Holz, the first violinist in the group that went to play for him.

One of Schubert's last musical decisions had been to take some counterpoint lessons with the renowned pedagogue Simon Sechter, who would later teach Henri Vieuxtemps and Anton Bruckner, two names you'd not ever expect to find linked. The American scholar Michael Griffel has suggested quite persuasively that Schubert hoped, by strengthening his contrapuntal skills, to acquire the skills for composing heroic finales in the manner of Beethoven— no more unfinished symphonies! In the event, there was time for just one lesson, on 4 November 1828. At that point he could survey his amazing accomplishments of that year and also look ahead at a future only he could imagine. At the same time he must have seen with inescapable clarity the likelihood of an early death.

In 1824, he had written to Kupelwieser about readying himself to pave the road toward the "big symphony." He meant a symphony in the manner and on the scale of one of Beethoven's, and in the next paragraph he mentions the impending premiere of the Beethoven Ninth. Was it to equip himself for further explorations of the road toward the "grosse Symphonie" that he went to Sechter? A week after that one lesson with Sechter, Schubert took to his bed for the last time.[1] When he died, he had made considerable progress on a D-major Symphony, and what he had achieved there suggests that this work, melancholic and visionary, would have surpassed anything he had done so far by way of large instrumental compositions.

And so we come back to Grillparzer and his "even fairer hopes." It is futile to speculate about the future that was cut off on the afternoon of 19 November 1828; at the same time, it is impossible not to think about it. Schubert would surely not have abandoned writing lieder, and I imagine him beating Schumann to Heine's Dichterliebe and all those Eichendorff poems, and setting Mörike thirty years before Hugo Wolf. He could have heard Brahms's First Symphony, unless his own symphonies, beginning with the great D major of 1829, had made Brahms even more nervous than he already was about Beethoven. As an old man, but not yet eighty, Schubert might have traveled to Bayreuth to see the first Ring.

Schubert had it in him to become a very great symphonist, and he might have come to enjoy the standing we now grant to Beethoven. In any case, the

---

[1] John Harbison has composed a moving tombeau for Schubert, using some of the material Sechter had given Schubert to work on. He calls it November 19, 1828.

view of Schubert would be very different for today's symphony audience, whose sense of him is now based on occasional encounters with six charmers and more frequent ones with one-and-a-half mature masterpieces. But Schubert's greatest chamber music, for instance the G-major String Quartet and the String Quintet, gives us a very good idea of his symphonic lungs. And of course, for us to take the measure of who Schubert was and what he could do, the late piano sonatas are essentials, as are the great song cycles. Happily, Schubert has been fortunate in his recordings, going back to the 1930s and the performances of the piano music by Artur Schnabel and those of songs by, among many fine artists, Gerhard Hüsch with Hanns Udo Müller. And if you can play the piano—you don't have to be a virtuoso—make the F-minor Fantasy, the A-flat Variations, the *Divertissement à l'hongroise,* and all those dances and marches your own.

Vast amounts of the works that most intensely illuminate who Franz Schubert was are unknown to most of us. The fairer hopes are fodder for our fantasy, but we do have the rich possession—on the page, on recordings, and sometimes (never often enough) in concert. That possession is enough to give us joy and pain, astonishment and ecstasy, for as long as we have our lives and our hearing.

—M.S.

Encountering Brahms

On a muggy August evening in 1966, shortly after my seventeenth birthday, I got on my bicycle and pedaled eight blocks across the Northwest Side of Chicago to the neighborhood shopping center. The charcoal clouds of a Midwest summer storm were building. From O'Hare, just minutes away across the subdivisions and parking lots, beyond an old farm acreage and a new hotel strip, the 707s lifted off and thundered against the low sky with Wagnerian grandeur. At Walgreen's I sorted through the bargain record bin—any record bin at Walgreen's was full of bargains. The fluorescent light above bounced back at me from the cellophane as I flipped through the titles. *The Chipmunks Sing. 101 Strings Play the Soul of Italy. Florian Zabach Goes Gypsy.* I stopped at an album whose cover bore a crude portrait of Johannes Brahms. It was a recording of the Third Symphony, with Erich Leinsdorf conducting an orchestra described on the front of the LP jacket as the Philharmonia and on the back as the Los Angeles Philharmonic. The recording cost ninety-nine cents. I bought it, biked home, and, as the rain began, put it on the turntable of the Grundig-Majestic console stereo in the living room of my parents' house. I have never ascertained which ensemble was featured on this recording—or, for that matter, whether Leinsdorf was the conductor. But since that evening I've determined that the music I was hearing was indeed the Brahms Third. Until that moment I had never heard the Brahms Third, nor had I heard any Brahms but the Lullaby, nor was I more than vaguely aware that Brahms had written anything *but* the Lullaby.

I had been listening to the classics—for me, that meant Beethoven—only for a few months. Now, in this symphony, I encountered things I had never imagined music capable of expressing—regret, and a yearning for what is past or for what might have been, which in either case is a longing for the impossible. As I write now, I realize the incongruities both of scene and situation, how this deeply serious and spiritual music completed on the banks of the Rhine in another century could console a love-forsaken teenager whom no one understood, not God himself, while the Boeings passing overhead pounded on toward Toledo and Denver, and in the other brown brick bungalows up and down the street the Chipmunks sang and the 101 Strings played the Soul of Italy and Florian Zabach went Gypsy. It was all, I would later realize, as implausible as Johannes Brahms himself, who had been born and raised in the more squalid parts of the squalid port city of Hamburg. Where did that music come from? You may as well ask how the world was created.

I have been dwelling on memories. I think that is the only way to convey the essence of Brahms—not the musical essence, but what the music implies. In "The Art of Memory," a wonderful essay on the composer in the September 1984 *Atlantic*, Richard Sennett, an accomplished amateur musician and author of the novel *An Evening of Brahms*, recalls that the pianist Rudolf Serkin dubbed Brahms "a memory artist." But all artists mold their shapes out of what they have. We create out of our experience. "Base your stories on what you know," young writers are advised. So why is it an interesting observation to call Brahms a "memory artist"? For this reason: because of what Brahms chose to do with his memories.

Biographical criticism of art is held in pretty low esteem in literary circles, but narrative fiction at least offers the opportunity to compare the details of plot with what is known about its author's life, and it's often evident how closely the art and the experience are intertwined—think of Thomas Wolfe, or Dickens, or Philip Caputo, or Jim Harrison, or Dave Eggers. Music allows no similar correlation. It may help us appreciate the music's emotional impact to imagine that Beethoven was raging against his deafness in the Fifth Symphony, or that in the *Pathétique* Tchaikovsky was trying to come to grips with being gay in a homophobic society almost a century before the term "homophobic" was coined. These biographical tidbits say nothing about the music itself, but they can arouse our interest. Brahms's biography includes nothing similar, no fate against which to rage or much of anything with which to come to grips.

He was born on 7 May 1833, the second child of Johann Jakob Brahms, bass player, violinist, and flutist, and Christiane Nissen. (Johann Jakob was twenty-four when they were married, Christiane forty-one.) Johannes began piano lessons at seven, and three years later he came under the tutelage of Eduard Marxsen, who had studied with Ignaz Seyfried, a pupil of Mozart's (and conductor of the first performance of Beethoven's Ninth), and with Carl Maria von Bocklet, a friend of Beethoven and Schubert. This is not to drop names, but rather to suggest that when Brahms came to think of himself as a descendant of this great tradition, he was basing that self-assessment on more than a high opinion of his abilities.

The story, told by Brahms himself (according to several sources who knew him), is that, as a young teenager, Johannes contributed to the family income by playing in the bars of Hamburg's red-light district. The American scholar Styra Avins has made the case that this sordid part of the Brahms legend never happened, while others maintain the opposite, as does Jan Swafford in his 1997 biography of the composer (*Johannes Brahms*, published by Alfred A. Knopf). Brahms did admit to playing in bars. The controversy seems centered on how old he was when this happened, and what, if any, psychological damage he sustained as a result. Both sides have merits and inconsistencies, and it may be that the complete facts will never come out—if, at last, they matter.

What seems true is that, besides any barroom entertaining he may or may not have done, the young Brahms also gave lessons and arranged music, and under a pseudonym he published light drawing-room pieces, just as a fledging novelist today might ghost-write romance fiction. When he was twenty he made a brief concert tour with the Hungarian violinist Eduard Reményi. At a stop in Hanover, Brahms met Joseph Joachim, who would become one of the century's greatest violinists and with whom Brahms formed a friendship that lasted—despite an extended silence arising from a serious misunderstanding—for the rest of his life. Through Joachim, Brahms was introduced to Robert Schumann, who was so impressed by the young man and his few compositions for piano that he hailed him in the *Neue Zeitschrift für Musik* as "the one . . . chosen to express the most exalted spirit of the times in an ideal manner, one who [sprang] fully armed from the head of Jove. . . . [A] youth at whose cradle the graces and heroes of old stood guard." "New Paths," Schumann titled his article. Perhaps he never imagined that praise like that could stop an artist. Perhaps he gambled on Johannes Brahms being equal to the challenge.

Schumann arranged for Brahms's first publications, and the young composer grew close to the Schumann family, even taking up residence with them at their home in Düsseldorf. But Robert had battled mental illness for years, and in 1854, exhausted by the struggle, he threw himself into the Rhine. He was dragged from the water, still alive. Death would not come for two more years, years he spent in an asylum. During this time, Brahms became confidant to Schumann's wife, Clara. She was thirteen years his senior, but Brahms had learned something about age gaps from his parents. Clara was also beautiful, kind, one of the most talented pianists in Europe, and a gifted (though neglected) composer. He could not have helped but fall in love with her. He did this with a completeness and an ardor characteristic not only of a young man but of a young Romantic artist. He was devoted to Clara, but their love, so far as we have any business knowing about such things, remained platonic. After 1856, they became best friends, literally friends to the death. At twenty-three, however, Johannes had experienced a major disappointment. He was powerfully drawn to Clara, but for one reason or another could not make the commitment, or was not allowed to. He was growing as a composer. He labored at his art regularly and with the concentration of a Michelangelo. He received ever greater recognition. At the same time, he claimed he wanted the steadiness he felt possible only by becoming the regular conductor of an orchestra. And though he settled in Vienna in 1869, he longed for his native city's recognition, but each time the Hamburg Philharmonic was in the market for a music director he was passed over. (An offer—which he declined—came at last in 1894, when he was sixty-one and had long since established his reputation as the greatest living composer of concert music in Europe.) He actually took a steady job in 1872, as artistic director of Vienna's Academy of the Friends of Music, but three years later he had had enough, and he quit and grew a beard. In 1876, at forty-three, he published his First Symphony, which inaugurated a series of large orchestral works that would indeed prove him heir to the great tradition. In 1895, when he attended the opening of Zurich's new Tonhalle, he saw on the ceiling his portrait alongside the portraits of Mozart and Beethoven. In 1896, shortly after Clara's death, he was diagnosed with liver cancer. He died on 3 April 1897.

By all accounts he was generous and openhearted. When an old friend asked him to use his influence to ensure that her daughter receive a scholarship to the Berlin Conservatory, he secretly paid the girl's tuition, taking care never to reveal what kind of "scholarship" this was. He could also be acerbic. A Viennese wit related the story—apocryphal, but telling—of how Brahms, standing in the doorway as he prepared to leave a dinner party, turned back to the guests at the table. "If there is anyone here whom I have not offended," he said, "I beg your pardon."

He was an artist who worked and reworked his material until he felt it was ready to present to the world. He burned the sketches for almost everything he produced. It has been estimated that he wrote some twenty string quartets before composing the first two of the three works he published in the genre. He kept close guard over his privacy, and late in his life he asked Clara to return the letters he had written to her decades before. When he had them in hand he destroyed them.

He adored music of the seventeenth and eighteenth centuries and was committed to the rigor and discipline of classical forms in an age when the school of Liszt, Wagner, and Berlioz had abandoned them. He wrote a rugged, concentrated music that, even when it seems to be an expanse of spontaneous melody, is built of the most tightly contained units arranged in the most economical of ways, as in the first movement of the Second Symphony or the last movement of the Fourth.

In outline, those are the facts, none of which I knew as I listened, for the first time, to my new recording of the Brahms Third Symphony. I recall in particular the third movement. Never had I heard music so tender—tender in the sense that a wound is sensitive to touch. This is the common ground that Brahms exposes in his art. His life, barren of sensationalism—as most of our lives are—was full of the kinds of domestic pleasures and disappointments to which we can all respond. His own world was not particularly tragic, but as a more or less rational, well-balanced individual who earned a good living, he had a clear vision of the larger world's essential sadness and his own essential loneliness in it. His experience was filled with melancholy, and as he looked back on that experience as he worked, it colored his art. He wrote about what he knew. Perhaps Frau Schumann will clarify all this.

Brahms's biographer Karl Geiringer has said that the composer adopted an increasingly "autumnal" style after the episode with Clara Schumann—those years between 1854 and 1856, when Brahms fell in love with her and when their relationship was consolidated in their resolution to be "good friends." In *Brahms: His Life and Work* (published originally by Oxford University Press in 1947), Geiringer speculates as to why, after Schumann's death, Brahms did not pursue Clara more aggressively:

> Certainly Clara embodied in every respect Johannes' ideal of womanhood, and he knew by experience how well suited they were to each other in all the lesser and greater affairs of life. As a man, then, he could not have wished for a happier fate than to be united to her, and the differences in their ages certainly did not dismay him. If, therefore, Brahms forcibly suppressed all the alluring dreams of union with Clara, and was content to remain her true friend for life, it must have been because the artist in him dimly felt that he must not definitely bind himself.

And Richard Sennett has said that, "If the two were not lovers in the physical sense after Schumann was confined to an institution, they acted as lovers in every other. The legacy of this affair was forty years of companionship, jealousy, and guilt between Clara Schumann and Brahms. The artistic effect on Brahms was entirely unexpected." Sennett marks 1855 as the year Brahms's music "suddenly changed gears." Geiringer comes to roughly the same conclusion. In 1856, he says, "the romantic exuberance of [Brahms's] first creations gradually vanished from his compositions. In his life and in his work a new period had begun."

The theory of Clara's effect on Brahms is tempting, stimulating, and too simple. Brahms in 1856 was twenty-three, hardly an age at which an artist's style is fixed. Nor is the change in Brahms's style as sudden as either Geiringer or Sennett suggest. If you listen for them, you will hear hints of typically "Brahmsian" melancholy in the D-major Serenade of 1857–1858 and the A-major Serenade of 1857–1860. But the Piano Concerto No. 1 of 1859 is a work that bears few of the characteristics we associate with the mature Brahms. And even the Piano Quintet, written as late as 1864, exudes more *Sturm und Drang* than regret. The Horn Trio of 1865 is a different story. Here we find what we have come to expect: haze hanging over a field on an October morning, the smell of burning leaves. Brahms was thirty-two when he wrote that music. He had been through Schumann's death, through the attraction-repulsion to Clara, through another similar episode with a beautiful young girl, Agathe von Siebold, for whom he even agreed to wear an engagement ring before breaking off the affair with the explanation that, as an artist, he needed his freedom. And then, in 1865, Brahms's mother died. He had loved her deeply. Of course it is possible to hypothesize that, with her death, he felt himself more a man in his own right than a son, and that as a result his music grew more assured, controlled, expressive—what followed almost immediately was the Requiem, and what followed that were the symphonies, concertos, string quartets, and finally the chamber works for clarinet and that music which sounds very often as though it had been written to accompany the transition to the other side, the last piano pieces. Yet to say that all this began in 1865, with his mother's death, is as dangerous as saying that 1856 marked the beginning of a profound change of style. Perhaps we need markers such as these to explain the obvious, for what we are really talking about is the simple fact that Brahms was maturing. The markers we point out are those of progressive steps. And at each progressive step, he had seen more of life. As reflective and perceptive an artist as he was, he was prepared to incorporate more of that experience in his work.

Certainly, Brahms can lead us to triumphs—the First and Second symphonies are familiar examples of this—but heartbreak and longing are never far away, and even in the Second Symphony, the melody that the orchestra embraces at the very end is a heroic transformation of one of the most poignant passages he ever wrote—which we first encountered, in the guise of the movement's second subject, as a reminder that all exaltation has a darker side. To call the first appearance of the theme a *memento mori* would be an overstatement; but its existence is one way in which Brahms tries to give us the complete picture, reminds us of the seriousness and clarity of vision we need to cultivate for any active encounter with the world. It is one of the things that makes him so great an artist.

In his biography of Brahms, Jan Swafford describes two remarkable scenes reported by the composer's friend (and first biographer) Max Kalbeck. They are remarkable because they offer glimpses of Brahms in private, behind the façade of the reserve he assumed in public. (The only other time he dropped the reserve was in his work.) Kalbeck presents these vignettes as images of

Brahms possessed by the demon of artistic creation, but, as Swafford suggests, they are more than that. I think they confirm what we sense in Brahms's music—that it speaks of the almost unbearable paradoxes and poignancies of life, the unfolding and receding in time of our experience, the simultaneous becoming and dying, so like music itself. Consider Kalbeck's observations. Neither is dated, but both were made at Bad Ischl—the Baden-Baden of Austria, as Kalbeck says, where Brahms spent nine summers between 1880 and 1896. Swafford has suggested that they might be from 1892 and have occurred in connection with the piano pieces of Opus 116 and Opus 117. Though we do not know where these scenes fall in the Brahms chronology, my thoughts are stimulated by Swafford's conjecture. I like to imagine that these moments are from 1893, the summer of the Opus 118 and Opus 119 Piano Pieces—miniatures that range in character from ghostly to heroic, and which say everything on the subject of Brahms's power to render a sense of the world's ungraspable beauty into sound. Perhaps it was the music of op. 118, no. 6—the Intermezzo in E-flat minor—that drove Brahms to the outbursts Kalbeck witnessed. (Kalbeck, incidentally, has taken his hits for occasional misreporting, but it is difficult to imagine him inventing material; and even if he did, these views of Brahms go to the essence.) Here is Exhibit A:

An early riser and nature lover just as he was, I went out for an early walk on a warm July morning. Suddenly I saw emerging from the woods and running across the meadow towards me a man whom I took to be a farmer. I feared I had trespassed and, even as I was anticipating all sorts of unpleasantness, recognized the supposed farmer as my friend Brahms. But in what circumstances he found himself, and how he looked! Bare-headed and in shirtsleeves, without vest and collar, he swung his hat in one hand and with the other dragged his stripped-off jacket after him in the grass; he was running fast, as if hunted by an invisible pursuer. Already from afar I heard him panting and groaning. As he neared me I saw how the sweat streamed down over his hot cheeks from the hair hanging in his face. His eyes stared straight ahead into emptiness and glowed as those of a predatory beast—he gave the impression of being possessed. Before I recovered from my shock he had shot past me, so close that we almost brushed against each other; I grasped immediately that it would have been awkward to call after him: He smoldered with the fire of creation. Never will I forget the alarming impression of elemental power that the glimpse of this sight left on me.

Exhibit B: On another day Kalbeck visited Brahms and heard him at work, trying out passages at the piano.

On a visit to the Salzburgerstrasse just before noon, I had climbed the outer steps in the garden and was about to enter through the wide-open door, when I saw that the door to the music room also stood open. I heard magical piano playing that bound me to the threshold. It sounded as though he were improvising, but I realized, as I heard the changes in certain frequently repeated passages, that Brahms was improving and honing a new composition that he had already worked out in his head. He repeated the piece several times part by part, then finally played it through without a break. The pleasure would have been complete and would have been even greater than the interest in the evolution of his work, had the solo not been transformed into a strange duo. The richer the shape of the work became, and the more passionate the performance grew, there rose up in increasing intensity a disconcerting growling, whimpering, and groaning, which, as the music peaked, degenerated into a loud howl. Had Brahms, acting completely against his nature, gotten himself a dog? That he would have tolerated the cursed animal in the room struck me as incomprehensible. After about half an hour the playing stopped, and with it the howling; the piano bench was pushed back; and I stepped into the room. No trace of a dog. Brahms seemed a little embarrassed and wiped the back of his hand over his eyes like a child who is ashamed—he must have been crying heavily, for the bright drops were still hanging in his beard, and his voice sounded soft and halting. I pretended I had just arrived and noticed nothing. Soon he was in good spirits again and ready to joke.

How can one composer's music suggest so much beyond itself? What is it about the sound of a composer's music—the sound that becomes his trademark, unfolding blossom-like from a combination of intervals, chords, and harmonies—that gives it its power to make us see? Brahms forces me to pose these questions that I cannot answer. Perhaps it is the sheer beauty of Brahms's sound that is so gripping—the beauty that conjures an ideal world, as lost and beyond our reach as Eden. For those lucky enough to have experienced some of life's satisfactions, such things as love and friendship and all that goes with them, the past holds rich memories, and to such memories and the intimacies and collisions that created them the amber glow of Brahms's music is consecration. In that sound, images are captured and suspended. Clara waits at the table, looking out across a Rhine that has started to catch the sunlight just now breaking through gray clouds. Joseph Joachim tunes his violin and glances at the freshly scribbled page that Johannes has given him. My mother puts an arm around a boy—he can be no older than three—and points across the meadow's tall grass toward the brook where, as a child, she hunted frogs with her brothers. As I draw back from these thoughts and this last scene, my eyes suddenly meet those of that small visitor from an earlier time. I am ambushed by the past—the past of others, and my own.

As surely as it takes me back forty years to an evening at the farther edge of my adolescence, Brahms's music is the music of memory. That is not an aesthetic statement. Of course all music depends to some extent on memory to make its effect, on our ability to assimilate the horizontal events of the music as they occur in time—the magnificence of the chorale theme played by the full orchestra at the end of the Brahms First Symphony is the more magnificent for our recollection of having heard it ten minutes earlier, played quietly by the trombones, in a different context. But in all that, Brahms is not unique. What makes him special, at least for an artist of his era, is his willingness to look back and say that, after all, we cannot always have things as we wish them. His music of the late 1890s has more in common with the terrible things to come in the next century than with the manic optimism of *fin de siècle* Europe. What would his art have become had he lived long enough, into his eighties, to see the Great War, the ultimate severing of present and future from past, the pain of a world remembering what has been, reenacting on a cosmic level our own personal regrets over an irretrievable past?

Somehow Brahms understood how music could render the sense of the past. The sound he creates is a sound always of parting, of that strange sense of suddenly realizing that the experience of the moment will never come again, let alone the experience of a year ago, or two years, or forty. It is the sound, for lack of a better word, of mortality. It is a sound that brings us back to ourselves.

—L.R.

Schoenberg, Brahms, and The Great Tradition

I n February 1931, Arnold Schoenberg, then fifty-six, wrote two essays on "National Music." Neither was published until 1950, the year before his death, when they were included in his book *Style and Idea*. Both are characteristically contentious and characteristically interesting. The second is also important as a piece of intellectual and artistic autobiography and self-evaluation because in it, neither for the first nor for the last time, Schoenberg seeks to establish his place in The Great Tradition of German Music—and nothing less than capitals will do.

"Nobody," he writes in a passage in the second essay uncomfortably reminiscent of Hans Sachs's harangue about *"die heil'ge deutsche Kunst"*—holy German art—at the end of *Die Meistersinger von Nürnberg*, "nobody has yet appreciated that my music, produced on German soil, without foreign influences, is a living example of an art able most effectively to oppose Latin and Slav hopes of hegemony and derived through and through from the traditions of German music." This, by the way, is a recurrent preoccupation of Schoenberg's: in the early 1920s, when he had formulated but not yet published his twelve-note method of composition, he let out the first hint by telling some of his students that he had made a discovery that would assure the dominance of German music for another hundred years.

Toward the end of that essay and in its most interesting part, Schoenberg goes on to support his claim for the Germanness of his work by stating proudly that his teachers "were primarily Bach and Mozart, and secondarily Beethoven, Brahms, and Wagner. . . . I also learned much from Schubert and Mahler as well as from Strauss and Reger." Aside from a few technical points picked up from his friend and quartet-partner, the astrologer Oskar Adler, and his future brother-in-law, the composer and conductor Alexander von Zemlinsky, Schoenberg was in fact self-taught; that is to say, what he needed to know he learned from studying the scores of his nine masters—and others.

With Mahler and Strauss, Schoenberg had considerable personal contact. Strauss didn't really like what Schoenberg was composing, but he recognized a real musician in his younger colleague. It was he who gave Schoenberg a copy of Maeterlinck's *Pelléas et Mélisande,* which led to the composition of his luxuriant tone poem on that subject. Later he encouraged Schoenberg to send him the Five Pieces for Orchestra, op. 16, though he did not in the end conduct them, explaining that he "feared to offer them to the conservative Berlin public." As for Reger, who died in 1916, he had nothing good to say about Schoenberg, and Schoenberg knew Reger only through his music.

Of Schoenberg's five primary and secondary teachers, Brahms, who was born in 1833, was the youngest. He and Johann Strauss, Jr., whom Brahms liked and admired so much, were Vienna's most eminent musical citizens while Schoenberg was growing up there. Schoenberg shared Brahms's delight in Strauss and made loving and delicious chamber arrangements of the *Emperor Waltzes* and *Roses from the South.* When Brahms died in 1897, Schoenberg was twenty-two and had been composing seriously for about five years. Beyond being aware of Brahms as a grand presence about town, he had shaken the great man's hand at the *Tonkünstlerverein,* the Society of Composers, which he had joined and at whose functions Brahms put in an occasional appearance. The Fourth Symphony, the Double Concerto, the D-minor Violin Sonata, the two Clarinet Sonatas, the Clarinet Quintet, the last piano pieces, the Four Serious Songs, the Chorale-Preludes for organ, all these the aspiring, intensely experiencing young man—who was even shorter than Brahms himself—had met as brand-new music. To the extent he could afford it, he went to hear them in concert, and as soon as they were advertised he hurried to Doblinger's to buy the scores in their handsome covers from Simrock in Berlin.

Characteristically mixing *Dichtung* and *Wahrheit,* invention and truth, Schoenberg recounted how his family subscribed to a multi-volume encyclopedia; as it was coming out in installments, he waited impatiently for the project to arrive at the letter S so that he could learn how to compose a sonata. But of course while that encyclopedia was slowly snaking its way through the alphabet, the growing boy with the big nose and the piercing eyes was not just twiddling his thumbs while waiting for P, Q, and R to go by. He learned to get around on the violin and viola, and eventually the cello as well. He began to compose marches and polkas and waltzes and ländler of the kind that inundated Vienna from every bandstand, café, and restaurant. Then, as his growing skill as a string player allowed him to play chamber music with friends, giving him direct access to a whole new world from the venerated Haydn to the modern and controversial Brahms, he had more and richer models to emulate.

The earliest piece by Schoenberg you are likely to encounter is the unnumbered String Quartet in D major that he wrote in 1897. In that charming work you can hear just how much of a Brahmsian the young Schoenberg was. You can also sense the always delightful presence of Dvořák—second-generation Brahms, so to speak. At that time musicians were either Brahmsians or Wagnerians, the gulf being wide and the differences bitter. (Brahms himself could not be bothered with this silly war.) That D-major Quartet was Schoenberg's last unambiguous statement of allegiance to Brahms. Two years later, in 1899, he composed *Verklärte Nacht (Transfigured Night)*, his first famous work and his first masterpiece. There we have entered another world. Schoenberg has tasted of the fruit of the Tree of Knowledge. Wagner has become part of his cosmos, and so has Richard Strauss, who had already written all of his tone poems except the *Symphonia Domestica* and *An Alpine Symphony*. By this time, moreover, the notion that one had to pledge fealty either to Wagner or Brahms, forever renouncing the other, had become absurd, and Schoenberg was one of the first composers to draw happily from both sources.

As he wrote in *National Music:* "I shut myself off from no one, and so I could say of myself: my originality comes from this: I immediately imitated everything I saw that was good, even when I had not seen it first in someone else's work. And I may say: often enough I saw it first in myself. For if I saw something I did not leave it at that. I acquired it in order to possess it. I worked on it and extended it, and it led me to something new."

Schoenberg's *National Music* pedigree is specific about his debts to Bach, Mozart, Beethoven, Wagner, and Brahms. Here is what he tells us he learned from Brahms: "Much of what I had unconsciously absorbed from Mozart, particularly odd barring, and extension and abbreviation of phrases." Among the other Mozartian virtues that Brahms confirmed for him are "coordination of heterogeneous characters to form a thematic unity. . . . The art of forming subsidiary ideas [and] the art of introduction and transition. . . . Plasticity in molding figures; not to be stingy, not to stint myself when clarity demands more space; to carry every figure through to the end. . . . Economy, yet richness."

All this has mostly to do with the concept of infrastructure and not with surface, with skeleton more than with skin, with idea rather than style. Schoenberg's music does not necessarily sound much like Brahms. Sometimes, to be sure, it can. The wistful slow movement of the Violin Concerto is an example, and the poetic opening of the Piano Concerto, hovering on the edge of a waltz, is a descendant of Brahms's late piano pieces. Maurizio Pollini used to play a recital program in which he juxtaposed some of those last Intermezzi with Schoenberg's Three Piano Pieces, op. 11. That must have opened many an ear to this relationship.

Pelleas und Melisande on the other hand is hardly likely to bring Brahms to mind at all except perhaps for the striding, virile, rhythmically complicated theme that represents Golaud. Wagner and Strauss are present, so is Mahler (the passage depicting Melisande's hair falling down the wall of her tower is a direct steal from the Sixth Symphony), and so is what is unmistakably the entirely new voice of the twenty-eight-year-old Arnold Schoenberg.

As the compositions of Fauré, Debussy, Schoenberg, and Sibelius show us, music for Maeterlinck's haunting play can go in many directions; I cannot, however, imagine a *Pelléas* by Brahms any more than a Brahms *Tristan*, nor for that matter a *German Requiem* by Schoenberg or Wagner. Schoenberg not only had the musical vocabulary to allow him to get us to feel Pelléas's erotic fever as Mélisande's hair glides over his face and hands, to sense his claustrophobic terror when he accompanies Golaud into the subterranean vaults, to see the scene darken when the servants, summoned by some sixth sense, enter the bedroom when Mélisande dies. He had the desire, the need to translate such moments into music. It was one of the places where he lived. Schoenberg's expressive range is not narrow, but he is most himself, and musically most brilliant, in a world of the possessed, a world in which utterance is rarely less than recklessly intense, a world of apprehension, angst, mystery, and pain, one where the border between dream and reality is blurred and where dream is more real than reality.

That is not the world of Johannes Brahms. Most of the time Brahms and Schoenberg, by virtue of their vast difference of temperament, are worlds apart in expressive intent, worlds apart therefore in the sound surface of their music. The physical sound of music and its expressive content, those are the things that reach us first. They are the only components really meant to reach us. The rest—*how* music is made—is of endless interest, but that is shoptalk, something for professionals.

On the question of what matters most, Brahms and Schoenberg would have found common ground. In a letter to the violinist and quartet-leader Rudolf Kolisch, Schoenberg stressed in passionate prose that for him the essential thing was to help people to see what an object *is*, not how it is *made*. "My works," he went on, "are twelve-note *compositions*, not *twelve-note* compositions." As for Brahms, whose fascination with and knowledge of technique was second to no one's, he was so concerned not to have anyone peek into his workshop, as he put it, that more than any other great composer he took pains to destroy his drafts, sketches, unfinished projects, and all works that did not meet his dauntingly lofty standards of professionalism.

Schoenberg said that he had learned from Beethoven "the art of being shamelessly long or heartlessly brief." Along with Bach it was Brahms who gave Schoenberg his most penetrating lessons in coherence, and in that sense he is a presence in everything valuable by Schoenberg, from the smallest (but never wispy) piano pieces of Opus 19 to the "shamelessly long" *Pelleas*. While neither Brahms nor Schoenberg wanted his listeners to dig for the sources of what Sibelius called "the profound logic" of music, both wanted their listeners to feel its power. Both knew that compositions are good when the *what* and the *how*, the idea and the style, are one. Both paid their listeners the compliment of assuming intelligence, alertness, an engaged memory, an open heart and mind, and thus of giving them lots to do.

In his later years, after he left his and Brahms's Vienna for good, Schoenberg twice more publicly engaged with Brahms. One of these engagements was truly public, namely his virtuosic orchestration of Brahms's G-minor Piano Quartet, op. 25. This is like the unexpected gift of a fifth Brahms symphony, and it has given delight to thousands of listeners as well as to most orchestral musicians. (A few string players are inclined to be sniffy about it.) The orchestration is analytical as well as exuberant, just as Schoenberg's Johann Strauss arrangements are at once scrutinous and affectionate. Brahms would have understood and liked that.

The other engagement was more specialized—an essay first worked out as a lecture for the Brahms centenary in 1933, then fully elaborated in 1947 and titled *Brahms the Progressive*. Even at that late date this was flying in the face of long-received opinion according to which "progressive" meant Liszt and Wagner while Brahms stood for "classical" and "conservative." The essay, also first published in 1950 in *Style and Idea*, is a brilliant demonstration that Brahms was more inventive in rhythm and bolder in the transformation of ideas than Wagner. To that extent Schoenberg saw Brahms as pointing toward himself and therefore regarded him as extraordinarily progressive. *Brahms the Progressive* is a statement that changed the course of Brahms criticism, and like almost everything that flowed from Schoenberg's pen it is an intensely passionate document—a declaration of love from son to father.

I should at last say the obvious, which is that Brahms too would have listed Bach, Mozart, Schubert, and Beethoven as his masters. I cannot imagine that he would have liked Schoenberg's music; he had enough trouble with Mahler's. I am sure, though, that he would have seen that Schoenberg's music was good, however alien its expressive intentions and its language, and that the composer of the Haydn Variations, the Fourth Symphony, and the Opus 119 Intermezzi would not have thought himself too superior or too grand to acknowledge Arnold Schoenberg as his pupil.

—M.S.

First-Rate Second-Class Composer

More than most music lovers, I suppose, I'm inclined to think of Johannes Brahms and Richard Strauss in the same breath. This is probably because, just as my father was born roughly three months before the death of Brahms, in 1897, I was born three months before the death of Strauss, in 1949. That is nothing more than obscure coincidence, but it makes a convenient place to begin talking about Strauss.

For Brahms and Strauss are names that belong together at the beginning. Strauss had started his career devoted to Brahms, but by the time he was twenty-one he had rejected the aesthetic principles to which that paterfamilias of all serious artists subscribed. Those principles also happened to be the intellectual coordinates that Strauss's father, Franz, first horn of the Munich Court Orchestra, used to plot out his life. Conventional wisdom, patterns of archetypal behavior, and hormones have pretty much determined that fathers and sons will come to a point where everything, possibly even the daily rising of the sun, is a potential source of disagreement. My own father and I, following the lead not just of Strauss senior and junior, but of Adam and Cain, could find no way around this tragicomic axiom of existence, so we embraced it.

Upset at what he believed was my lowbrow taste in music—Elvis, the Top Forty, the original soundtrack albums of *Exodus* and *How the West Was Won*, and stuff that makes even me wonder today, like *The Music Man*—upset by all this, my father "encouraged" me in the direction of Beethoven and Mozart. To him these were just a little more than names. Yet in steering me their way, he had no idea of what he was starting. My teenage hormones were ready to respond to Beethoven, and in Beethoven I discovered a new musical obsession. Soon my father was asking rhetorical questions: "Don't you find those symphonies a little long?" and "How can you sit through a whole concerto?"

But if my father thought the Beethoven Seventh was a lengthy excursion, he was hardly prepared when I loaded the phonograph with *Der Rosenkavalier*, four LPs' worth of an opera whose span crosses at least four time zones. By turns he derided and patronized the music. He was especially amused by the scene immediately preceding the presentation of the rose. The duenna Marianne is at the window, watching the crowds surround the carriage of Octavian, the emissary come to deliver Baron Ochs's token of betrothal—the Silver Rose—to Marianne's charge, the seventeen-year-old Sophie. Marianne can barely contain herself as she reports on the scene in the street. At its climax she sings "*Sie reissen den Schlag auf! Er steigt aus!*" (They fling open the doors of the carriage! He gets out!) Those three words—"*Er steigt aus!*"—are set to the three rising tones of Octavian's theme, a virile, passionate fanfare, resplendently scored. It's a great moment. My father thought it was silly. "*Er steigt aus!*" he would say, with a sarcastic chuckle, as though a phrase so mundane were unworthy of a place in an opera, and certainly unworthy of such music— which, tied as it was to an admittedly routine line, I suspect he considered a little pompous (what he did not know was that, a few times, Strauss was as excited as some of his characters, and unwittingly set Hugo von Hofmansthal's stage directions to music). My father was in his early seventies then—too old, he would have told you, to acquire an appreciation of a composer who had not figured among the operatic demigods he had discovered in his youth—Flotow, Donizetti, Meyerbeer, early Wagner—when, as a baker's apprentice, he would patiently save his *pfennigs* for standing-room tickets at the opera house in Braunschweig, a small dark city in Northern Germany.

By now you may realize that my father was a music lover—not a sophisticated one; but lovers, like doctors, composers, and bakers, come in all varieties of competence. He never did learn to appreciate Strauss, despite my efforts to bring him over, and almost to his dying day he would repeat that phrase, "*Er steigt aus!*" with a laugh whenever I mentioned Richard Strauss or his music. (To his credit, he did not do that when a soprano friend of my wife's sang Strauss's song "*Morgen*" at our wedding.) He may not have realized it, but he was on to something in his criticism of one of my favorite composers.

Almost from the beginning, Strauss was attacked for the not always peaceful co-existence in his music of the sublime and the ridiculous. Barbara Tuchman, in *The Proud Tower*, her 1966 history of pre–World War I Europe, quotes the American critic Lawrence Gilman, who in 1914 attempted to sum up the composer's career thus far, when Strauss had already written not just

Rosenkavalier but, before that, his groundbreaking operas *Salome* and *Elektra*, and the tone poems for which he is still most admired. While Gilman found Strauss's best work sublime, he faulted the composer's capacity for mind-boggling bad taste and a tendency to be aggressively "commonplace."

Other writers have not been as kind as Gilman. Tuchman is one of them. She takes special pleasure in stories that cut the composer down to size, especially stories about the Strauss domestic scene, dominated by Frau Strauss—the soprano Pauline *née* de Ahna, famously bitchy but in Tuchman's account reduced to a character Madeleine Kahn might have portrayed opposite Gene Wilder's Strauss in a Mel Brooks comedy. The Strauss household as depicted in *The Proud Tower* shelters a composer who worked in response to a nagging shrew's harangues, not to a muse's inspiration. He is more clerk than artist, a nine-to-five drudge with a tidy desk and meticulously kept files. All this manifests a common attitude about Strauss. Yes, of course his music sounds glorious, but is it really art? Shouldn't art be born out of sweat rather than a desire to put food on your family's table? Tuchman goes so far as to chide Strauss for his comfortably bourgeois appearance, which is Brooks Brothers smug in comparison to the scowling, tortured Beethoven with his gravy-stained shirts or the sensitive, greasy-locked Schumann. After all, hasn't every artist you've ever known had a horrible concept of personal hygiene, and aren't deafness or insanity prerequisites to the composition of great music? *"Er steigt aus!"* Strauss was no less tidy on the podium. He conducted with the most economical and understated gestures, which seemed always to result in impassioned responses from the orchestra. He maintained that the audience should have the damp palms, not the person holding the baton.

When Strauss's critics ask how a guy like this can be taken seriously as an artist, they may be voicing some fascination at a seeming perversity, one best summarized by George R. Marek in the introduction to his 1967 *Richard Strauss: The Life of a Non-Hero* (published by Simon and Schuster). "How," Marek asks, shall we "reconcile the punctilious businessman—and Strauss was a good businessman—with the composer of *Don Quixote*? How are we to explain the difference between the dry dignitary, correct in dress and demeanor, and Strauss, the composer of the final scene of *Salome*? The man who saw the sun rise on Zarathustra's mountaintop—how could he be content with three-room domesticity? . . . The man who was able to organize the tour of an orchestra and was aware of the last penny of expense that such a tour entailed, and the composer of mystic, dream-drenched songs, exquisite in their musical poetry—how could they have been one and the same?"

The very fact that Stanley Kubrick appropriated the "Sunrise" from *Also sprach Zarathustra* for the opening of *2001: A Space Odyssey* was confirmation to some that Strauss's music had found its proper place, introducing a quasi-philosophical film with an overrated sense of its own importance. ("See it stoned," friends urged one another in 1968, which says as much as anything about the appeal of this movie, which will always be associated with *Zarathustra*—by the composer who once in all seriousness described himself as the Tintoretto of music.)

Strauss's reach sometimes did exceed his grasp. Often he is criticized for supplying the public with what he thought it wanted rather than forming public taste with the power of his art. He did both. His style did not develop significantly after *Rosenkavalier* and *Ariadne auf Naxos*—that is, after 1912, though in the 1945 *Metamorphosen*, a lament over the destruction of the world as he knew it, one senses the distancing devices are gone, making way for a new, more direct way of communicating. Neither *Metamorphosen*, however, nor *Rosenkavalier* nor *Ariadne* tells us much about the Strauss who was once known as a great radical. Almost by definition, he was walking dangerous ground. As the composer who discarded traditional patterns of composition and stretched the tone poem as far as even that elastic genre could go, he had committed himself to a treacherous task, to writing music that tells stories—stories of Don Juan, of Till Eulenspiegel, of a hero's life, of a man's death and the subsequent transfiguration of his soul. Brahms and his school maintained that such a thing was not possible—that music is an abstract art with no meaning beyond itself. Writing out scenarios to guide his listeners through the tales his scores attempted to depict (though the more he resorted to external programs to sharpen his music's focus, the more he diffused its effects), and resorting to ever more "realistic" means of portraying his subjects, until he found himself writing for a wind machine in one of his last tone poems, *An Alpine Symphony*, Strauss saw that the logical continuation of his life's work was not in orchestral music but in what he had started back in 1894 with *Guntram*. Opera was where his future lay. In committing to that direction, he acknowledged that there are limits to the stories music can tell without relying on the human voice for help.

Strauss always ran the risk, as do all public figures, of being misunderstood, and the professional jealousies provoked by his enormous success may have doomed his contemporaries' efforts to figure out this irritating man whose personal and artistic personas were so at odds. At the turn of the twentieth century, he may have been the most famous living composer in the world; certainly he was the most talked-about and probably the most highly paid. As this acclaim had come rather easily, the question was whether the Tintoretto of music had a proper respect for his gift. "The puzzle of Strauss," wrote the conductor Fritz Busch, "who in spite of his marvelous talents is not really penetrated and possessed by them like other great artists, but in fact simply wears them like a suit of clothes which can be taken off at will—this puzzle neither I nor anybody else has yet succeeded in solving: his decided inclination towards material things; and with his complete disinclination to any sacrifice, the sworn enemy of social change." "*Er steigt aus!*"

A more sympathetic Strauss biographer, Michael Kennedy (in his 1976 biography of the composer in Dent's Master Musicians series), gives us a more balanced insight into the composer's legendary preoccupation with money. Strauss, he says, "saw no reason why a composer should not be well remunerated for his work and persistently championed his colleagues' rights in this respect as well as his own." Beginning in 1898, he waged a successful seven-year campaign to reform German copyright laws.

He was generous with the influence he wielded, and he became the champion of Elgar, Sibelius, Mahler, and other contemporaries. Much has been made of his ties to the Nazis before and during the Second World War, but his presidency of the Reichsmusikkammer had been conferred upon him by Goebbels in 1933 without his knowledge. As for his being "the sworn enemy of social change," Strauss simply wanted nothing to do with politics. Yet if he was apolitical, he arrived at a firsthand understanding of Nazi tyranny. Stefan Zweig, his librettist for the opera *Die schweigsame Frau*, was Jewish, and when the work was scheduled for its first performance, in Dresden, Strauss learned that Zweig's name had been omitted from the posters. He demanded that it be restored. It was. But, as Kennedy tells us, "Hitler and Goebbels, who had promised to attend the premiere, stayed away, and after four performances the opera was banned throughout Germany. At the same time Strauss was ordered to resign his presidency of the Reichsmusikkammer on the grounds of ill-health. Strauss then wrote an obsequious letter to Hitler, but he was now desperate to protect not himself but his daughter-in-law Alice, who was Jewish, and her children."

The image of Strauss the Nazi sympathizer continues in popular mythology, and even so fine a writer as Roger Kahn, in his 1993 baseball history *The Era*, refers to "Richard Strauss, who was still alive [in 1947] and busy explaining why he had not been—to put this charitably—more passionately anti-Nazi." True, a disturbing photo from those years shows Strauss enthusiastically shaking hands with Dr. Goebbels, who displays his swastika armband prominently for the camera. But is it really so remarkable that an eighty-year-old man might conclude that protecting his grandchildren was more important than taking on the Führer? Someone else in Strauss's position might have acted differently, and the entire question of his moral responsibilities during this time is complex. He was not the hero we might wish him to be, but others in other times have also fallen short on heroics. Whether the politically naïve Strauss comprehended what the Nazis really were is anyone's guess. A nation is slow to acknowledge any sense of its own culpability. The more outrageous the transgressions of political leadership, the less ready are the governed to call their leaders to account, for just as we are inclined to deny that a friend or family member might be guilty of theft or murder, we refuse to believe that great incompetence and wrongdoing can exist at such high levels of the state. Wouldn't someone have exposed such criminal leadership by now? Since no one has, all must be in order. The Germans discovered that such thinking can lead to disaster. While it would do every nation well to heed Germany's example, perhaps Strauss was just like so many of us, waiting for someone else to set things right. In any case, to have been more publicly anti-Nazi would have been dangerous to those Strauss loved. It would also have been out of character. All we can say for certain on this subject is that Richard Strauss himself was no Nazi.

Facts and sympathies aside, the basic dilemma about Strauss remains. "How reconcile the punctilious businessman . . . with the composer of *Don Quixote?*" And why, at this point, do some writers still feel it necessary to belittle Strauss while others feel an equal need to come to his defense? Strauss himself was pretty secure in his reputation. "I may not be a first-class composer," he once said, "but I *am* a first-rate second-class composer." Part of the reason for our discomfort with him comes back to that phrase my father took such pleasure in throwing at me whenever I mentioned Strauss. "*Er steigt aus!*" That phrase, and the music to which it is set, sums up Richard Strauss, who brought the commonplace and the wondrous together in the most surprising—though not always the most appropriate—ways. Today, it is difficult to grasp just why Strauss was considered so ultramodern at the outset of the twentieth century. He left no artistic heirs, and it seems to us now that his music represents not the beginning of a new era but the culmination and conclusion of an old one. The era from which it emerged ended abruptly with World War I. The opulent textures of his music belong more to the nineteenth century than to any other, yet that opulence was always a part of his work, right up to his death. It is that opulence in Strauss that we treasure, although some listeners will equate it with vulgarity, and sometimes they will be right. The big gestures and encompassing sounds of his music represent a *Weltanschauung* whose validity was called into question by the Great War, and in the past few years I have wondered whether my father's resistance to Strauss's beauties was solidified by his memories of trenches in the Ardennes, for his youth was conditioned by that, too, not only by what went on in the opera house in Braunschweig.

Yet today, as cities burn and the innocent die in the crossfire, Strauss's music seems more and more necessary and utterly valid. Beethoven and Bach help us envision a perfect world in ethical terms. Strauss's music is not about ethics and morality. It is not even about heroes, prophets, pranksters, or death and transfiguration. It is about beauty itself, first-rate beauty: pleasure, which is its own reward.

—L.R.

Sibelius and Mahler:
What More Could There Be?

Musicology doesn't often lend itself to the "what if" questions that haunt history and our personal chronicles. It's compelling to imagine what the world would look like today if JFK had canceled his trip to Dallas, and we all have our own stories of roads taken or avoided, for better or worse. Music's intrigues are confined to the music, but not always. So here is a question that can have as much or as little to do with music as you choose to make of it: When is a composer's work complete? Take, for example, Gustav Mahler and Jean Sibelius. What if Sibelius, who lived until 1957—his ninety-first year—had continued to compose after the late 1920s? What if Mahler, who died just before he turned fifty-one, in 1911, had lived as long as Sibelius and had continued working with his customary energy? What would twentieth-century music have become? How different would our concerts sound?

They were contemporaries. Mahler, born in 1860, was only five years Sibelius's senior. Mahler completed his First Symphony in 1888 and his last in 1910—nine symphonies in twenty-two years. Sibelius completed his First Symphony in 1899 and his last in 1924—seven symphonies in twenty-five years. You could do the math and calculate that if each of them had continued working at approximately the same pace—had Mahler been given the time and Sibelius the inclination—they might have left us another twenty-odd symphonies between them.

Such speculation might be more suited to the late hours of a cocktail party. For in an eerie way, the body of work each composer left us seems complete, as though nothing more was left to be said. It is difficult to imagine Sibelius going beyond the Seventh Symphony and *Tapiola*, difficult to imagine Mahler going beyond the Ninth Symphony or what we know of his Tenth, which he did not live to complete. And if this seems a tautology—if it seems I'm saying that their work defines these composers because their work is all we know of them— think of others about whom we can't say the same: Mozart, for instance, or Schubert, or Schumann, who were all reaching stride but who don't seem to have tapped their reservoirs fully. Ask yourself: What more could we have expected from Sibelius and Mahler?

Perhaps this is just a failure of my imagination, or perhaps they were such powerful individualists that only they could suggest anything beyond what they had already done. Conceiving of what they might still have written is difficult because each evokes a sound world uniquely his. Early Sibelius is unmistakably Sibelius, for all the influence of Tchaikovsky, and as different as the expansive Second Symphony of 1902 sounds from the concentrated, densely packed Seventh of 1924. And Mahler, even in his Symphony No. 1, appears to have sprung from nowhere with that strange and wonderful concoction of folk song and epic, ditty and declamation, that is a hallmark of his style. Yet even though these two were completely their own men, working in an era that saw composers searching for a language that would take them out of the nineteenth century into the twentieth—beyond Liszt and Brahms and Wagner—they shared a common passion: to capture in their music a sense of what it means to be alive. How they pursued this tells us a lot about music, and about why we listen.

In late October 1907, Mahler was in Helsinki for a guest-conducting engagement. Based in Vienna, he was one of Europe's most prominent conductors—he was known in those days as a conductor who also composed, though he already had six symphonies and an as-yet-unperformed seventh symphony to his credit. Sibelius was a composer who also conducted, and he was hoping to carry his music beyond his native Finland. Although only five years separated them, Mahler was a colleague far more senior than that age span suggests, someone whose work on the podium and off had already won him international stature. In the course of Mahler's Helsinki trip, the two sought each other out and engaged in a now-legendary dialogue. Sibelius's biographer Erik Tawaststjerna offers the composer's recollections of his talks with Mahler (in Volume II of *Sibelius*, translated by Robert Layton and published by the University of California Press in 1986; this is the source of all the quotations pertaining to Sibelius in this article). Writing twenty-five years later, Sibelius remembered "a number of walks together, where we discussed all of music's problems in deadly earnest. When our conversation touched on the symphony, I said that I admired its style and severity of form, and the profound logic that created an inner connection between all the motives. This was my experience in the course of my creative work. Mahler's opinion was just the opposite. 'No!' he said, 'The symphony must be like the world. It must be all-embracing.'"

Sibelius had been struggling toward his position. Just a month earlier, his Symphony No. 3 had premiered. In its tautness, its clean lines, and its lean textures—its "profound logic"—it departed radically from the Second Symphony, which was one of those richly colored works, painted on a broad canvas, that helped make Sibelius a national figure. For Sibelius, that status was a double-edged sword. Finland was chafing under Tsarist domination. The country needed heroes. Even a composer could assume the role, especially one who gave the people works like *Finlandia*, the Legends from the national epic the *Kalevala*, and a symphony such as the Second, inspired now and again by folk song and conjuring visions of northern forests. But Sibelius hated being described as a nationalist. He had higher aspirations, and when he outlined his symphonic aesthetic to Mahler, he was talking about a way to realize those aspirations. His new Third Symphony was an example of the Sibelian aesthetic at work. As Tawaststjerna says, the Third Symphony was a foray in an international direction, in which the composer moves from the overtly "Finnish" toward the universal. Yet the Third also showed that he "was totally out of step with the times"—times that saw orchestral music expanding in size, in works such as Richard Strauss's tone poems and Mahler's symphonies. While Sibelius saw "profound logic" as a means to his ends, Mahler, at least initially, took the opposite path.

Mahler said the symphony had to be "all-embracing," and he lived that conviction. Consider the way he operated right from the start, in his First Symphony. There he references a few melodies from his own songs, quotes "*Frère Jacques*" and scores it for an ensemble that suggests a Klezmer band, works up a lather with an Austrian country dance, and ends with a finale of continually changing character, from violence to tenderness, culminating in crashing cymbals and blasting brass as the eight horn players are directed to stand with the bells of their instruments raised, pouring out the sound. You can't fail to get the point. Some listeners still think of Mahler more as a collector of found objects, who gathered bits and pieces from life and expected them to reflect life. He never worked in that simplistic a way, yet Mahler can't often be accused of subtlety, especially not in the early symphonies. Mahler's subtlety grew over the years, grew awesome at the end, but he always remained a composer of large gestures. And from the start, his control of vast orchestral forces and vast spans of musical time integrates those gestures in a way that saves them from being histrionic. He goes to the edge of what's acceptable, always risking overstatement but never quite crossing the line that separates artistic genius from artistic blunder. That great daring continues to draw us into his music.

Unlike Sibelius, Mahler was no national hero, and he once described himself as homeless three times over, as a Bohemian among Austrians, as an Austrian among Germans, and as a Jew everywhere. But if Mahler is the outsider, it is Sibelius whose sound has served so rarely as a model to others (though a composer as recent, and as different-sounding, as John Adams has acknowledged his debt to Sibelian artistic strategies). In fact, the one composer whose sound occasionally recalls that of Sibelius is New Zealand's Douglas Lilburn, author of engaging music that has not yet made it into the world arena. Mahler's influence, on the other hand, was felt for many years into the twentieth century in the work of his closest spiritual compatriot, Dmitri Shostakovich, who learned from Mahler the tactic of fusing the quirky march with the stirring hymn, the ridiculous and the sublime, and who not only enjoys an international reputation but is a hero to Russians. Sibelius and Mahler left legacies that went in unexpected directions.

Yet if Sibelius and Mahler seem dissimilar at first, their methods tended to converge as they continued to pursue their common goal. Mahler believed that a symphony "must be like the world," while Sibelius called composition "a quest in the infinite recesses of the soul." Any attempt to identify differences that might make one the greater composer is to quibble—to relegate the eagerly encompassing Mahler to one corner of the ring and the calmly probing Sibelius to another. The point is that each of them approached his art as something that, in some sense, was *all-embracing*. Mahler works toward that end in a more obvious way than Sibelius, but Sibelius's music can also have that encompassing appeal. As Tawaststjerna points out, the Danish composer Carl Nielsen, another "nationalist" whose art goes beyond national boundaries, described the Sibelius Second Symphony in exactly those words: *all-embracing*.

What motivates an artist to embrace all, or to explore depths, and in either case to keep on working, even if your listeners don't grasp what you're about?— and both Mahler and Sibelius encountered puzzled, hostile audiences. One answer is obvious: the sense that the Muse's offer of inspiration is good for a limited time only, that if you fail to Act Now or don't Respond by Midnight, the deal might be off. How Sibelius and Mahler responded to this sense of encroaching time says something about the way they primed themselves. Sibelius, plagued by self-doubt, was always on the lookout for disasters that might cut his time short. He imagined he had hearing problems. He feared he had diabetes (a fancied ailment that led him to a doctor who remarked on his "fine physical condition and outstanding hypochondria"). He smoked too much. He drank way too much and tortured himself for his weakness. ("I am now in my prime," he wrote in 1907, "and on the threshold of big things, but the years could easily melt away with nothing to show for them, unless I am taken in hand—above all, by me. This drinking—not that I don't enjoy it—has gone too far.") At last, in 1908, he encountered the real thing. He was diagnosed with a throat tumor and underwent surgery. The growth was benign, but the thought of what could have happened was terrifying enough to keep him away from cigars and alcohol for the next seven years. It was a time during which, as Tawaststjerna says, he "redoubled his activity" in the face of an early death. It was in this period that Sibelius created one of the great symphonies of the twentieth century, or any century, his Fourth.

This bleak, probing music, says Tawaststjerna, "with its soundings of the innermost spiritual condition, is one of the most remarkable musical documents of the Freudian era." He continues:

> Sibelius portrays his inner landscape with a discretion born of discipline or, to put it another way, with the objectivity of the greatest artists. . . . Indeed, though it may be a "psychological symphony," it is far from being a purely autobiographical document, a record of his inner life, for once the symphony was in the process of gestation, it *became* his life. This interaction makes the Fourth particularly fascinating: the symphony itself and his inner life reflect each other. Here we have a tense yet ultimately harmonious balance between art and life.
>
> Much the same might be said of another work being composed at this time: the Ninth Symphony of Mahler, again written in the shadow of death.

Mahler's Ninth has often been called a "farewell" symphony, but, as Michael Steinberg has written in his commentary on the work, it is not the product of a man preparing to leave the world. Nevertheless, as Mahler grew older, he was forced to confront mortality in the most immediate terms. He was acquainted with death. Seven of his thirteen siblings died in infancy, and his favorite brother died at thirteen. None of this, however, prepared him for the death of his daughter Maria in 1907, when she was not yet five. That catastrophe was followed several days later by another, when Mahler himself was diagnosed with a heart condition that forced him to scale back the physical activities such as hiking and swimming that gave him such pleasure. The grandiose Eighth Symphony, that all-embracing hymn to the *Creator Spiritus*, had been completed in the summer that Maria died, a few months before Mahler declared his symphonic credo to Sibelius in their Helsinki talks. In *Das Lied von der Erde*, commenced shortly thereafter, a new atmosphere fills Mahler's music, more reflective, a little bewildered by life, sometimes defiant, ultimately accepting. It is an atmosphere that comes to fuller fruition in the Ninth Symphony, and that continues in the Tenth.

The Mahler Ninth, and what we know of the Tenth—the composer completed only the first movement, almost finished the third, and sketched out the rest— offer music of almost incomprehensible poignancy. These are works that moved Arnold Schoenberg to comment, rather melodramatically, on the subject of *Ninth Symphonies* in general: "It seems that the Ninth is a limit. He who wants to go beyond it must die. It seems as if something might be imparted to us in the Tenth which we ought not yet to know, for we are not yet ready."

Mahler shared a superstition about Ninth Symphonies, but he seemed to have no misgivings about completing *his* Ninth. Once again, intuiting the Muse's offer and perhaps fearing its withdrawal, he went from the Ninth straight into the Tenth. And in the Tenth he continues and adds to what he had started in the preceding work. For the Ninth concludes with an adagio, which is how the Tenth begins. (Virtually no precedent exists for such an opening. Although some Haydn symphonies do indeed begin with slowly paced movements of more than usual gravity, such as nos. 22 and 49, these are exceptions so rare as to make Mahler essentially alone in starting a symphony the way he begins his Tenth, and the Tenth's opening is of a different expressive world than anything in Haydn.) Perhaps I'm reading too much into this, but I choose to believe that Mahler's odd decision to open a symphony with a slow movement was prompted by his need to keep exploring the expressive possibilities he had created in the Ninth. Those possibilities developed from a great leap forward he made in architectural mastery and in the wisdom with which he propelled his music; they developed from what seems a new understanding of dramatic transition, in which the movement from event to event is as seamless as the movement of life, self-contained within terms more abstract than any he had ever conceived. In terms of today's New Age thinkers, we might say that Mahler gives us a sense of The Journey. As I said, almost no symphony until then had opened with an adagio, but at least two—Tchaikovsky's *Pathétique* and Mahler's own Ninth—had closed with adagios. In such a context, the Adagio of the Mahler Tenth sounds more like a concluding movement. (Mahler's sketches also show the Tenth ending in a long adagio.)

Mahler and Sibelius, like so many other artists, were driven by fear that they would not live to complete all they set out to do. Let us, though, assume for a moment that Mahler did indeed finish what he had intended to complete. It's not a question we will ever be able to answer; yet his Ninth Symphony, and the Adagio from the Tenth, have their counterparts in works with which Sibelius effectively ended his composing career, the Seventh Symphony and the tone poem *Tapiola*. These are works in which Sibelius realized his symphonic ideal. He mastered—as did Mahler, in his own way—the art of transition within a new concision of form, at the same time creating a sound world entirely abstract and self-referential even while it suggests nature's vastness and huge interior spaces. I don't mean to suggest that Sibelius is engaging in musical landscape painting. His music moves—as does Mahler's—with an inevitability and force equaled only in the world of forests, gathering thunderclouds, oceans, and upward-thrusting peaks. When he finished *Tapiola*, in 1926, Sibelius had thirty-one years left to live. Scholars have speculated on why he simply stopped composing. He was at work on an eighth symphony as late as 1943, but before the 1940s were over, he had burned his sketches for that work, along with a bundle of other music. He had said what he had to say.

They had little in common, Mahler and Sibelius, and they were different in their approaches to their art. Yet they realized every artist's goal: they attained ultimate control of their craft, using it to render a complete sense of life as though no art were involved in the rendering. The sense of life they communicate reaffirms why we continue to turn to the greatest music. For the greatest music is a world unto itself, a world that shows us the ideal, a world of honesty, a world free of pettiness. It is that place we envision in contemplation, when time pauses, when the sun drops below or rises above the horizon, igniting the clouds, and we can think of nothing but gratitude for whatever has allowed us a moment at the center of things.

So what more would Mahler and Sibelius have given us, had Mahler lived to be ninety-one, or had Sibelius continued to compose? Those are questions for the late hours of a cocktail party, to be posed and then forgotten. In the time allotted or in the time they chose to use, each of them, in different proportions, used all-embracing strategies and profound logic to search. They were searching for an ideal world, and when the search was over, they had arrived.

—L.R.

Remembering Rachmaninoff

A doorbell rings in Hollywood. Answering, the owner, five foot one, has to tilt his head back to look into the face of his unexpected and tall, tall visitor. A "six-and-a-half-foot scowl" is how Stravinsky described Rachmaninoff. But on this spring evening, Rachmaninoff is not scowling. He has come to present an immense jar of honey to his fellow-expatriate and fellow-composer. What a shame that Vera Stravinsky is not on hand with her camera to capture this moment. (And by the way, there are pictures of Rachmaninoff smiling most winningly.)

The date of this scene is 1942. If I were making a movie about Rachmaninoff or Stravinsky, I would cheat and say this was their first meeting in umpteen years, but it wasn't quite. I don't know how much time had elapsed between their last encounter in Europe and their first in California, which preceded this one by some days. In any case, as a result of the upheavals in Europe they had both landed in Hollywood, Stravinsky in 1940, Rachmaninoff two years later.

Greater Los Angeles and Hollywood in particular had become the magnet not just for expatriate actors, but for musicians, writers, and intellectuals, some of them among the most brilliant in their generation. The climate was kinder than any they had ever known, the heating bills were low, and besides, there was always the hope of work in the studios. Many of these new Californians at once split into cliques and cabals, not speaking to but ever ready to badmouth each other, feeding and watering all the aesthetic and political differences that had separated them in Europe.[1] Rachmaninoff and Stravinsky were on opposite sides of the fence that separated the modernists from the anti-modernists. Rachmaninoff regarded *The Firebird* and *Petrushka* as works of genius but had no use for Stravinsky's later compositions; Stravinsky had no interest in Rachmaninoff's music at any time.

But Rachmaninoff was not a petty or a jealous man. Thinking about Stravinsky, he saw a Russian, an honorable (if wrong-headed) musician, and above all, a father whose children, like his own, were caught in occupied France. He telephoned his biographer, Sergei Bertensson, and said: "As I know how much Igor Fyodorovich has always disliked my compositions . . . and he must know my attitude to modern music, I'm not sure whether I could invite him and his wife to my house—which I'd love to do—because I don't know how he would receive my invitation. Would you be so kind as to send out a feeler?"

Vera Stravinsky's response was positive and led to cordial dinners at both houses. One can imagine the atmosphere, the passage back and forth across the table of the stately and sonorous patronymics—Sergei Vasilyevich, Igor Fyodorovich, Natalia Alexandrovna, Vera Arturovna. At the first of these dinners, Stravinsky mentioned his fondness for honey; hence Rachmaninoff's surprise visit a few days later. Bertensson, who was also one of the dinner guests, writes that "besides comparing notes on their families in France, they had a very lively discussion of musical matters—but not a word about composition. They talked about managers, concert bureaus, agents, ASCAP, royalties."

Common ground on which they did not touch—and it is understandable why not—was what it felt like to be composers who seemed to have lost their hold on their audience. Stravinsky, then far from being the adored and prosperous media figure he became in his old age, was resented by the public and battered in the press because he had moved on from the style of his great pre-war dance scores, *The Firebird*, *Petrushka*, and *The Rite of Spring*.

As for Rachmaninoff, since the end of World War I and except for the Rhapsody on a Theme of Paganini in 1934, his compositions had been rejected by those who yearned for more of the lushness of the Piano Concerto No. 2 and the Second Symphony. When audiences coughed restlessly during his Variations on a Theme of Corelli, which he wrote in 1931, he would leave out the next variation; on one tour he was able to play the entire set just once. Of his Symphony No. 3, whose final version came out in 1938, he said that he did not need all the fingers of one hand to count its admirers, who were himself, the violinist and composer Adolf Busch, and the conductor Sir Henry Wood. Moreover, Rachmaninoff was in a double bind. As an almost exact contemporary

---

[1] There is a large and entertaining literature on this period in Hollywood. Try Otto Friedrich's *City of Nets* or Anthony Heilbut's *Exiled in Paradise,* and for a view from the inside, Salka Viertel's *The Kindness of Strangers* or Thomas Mann's *The Story of a Novel.*

of Schoenberg and a slightly older colleague of Bartók, Stravinsky, Webern, and Berg, he had come to think of himself as an absurd and useless anachronism.

Rachmaninoff's conservatism as a composer is a prime fact about him, and it is central to his reputation. The public loves him, and in recent years its love has become more embracing of at least some of his later music: the Symphonic Dances, for example, have become a repertory piece and a major hit. On the other hand, the academy and most professional criticism thinks little of Rachmaninoff. In *Me of All People,* a book of conversations with Martin Mayer, Alfred Brendel speaks of "a Bermuda triangle between Puccini, Rachmaninoff, and Lehár, in which primary, genuine, noble emotions [are] in dire danger of being sucked away." I don't recall hearing one word about him in any music course when I was a student, and I did no better in the music history classes I myself taught later. I loved to listen to his music, but it was the love that dared not speak its name, and I kept it private. A bit of unsystematic inquiry suggests that, overall, the situation in schools hasn't changed much.

Rachmaninoff is one of many composers we know too narrowly. Once, when I gave a talk on Rachmaninoff, I titled it "Beyond *Full Moon and Empty Arms*" and began by playing Frank Sinatra's 1945 recording of the song Buddy Kaye and Ted Mossman concocted from the last movement of the Piano Concerto No. 2. It is a great tune in a style Rachmaninoff had learned from Tchaikovsky, and it is the kind of generous, heart-on-sleeve music that first comes to mind when you hear Rachmaninoff's name.

Coming up with such tunes is a rare gift, but Rachmaninoff could also invent more subtle melodies that don't stick to the ear quite so immediately. One that stuns me every time begins the slow movement of the Symphony No. 2. Violins lead off with a yearning phrase. Then the clarinet unwinds a long thread of melody, a quiet musing on just a few notes. The violins continue it, turning the heat up, until they come back to the yearning phrase from the beginning. By this time, nearly four minutes have gone by, four minutes of continuous melody in which Rachmaninoff never repeats himself. How often do you find something like that?

In part it is the quiet of this passage that is so moving. Often, the Rachmaninoff we think of is the splashy last pages of his concertos or the Second Symphony. He can pull that sort of thing off to a fare-thee-well, but he also knows the beauty of restraint. You hear that in his songs. His range in that world is remarkable, and being restricted to one voice and two hands on a keyboard stimulates his invention. The piano is a fully participating partner, now leader and inciter, now unobtrusive but firm and essential lender of support, and in the most exquisite moments—and always supposing the right pianist— the magical second singing voice. The great Russian bass Fyodor Chaliapin, who gave many recitals with Rachmaninoff, said that it was never a matter of "I am singing" but always of "we are singing."

In his later years, Rachmaninoff came more and more to like lean music with sharp outlines. The Rhapsody on a Theme of Paganini has its irresistible Variation 18—"This one is for my agent," he said of that expansive tune—but most of that work is crisp and spare. It is witty, too. An especially charming touch in its opening pages, cadaverous as Paganini himself, is the image of one of the world's great pianists playing just a few notes—sixteen measures of a Rachmaninoff concerto that anyone can play!

And listen to a much earlier piece, the E-minor Prelude, op. 32, no. 4, of 1910, in which the most diverse ideas interrupt each other and are intercut in a dazzling sequence of delicious unpredictabilities and productive discontinuities. Here is music that seems to look ahead to the Stravinsky of the *Symphonies of Wind Instruments*.

What will amaze someone brought up on Rachmaninoff's concertos and symphonies, his Preludes and *Études-Tableaux*, and the songs, is the first encounter with the *All-Night Vigil*. This is more than an hour of music for *a cappella* chorus, intended for a night-long service in Russian Orthodox churches on the eve of holy days. The world of secular yearning, melancholia, and virtuosity is far away. This rapt masterpiece was Rachmaninoff's own favorite among his compositions. One of its *alleluias* finds its way into the Symphonic Dances, and he asked to be buried to the sound of its fifth hymn, "Now lettest thou thy servant depart in peace."

It is only by fortunate chance that we have these compositions at all. The premiere of the Symphony No. 1 was a disaster, the performance terrible, the reception brutal. Rachmaninoff, just about to turn twenty-four, ran from the hall and soon destroyed the score. After his death, someone in Russia found first a two-piano reduction and later the orchestral parts that he had not stayed to collect on that terrible evening in 1897. The symphony was reconstructed, and to many who now know it, it is the most powerful of his three. The catastrophe of that premiere left Rachmaninoff convinced he could not compose again, and only a course of psychotherapy and hypnosis with an exceptionally understanding doctor released him to emerge with the Piano Concerto No. 2.[2]

Rachmaninoff the composer was only one of three Rachmaninoffs. He was one of the great pianists in history and, by all accounts, hardly less remarkable as a conductor. He did a lot of conducting in his early years, opera as well as concert, and was highly regarded enough to have been asked to take over both the Boston and Cincinnati symphonies. But in fact he rarely conducted after leaving Russia for good in 1918, when, sacrificing time he would have liked to use for composing, he became virtually a full-time pianist to support his family.

---

[2] Diane Ackerman has written a touching poem about Rachmaninoff's encounter with Dr. Dahl, *Rachmaninoff's Psychiatrist* (in *Origami Bridges*, HarperCollins, 2003).

The concentration, clarity, nobility of style, and beauty of sound of the few recordings he made as a conductor, all with his favorite orchestra, the Philadelphia (the great Philadelphia of the Stokowski and early Ormandy years)—*The Isle of the Dead*, the *Vocalise*, the Symphony No. 3—make believable every superlative one reads about his work on the podium.

On the other hand, Rachmaninoff the pianist is well documented. All the recordings he made for Victor, including those of his conducting, are available, plus transfers of some piano rolls. They include his four concertos and the Paganini Rhapsody, sonatas by Beethoven, Schubert, and Grieg with his friend Fritz Kreisler, and a large sampling of solo works. Unfortunately, he was allowed to record only two of the big pieces in his solo repertory, Chopin's *Funeral March* Sonata and Schumann's *Carnaval*. The dozens of little pieces include many transcriptions by himself, his cousin and teacher Alexander Siloti, Liszt, Rubinstein, Tausig, and others. And, in Mount Rushmore–sized majesty, there is even a *Star-Spangled Banner*, with which he would have begun every recital during the war years.

Rachmaninoff the transcriber made dazzling solo piano versions of movements from Bach's E-major Partita for Unaccompanied Violin (of which Bach himself had made a singularly bold version for solo organ with full orchestra), Schubert's *Wohin?*, the Scherzo from Mendelssohn's *Midsummer Night's Dream* music, *The Flight of the Bumblebee*, and wonderfully inventive, larger-than-life ones of Kreisler's *Liebesfreud* and *Liebesleid*—all of them startling us with harmonies that were not in the vocabularies of their original composers. Yet these excursions never fail to highlight something salient and characteristic in the pieces. They have all the special charm of hybrids, but they never betray the original composition. Even when his conscious aim was only to provide himself with spectacular or charming encore pieces, Rachmaninoff always thought as a composer.

Much of what makes Rachmaninoff so extraordinary a pianist is that there, too, his perceptions and choices are those of a composer. He sometimes takes bold liberties with the text—by our standards, not by those of his day, when he was thought a rather severe interpreter. For instance, he invents a completely new distribution of louds, softs, and crescendos for Chopin's Funeral March, and it makes so much sense and is so convincing that some pianists today really wish they dared emulate him. On both recordings of Chopin's *Minute Waltz* he pulls up to a stop on the B-flats at the tops of the melodic curves. The gesture is extreme, but the B-flat *is* the top of the phrase, and so, even though he exaggerates, he is not just arbitrarily messing around, but drawing our attention to one of the "facts" of the piece.

Rachmaninoff is among those performers who always give you the sense that, preparing to sound the first note, they know exactly when and how the last is to arrive—and that the closing event is already implicit in the first. The characteristics of concentration, clarity, nobility of style, and beauty of sound that I pointed to as hallmarks of his conducting are equally present in his piano playing. He had an encompassing technique when it came to power and marksmanship. That he could play what he himself wrote attests to that. His rhythm was phenomenal. The little sequence of chords with which the piano responds to the orchestra's proposal of a new theme in the first movement of his Third Piano Concerto has, as he plays it, an incredible panther-spring. No other pianist has come close, not even Horowitz, whose performance of that concerto Rachmaninoff thought better than his own.[3]

His playing of the transcriptions I mentioned earlier is electrifying in its energy and the sharpness of its outlines. But I find myself returning most often to the performances of the quietest pieces, Liszt's transcription of Schubert's Serenade, Siloti's of the Saint-Saëns Swan (something every cellist needs to hear), and Sgambati's of the Dance of the Blessed Spirits from Gluck's Orpheus. Rachmaninoff casts a spell. The playing is amazing as a lesson in how to make a percussion instrument sing, how to make us forget that there are hammers in this machine. Chaliapin's "we are singing" comes to mind again. The melodies move from beginning to end with an uncanny tensile strength, and they are supported by accompaniments exquisitely responsive to each fluctuation in the harmony. Always expressive, he is never sentimental or affected, not in his own music, not in anyone else's. So many pianists use Rachmaninoff's concertos as showcases for vulgarity, but when he himself played them they were one more surface that reflected his own nobility of mind and spirit.

The musical world has changed so much that it is startling to realize it is not much more than sixty years since 28 March 1943, when Rachmaninoff died of a rapidly progressing melanoma. When he went, the world lost a man and musician of uncommon human and artistic integrity, sincerity, and decency. "My poor hands," he said on one of his last days. Perhaps he would no longer be surprised—just happy—that he was not swept away by history after all, and that, thanks to what those hands did, whether they held a pencil or touched keys of ivory and ebony, he is still a presence among us, vivid, exciting, and commanding our love.

—M.S.

[3] Acknowledging the brilliance of Horowitz's first two recordings of this work, particularly the first (1930, with Albert Coates and the London Symphony), I am still not convinced by Rachmaninoff's generous evaluation. Nobility was not in Horowitz's expressive vocabulary. One piece, though, where Rachmaninoff is, to my ear, bested by another pianist is his arrangement of Mendelssohn's Midsummer Night's Dream Scherzo. The champion here is Benno Moiseiwitsch, whom Rachmaninoff regarded both as an esteemed colleague and a good friend.

Erich Wolfgang Korngold: A Meditation

On a gray Vienna morning in 1954, Erich Wolfgang Korngold sits in a hotel room, trying to figure out what went wrong. He is fifty-seven—too old to be a Wunderkind, as he said when he left Warner Brothers. Twenty-five years ago a newspaper survey of Viennese music lovers named him one of the two greatest living Austrian composers, along with Arnold Schoenberg. Last night he attended the world premiere of his Symphony in F-sharp. He had worked on it for five years, and to hear its first performance here, in the city that had nurtured and adored him, should have been the crowning moment of his career. Now he is writing to the Austrian Radio network, requesting that the tape recording of the performance be suppressed—a request that will be ignored. He had expected better and had thought he had a right to. But five years ago, when he had returned to Vienna for the first time since before the war, he had been through the same thing. The Staatsoper premiere of his opera *Die Kathrin* had filled him with high hopes, but *Die Kathrin* was withdrawn after only six performances, performances as poorly attended as the rehearsals were unfriendly. "Unfriendly" was a gentleman's word, and he was a gentleman in everything but his music, which was the work of a man whose honesty would allow him to say nothing but what he believed, for better or worse. He had learned his manners, along with his art, in another era. Maybe that was part of the problem.

He knew what the other part of the problem was. It was called Hollywood. Flashback. The screening room. Erich Wolfgang Korngold sits at the piano. The reel begins to roll. Erroll Flynn and his crew of British pirates have broken the chains that held them prisoner in the hold of a Spanish galley. They take the deck. They climb the riggings. They wrest control. They strike for the shores of Dover. "Once more, please," says the composer. He has watched this *Sea Hawk* footage eight times already, and he scribbles a few more notes. Again Flynn and the sailors break their chains. Now, as they leap to the deck, the piano explodes, and when the music reaches the edge of ·frenzy, another inspiration flashes through Korngold's inner ear. He hears a male chorus pick up the melody and carry it beyond the boundary of excitement. To him, that is what movies are all about. To him, they are operas—hadn't he once told his orchestrator and his fellow film composer Hugo Friedhofer that *Tosca* was the greatest movie score ever written?

He had loved the movies, though it took Warners some doing to convince him to write for them. Maybe his detractors should know that. But he had always had detractors in one form or another. As we watch him now, we have the advantage of knowing what he cannot know. That within three years he will be dead, that his life will end in Hollywood when he is only sixty—hardly an advanced age even by 1957's standards of life expectancy for prosperous males in nonhazardous occupations, and that though the cause of death will officially be heart failure it is almost certain that heartbreak has been a contributing factor. We know that few will take special notice of his passing, and that fewer will understand how really hazardous his occupation has been. We know that German-language critics, from whom a good word would have brought special pleasure and who seem convinced that his reputation had long since started to rust, will nonetheless go the extra distance to try to corrode his memory. In an obituary published in *Musica* in February 1958, Karl Robert Brachtel will say that "it was a much-discussed question, whether his father's position opened the way for the young Erich Wolfgang or not. . . . Today one encounters Korngold's name primarily as the arranger of classic Viennese operettas . . . or as composer for various American films. . . . The bulk of Korngold's output lies qualitatively and quantitatively in his youth. His voice was hardly original—the premature heralds of his supposed importance placed him next to Richard Strauss and Pfitzner. . . . He did not stand next to them, but in their shadow." We know that for every moviegoer who had written in 1942 to ask him if his score for *Kings Row* would ever be recorded, millions more, though they had been seduced by his music into embracing the worlds of *Captain Blood, The Adventures of Robin Hood, The Sea Wolf,* and *Deception,* knew his name only as a sonorous mouthful of syllables.

The third and fourth of those syllables were significant. Erich Wolfgang, born in the spring of 1897 in the old Austro-Hungarian empire, owed his middle name to his father's love of Mozart. His father was Julius Korngold, Vienna's most revered and most feared music critic since Eduard Hanslick, whom he had succeeded at the *Neue Freie Presse*.

Like Mozart, Erich Wolfgang was a prodigy. He was also a musical dramatist from the start, improvising themes at the piano for imaginary scenes that his father described. Erich was a regular boy, said Julius, except when he was composing or playing the piano. At those times, he seemed to enter a trance. In hours presumably less trancelike he studied some counterpoint with Robert Fuchs, who had been a friend of Brahms's, and at ten he played an excerpt from his cantata *Gold* to Gustav Mahler, who called him a genius and arranged for Erich's studies with Alexander von Zemlinsky, himself a composer of gorgeous late-Romantic scores. (That Zemlinsky was also Arnold Schoenberg's teacher—and future brother-in-law—says something about the size of fin-de-siècle Vienna's music world.)

Everything came easily. In 1909 Korngold's op. 1, a piano trio dedicated to "my dear Papa," was given its world premiere by Arnold Rosé, Bruno Walter, and Friedrich Buxbaum. What are musicians such as these doing with the music of a twelve-year-old? We can be certain that dear Papa's influence never hurt, but we also know that the muse who visited Korngold during those creative trances was no pre-teen spirit. In 1910 he emerged from a trance to find himself in the middle of the Vienna music scene. His ballet-pantomime, *The Snowman*, orchestrated by Zemlinsky, had been given a command performance at the Court Opera for the Emperor Franz Joseph. The success was complete, and the work made its way throughout Austria and Germany, onto the stages of forty opera houses, where audiences talked of this young composer as though he were a young god. In 1972 the German writer Jodok Freyenfels, in the *Neue Zeitschrift für Musik*, looked back on those days and recalled talk of another kind in Vienna's coffeehouses and salons: rumor that Zemlinsky had not only orchestrated *The Snowman* but that he had composed it and been paid for this project by the father. "Thus the thirteen-year-old Erich Wolfgang, on the day of his first success, was already the victim of backbiting and envy that arose from extra-artistic motives. And this fate was to pursue him throughout his life, again and again." The world of the arts, like that of academe, seems inclined to interpret rapid success as evidence of inferior talent, to mask jealousy behind a commitment to "standards." Freyenfels has a name for this tendency as it applied to Erich Wolfgang. He calls it The Korngold Case.

The Wunderkind could not escape a less malignant form of natural resentment, either. What, after all, gives any thirteen-year-old the right to enjoy glory when those three and four times his age are sitting around in the obscurity of Vienna coffeehouses, debating the authenticity of a child's music? Certainly this child's music—full of big melodies and easy to hum or whistle— sounded as though it had been written by someone older, someone who looked back to the previous century. Contemporaries such as Berg and Schoenberg were headed in very different directions. They thought little of Korngold's work—and that, said the coffeehouses, was why Papa Julius thought little of theirs. Artists who embraced Erich Wolfgang were accused of using the son to curry favor with the father.

But though he was assailed by various contingents whose attacks sprang from envy, or skepticism, or artistic differences, Korngold throughout the teens and into the 1920s became one of Europe's most cherished composers, his music championed by such artists as Arthur Nikisch and Felix Weingartner, Carl Flesch and Artur Schnabel. In Berlin, at a performance of the Korngold Sinfonietta, Richard Strauss sat next to the seventeen-year-old composer, declaring himself "protector of his young colleague." In 1916 Bruno Walter introduced Korngold's first operas, a pair of one-act dramas called *The Ring of Polycrates* and *Violanta*. In 1920, Korngold enjoyed what would prove to be the greatest success of his life when, on 4 December, the opera *Die tote Stadt* (*The Dead City*) was given its world premiere simultaneously in Hamburg and Cologne. Within a year the work was presented on eighty different stages and made its way to the Met, the first German opera to be presented there after the Great War, with Maria Jeritza singing the female lead.

Memories. Korngold smiles as he looks out at the Vienna morning, the city coming to life. He is not consoled by the recollection of cheering audiences. In retrospect, casual encounters seem so loaded, aimed at the target of the future. There was the day he began working with director Max Reinhardt, rescripting and reorchestrating Strauss operettas. Some thought he was in it only for the money, but *Die tote Stadt* had been a tough act to follow. And while he was working on the Strauss he was writing what he thought of as his operatic masterpiece, *Das Wunder der Heliane*. *Heliane*'s music is slow-cooked and densely flavored, and there is plenty of it, maybe a little too much, for under its weight the plot's ingredients are in constant danger of separating. Though the opera contains much to please the ear, it disappointed more than it pleased when it appeared in 1927, and among the unhappy were those in the marketing department of the Austrian tobacco monopoly, who, expecting a hit, had just introduced a high-end cigarette called "Heliane."

This morning, the memory of Max Reinhardt is haunting. It was because of Reinhardt that Korngold first came to Hollywood. That was in 1934, when Reinhardt shot a film version of his Hollywood Bowl production of *A Midsummer Night's Dream* and invited his old collaborator to supervise the music. The following year Korngold was back in California, working on a now-forgotten Paramount musical, *Give Us This Night*. He remembers when Warners approached him. Would he contribute an original score for *Captain Blood*? He would not. But Korngold was a *name*, and Warners wanted his prestige. Someone—he can't recall who—persuaded him to attend a screening of the film, and that was really all it took. He found the movie absorbing, and it inspired his first great original film score. Yet home remained Vienna, and his artistic home remained the opera house and concert hall. He agreed to score other films as they were offered, if they happened to appeal to him—*Anthony Adverse* was one, and *The Prince and the Pauper*—but he continued to refuse a long-term contract. Then, in 1937, he began to grasp that his days in Europe were numbered. He was a Jew. Hitler had forbidden the staging of his latest opera, *Die Kathrin*, and Austria and Germany were drawing ever closer, two countries on the verge of becoming one. What choice had he but to move his family? The logical place to go was where work was waiting. He bought a house in Hollywood. Even Papa had a room in it. Then he settled in with Warners. On his terms.

No major composer had ever had an extended contract with a studio. Warners, so eager for Korngold's services, let him dictate conditions that no other film composer had ever enjoyed. Korngold was required to score only three pictures every two years. He could decline any project offered him. To get an idea of just how good a deal this was, consider the fact that "in his twelve years with Warners"—this is according to William Darby and Jack Du Bois in their 1990 study *American Film Music* (McFarland & Co.)—"Korngold worked on twenty films, four of which were essentially arranging assignments, and sixteen of which were largely original compositions. In that same period Max Steiner, who worked under more typical studio pressures, was the principal composer on more than one hundred films."

Most film music ends up the product of committee approval. Not Korngold's. "In none of my assignments have I ever 'played' my music first to either the [studio] music-chief, the director or the producer. And the studio heads never make the acquaintance of my music until the day of the sneak preview." That was what he said in 1940, in *Music and Dance in California*.

And what music he wrote. To him, a film script was a libretto. The main title music, accompanying the opening credits, was an overture. A love scene was a duet. Listen to some of those main title sequences, and from their strongly defined themes you will draw an immediate impression of the nature and mood of the dramas they introduce—the sweeping minor chords and broken phrases of *Of Human Bondage* herald its protagonist's debasing struggle, the crashing dissonance of *The Sea Wolf* warns us about the sadistic Captain Wolf Larsen, the noble fanfares of *Kings Row* announce a tale in which love and good are triumphant. This is music aimed for the heart, grand and tender, generous of spirit and inexhaustible in its wealth of melody—inviting, open, friendly. He had learned to write this way in Vienna, and the richness of that tradition glowed in every passage he scored. Taken as a whole, Korngold's film music is a good example of what R. S. Hoffmann, his first biographer, identified as the composer's "optimism."

Besides, films were exciting. And he was proud of what he contributed to them. "When, in the projection room, or through the operator's little window," he wrote, "I am watching the picture unroll, when I am sitting at the piano improvising or inventing themes and tunes, when I am facing the orchestra conducting my music, I have the feeling that I am giving my own and my best: symphonically dramatic music which fits the picture, its action and its psychology, and which, nevertheless, will be able to hold its own in the concert hall. . . . Never have I differentiated between my music for the films and that for the operas and concert pieces. Just as I do for the operatic stage, I try to invent for the motion picture dramatically melodious music with symphonic development and variation of the themes."

Korngold scored a movie as though it were a musical drama, assigning individual themes to characters and putting those themes through the permutations that would reflect and advance plot. You have only to listen to his score for *Kings Row* to get some idea of how his music worked. Every principal theme is introduced within the first ten minutes of the film. During the two hours that follow, the music's ebb and flow, accelerations and sudden disintegrations, will add a third dimension to the performances, and when Betty Field tries to seduce Robert Cummings, Korngold is helping them convince us that they really are Cassie Tower and Parris Mitchell.

Instead of stunting his growth as a composer, films gave him the opportunity to develop along the lines he had so clearly marked out for himself in a work such as *Die tote Stadt*, full of memorable melodies in the manner of a Viennese Puccini, taut drama, and lush orchestral sound. "It says much for Korngold's imaginative powers," says Christopher Palmer in *The Composer in Hollywood* (published by Marion Boyars in 1990), "that although he grew up steeped in the traditions of an era already moribund at the time his own musical personality was developing, the conventions he inherited often seem in his hands not the empty mockery of a decaying impulse but the noble expression of one still living. . . . The combination of a certain spiritual *naïveté* with the most fantastic flights of melodic, harmonic and orchestral imagination equipped Korngold superbly for the medium of the film score." Korngold might have been amused by that reference to his "spiritual naïveté." Yet this morning, in Vienna, it is exactly his naïveté that he is lamenting.

Was it naïveté that made him think he could have it both ways, that his music could star both in Hollywood and the concert hall? By 1946 Korngold was beginning to feel as though he had to choose between the two worlds. He felt he was at the end of the road in Hollywood. Some said that his recent scores were not up to the standards he had set himself in his earlier days. (He agreed: "When I first came here, I couldn't understand the dialogue—now I can.") Max Steiner told him he thought his own music was getting better while Korngold's was in decline. ("Maxie, my dear, you're absolutely right.

And I'll tell you why—it's because I've been stealing from you and you've been stealing from me.") When he finished work on the 1946 *Of Human Bondage*, a film he did not much like, he decided to have a look at the original, produced a decade earlier. One day on the lot he spotted Bette Davis, who had starred in the first version. He told her he enjoyed the film, but that he thought ten years had dated certain scenes, which now seemed a little ridiculous. "Of course," he added, "this new film is ten years ahead of its time. It's ridiculous already." For those who did not understand his growing disenchantment, he made it as clear as possible: "A film composer's immortality stretches all the way from the recording stage to the dubbing room."

The war was over. His father was dead. "I feel I have to make a decision now if I don't want to be a Hollywood composer for the rest of my life." It was time to reassess things—time, perhaps, to go home. He scored one more film, the 1947 *Escape Me Never*, whose main title theme is a long-breathed, soaring Viennese melody that tells us how much his native city was on his mind—and which, a year later, he used in his song "*Sonett für Wien.*" Then he called it quits. He "once again gathered his powers," says Jodok Freyenfels, "with the intention of ending his life work as meaningfully and as fruitfully as possible."

He was happy writing concert music again, and pleased that his Violin Concerto, which he had finished even before leaving Warners, was giving audiences much pleasure. By 1949 it was time to pursue the future by returning to his past. It was time to take his music back to Vienna.

Yet the Vienna he had left more than ten years before was itself a *tote Stadt*. One thing that remained from the past, however, was The Korngold Case. In 1950, *Die Kathrin* was sacrificed on its altar. Freyenfels sums up the attitude of Viennese critics: "If Korngold's opera fails, we can with good conscience reject the many pieces he has submitted for the purpose of redeeming himself artistically." He could not have it both ways.

Korngold pushed ahead—courageously or naïvely. He was determined to reenter Viennese musical life. In 1954 he arrived in Vienna like an excited child, carrying his Symphony in F-sharp with him. He did not know he was entering a personal twilight, where appearances and sometimes even friends are deceiving. Was he aware of a conversation supposed to have taken place some years before between Otto Klemperer—the same Klemperer who had led the Cologne premiere of *Die tote Stadt* in 1920—and Heinrich Kralik of Austrian Radio? Kralik asked Klemperer, who was no stranger to the United States and who had even spent time in Los Angeles as music director of the Philharmonic, what Korngold was up to in America. "He's doing well," Klemperer said. "He's composing for Warner Brothers." Kralik thought it was a shame that such a talent should be spent on film music. "Oh, well," Klemperer replied, "Erich Wolfgang has always composed for Warner Brothers. He just didn't realize it."

At its premiere, the Symphony was a disaster, victim of uninterested performers and insufficient rehearsal time. And so, says Freyenfels, "Korngold was finished off like a film composer from Hollywood."

Possibly no one who heard that first performance of the Symphony caught a poignant reference that the composer had inserted into the final movement. There, a theme from *Kings Row* suddenly appears—tender music associated with Parris Mitchell's grandmother, a frail and dignified woman who tries to maintain the values of the Old World in which she grew up. In the film, as she nears death, a friend speaks this passage while the "Grandmother" theme— the one that shows up in the Symphony—is played softly under the words: "When she passes, how much passes with her. A whole way of life—a way of gentleness, and honor, and dignity. These things are going, . . . and they may never come back to this world."

For Korngold, who found himself so out of step with a world that had moved in a different direction from the one he had taken, these words could be an epitaph. He smiles once more. There is no self-pity here. Wasn't it a calculated irony, and a calculated risk, to include a film theme in a concert work for the serious Viennese? He was honest with himself, and he was honest about himself with his audience.

Now, as he sits in his room, the price of honesty must seem steep. He knows he is out of fashion. We look ahead and see that he will become almost as good as forgotten, though there is always a small contingent that refuses to forget him, and for whom Hugo Friedhofer, who had orchestrated most of his film scores, speaks: "I know there is a tendency in some quarters to be rather derogatory about his music but I don't think that anybody with any spark of feeling can listen to Korngold and not agree that here was a man who knew exactly what he wanted to say and said it beautifully."

And we look ahead farther still—to 1972, when RCA takes a gamble and releases two Korngold albums, a collection of film music with Charles Gerhardt conducting the National Philharmonic, and the Symphony, with Rudolf Kempe and the Munich Philharmonic. Both recordings are produced by Korngold's son George, and both capture brilliant performances in sound that at last communicates the breadth and depth that never came through the speakers while *Anthony Adverse* or *The Sea Hawk* flickered on late-night TV. The public hears the real sound of Korngold, and his music begins to come back from the dead. Today, "Korngold" may not be the household name it was in the earlier years of the twentieth century, yet it is possible to hear more of his music— both the film music and the concert works and operas—than it has been since the late 1940s.

"Only what is bad gets totally discarded," Christopher Palmer says in *The Composer in Hollywood*. "What is good may go out of fashion in its more superficial aspects, but the principle, the essence, the core of quality—star quality—remains as a vital regenerative force." Korngold's music, it is clear at last, will be with us for a long time. His spirit need no longer brood in a strange room in an unfriendly city. In the larger world of music, The Korngold Case is closed.

—L.R.

Tchaikovsky's Mozart (and Others')

> The reason pictures slumber for generations is
> that there is no one to see them with the experience
> that awakes them.
>
> —Elias Canetti, *The Torch in My Ear*

D riving on Route 101 south of San Francisco, I picked up on my car
radio something by Mozart that I could not at first identify. Before
long, a couple of strange bass notes made me suspicious, and then I
realized I was making a mistake that I had made before: this was not Mozart at
all, but the Mozartian pastiche in the masquerade scene of Tchaikovsky's *The
Queen of Spades*. I thought how delighted Tchaikovsky would have been at
taking someone in at his own *ballo in maschera*, so to speak, and I tried to
imagine the joy he must have had writing this substantial patch of "eighteenth-
century music."

Artists find many kinds of joy in their work. Writing the *Pathétique*, a
consummate and original masterpiece, must have given Tchaikovsky the kind
most easily understood by the outsider. Another, more special, is that which
comes from using all one's art in an act of homage to a great and beloved
colleague, living or dead. Writing *Eugene Onegin* and *The Queen of Spades*,
Tchaikovsky felt particular emotion because it was a form of communing with
Pushkin. It was with an even more intense devotion that, in the summer of
1887, he made *Mozartiana*, delicately crafted, apt orchestrations of the
following: two of Mozart's most idiosyncratic piano pieces (the Gigue, K.574,
and the Minuet, K.355); the more centrist Variations on a Theme by Gluck, a
composer for whom Tchaikovsky "felt sympathy . . . in spite of his meager creative
gift"; and, by an interesting Romantic detour, Liszt's organ transcription of the

Ave verum corpus. (In 1893, the last year of his life, Tchaikovsky turned part of Mozart's C-minor Piano Fantasy into a vocal quartet!) But how still more delicious it must have been for him, in the *Queen of Spades* masquerade, actually to slip into Mozart's clothes!

For Tchaikovsky adored Mozart. To his patroness, Madame Nadezhda von Meck, whose taste in music—except insofar as it led her to support him generously for thirteen years—drove him to despair, he wrote in 1878: "I don't just like Mozart, I idolize him." *Don Giovanni*, he tells her, is for him "the most beautiful opera ever written" and Donna Anna "the most superb and wonderful human portrait ever achieved in music. . . . I am so much in love with the music of *Don Giovanni* that even as I write to you I could shed tears of agitation and emotion." Whenever he has heard Ferdinand Laub's quartet play the Adagio of the G-minor Quintet, he has had "to hide in the farthest corner of the room so that others might not see how deeply this music affects me. . . . I could go on to eternity holding forth upon this sunny genius, for whom I cherish a cult." He concludes: "If I could do anything to make you change your mind, that would make me very happy. If ever you tell me that you have been touched by the Adagio of the G-minor Quintet I shall rejoice."

In this letter Tchaikovsky suggests an explanation for this "exclusive love" of his. "The music of *Don Giovanni* was the first that stirred me profoundly. . . . It is thanks to Mozart that I have devoted my life to music. He gave the first jog to my musical powers; he made me love music above all things in this world." Perhaps because it sounds a little too homespun for the tone of their correspondence, he does not tell her that this came about because the Tchaikovsky family owned an orchestrion, a mechanical organ that imitated orchestral sounds and for which one acquired "records" in the form of perforated discs or pinned cylinders. This particular orchestrion had in its repertory excerpts from *Don Giovanni* as well as from operas of Rossini, Bellini, and Donizetti. Later, when he was twelve, Tchaikovsky's Aunt Ekaterina took him through all of *Don Giovanni* at the piano.

But in a letter to Madame von Meck written two weeks after his first, expansive outpouring about Mozart, Tchaikovsky suggests a more interesting reason for his love, obviously in response to her reaction: "You say that my worship of [Mozart] is quite contrary to my musical nature. But perhaps it is just because—being a child of my time—I feel broken and spiritually out of joint, that I find consolation and rest in the music of Mozart, music in which he gives expression to that joy in life that was part of his sane and wholesome temperament, not yet undermined by reflection. It seems to me that an artist's creative power is something quite apart from his sympathy with this or that great master."

To this last sentence one might add an aside: interpreters of Tchaikovsky do well to remember Tchaikovsky's love of Mozart, just as Berlioz conductors should not forget Berlioz's adoration of Gluck (which Tchaikovsky cites as an instance of "glaring inconsistency"). What music a composer knew, admired, and loved is always a good question for a performer to ask.

On later occasions, Tchaikovsky returns to this theme of innocence, for example, in July 1880, when he writes to Madame von Meck: "Mozart is a genius whose childlike innocence, gentleness of spirit, and virginal modesty are scarcely of this earth. He was devoid of self-satisfaction and boastfulness: He seems hardly to have been conscious of the greatness of his genius." And again three months later, when he has begun to study *The Magic Flute* (to him a wedding of a "senseless and idiotic" subject to "captivating music"): "You would not believe, dear friend, what wonderful feelings come over me when I surrender to [Mozart's] music. It is something altogether different from the stressful delights awakened in me by Beethoven, Schumann, or Chopin. . . . My contemporaries had the spirit of modern music instilled in them from childhood, coming to know Mozart only in later years . . . but happily, fate decreed that I should grow up in an unmusical household, so that as a child I was not fed the poisonous food of post-Beethoven music. . . . Do you know that when I play Mozart I feel brighter and younger, almost like a young man again?" He had just turned forty.

Under the spell of *Carmen*, he suggests to his brother Modest that Mendelssohn, Chopin, Schumann, and Glinka were "the last Mohicans of the Golden Age of Music" (and that Bizet, in his innocent pursuit of *le joli*, has captured some of their spirit) until it occurs to him that "in their music, too, you can see a move away from the great and beautiful to the 'tasty.'"

Tchaikovsky is offering not music criticism nor even declarations of love—not that these two categories have to be mutually exclusive—as much as nostalgia. For one thing, in common with most nineteenth-century musicians (except for the occasional antiquarian like Brahms), Tchaikovsky did not really know very much Mozart; when you track down the references in the correspondence and the diaries, you find him returning over and again to the same few works—above all *Don Giovanni*, for which he shared a passion with most Romantic artists, the *Jupiter* Symphony, *The Magic Flute* (but rejecting, as we saw earlier, the *raison d'être* for the music), and parts of the Requiem. His offbeat choices in *Mozartiana* are as surprising as they are delightful. And in spite of his enthusiastic commendation of the string quartets in a letter to Madame von Meck, he writes elsewhere that he finds the one in D minor "rather watery."

Tchaikovsky also does not draw any musical conclusions from his study of Mozart, neither in the shaping of his operas nor in the facture of his orchestral works. Haydn and Beethoven and Schubert all learned from Mozart, and so did Brahms and Strauss, Schoenberg and Stravinsky, but Tchaikovsky's adoration of him—except in special situations like *Mozartiana* and *The Queen of Spades*—found its place outside his composing life.

What fascinates Tchaikovsky is not so much Mozart's music as the idea of Mozart, the idea of naïve, spontaneous, "sunny" genius, of "childlike innocence . . . not yet undermined by reflection," of "virginal modesty," the idea of a lost Golden Age. Tchaikovsky's Mozart is a pre-Freudian child, his early death undeniably a compelling part of the whole Mozart phenomenon; Tchaikovsky's worship of this child is a game of make-believe.

The make-believe image of Mozart-the-Child persists. Mozart-the-Plaster-Cast, as we see him on the wrappers of Mozart-Kugeln, is with us yet. All this has a musical correlative in a certain approach to performance that I have heard musicians refer to as the Mozart-Never-Had-an-Erection style.

Against these things, we might, as the critic Patrick J. Smith has suggested, set such revisionist manifestos as Peter Shaffer's *Amadeus*, which has shown admirable power to enrage as well as, less usefully, to provoke blank denial: "He just *can't* have talked that way or crawled around on the floor like that." Like the German novelist and playwright Wolfgang Hildesheimer, who published a stimulating Mozart biography in 1977, Shaffer shows how the unity of man and artist is complicated: Mozart did not behave the way the Adagio of the Serenade in B-flat, K.361, sounds, an uncomfortable idea for those who would prefer a more simply arranged world in which wonderful music is written by wholly wonderful people.

Hildesheimer looks with sympathy and insight at the problem of a pampered and exploited child prodigy who needs to grow up and become a man. Particularly, he questions the reliability of Mozart's letters, especially those to his father, the most important and the most problematic person in his life, as guides to what was going on in his life and mind.

The prodigious child seemed, to those who encountered him, not just to be making magic, but to be a magical personage himself. He was more than your ordinary extraordinary kid. Once he was grown and wrapped in a physically unprepossessing package, that sense of numen was available only to those who could hear it in his music. In that respect the Viennese, when they had tired of him as a "sensation" and were ready for the next marvel, failed him. But he always provoked reactions out of the ordinary—sober Haydn saying to Leopold Mozart, "I tell you before God and as an honest man that your son is the greatest composer I know, personally or by reputation"; Beethoven saying to his pupil Ries at a rehearsal of the C-minor Concerto, "Ah, we shall never be able to do anything like that"; Rossini putting it in his own wry way, "Beethoven of course is the greatest of composers, but Mozart is the only one"; and, to step outside the fraternity for a moment, Kierkegaard in *Either/Or*, "I have you to thank that I shall not die without having loved."

For the Viennese, he became too complicated. "Too many notes," said Emperor Joseph II about *The Abduction from the Seraglio*. For the Romantics, for whom he had already been embraced by "the pathos of time," he was near to divine because of his simplicity, his "childlike innocence." They canonized him, a process begun with the changing of his name from Amadè to the more solemn Amadeus. As for their relationship to his music, they tended to value works like *Don Giovanni* and the D-minor Concerto that most nearly approached their own sensibility or those that embodied their ideal of simplicity, the *Coronation* Concerto, for example, and even a forgery like the notorious "Twelfth Mass," pieces rather bland for current taste. Of the two misunderstandings, we sympathize more readily with the Emperor's. And Artur Schnabel was precisely on target when he said of Mozart's piano sonatas that they were "too easy for children and too difficult for artists."

"To be great is to be misunderstood," said Emerson. There is more wit and, for that matter, more truth in Rilke's remark that "fame, after all, is nothing but the sum of all the misunderstandings that gather about a name." Writers celebrating the Mozart tercentenary in 2056 will no doubt find late-twentieth-century views of Mozart as expressed in performance and criticism as blinkered as those of our predecessors seem to us. Surely, in the realm of performance we shall be charged with want of humor and—who knows?—of innocence: we know the humor is there but are inhibited about bringing it out. We do have some feeling for his emotional range, for the thin line between laughter and tears, for his dissonances and his rhythmic oddities (those five-bar phrases I never heard about at school), for the color of his sound. We have heard a wider range of his music than any generation since his own, we have some sense of historical context for him. We know that he too worked hard and sometimes had trouble making pieces come out right.

I want to see him without even a trace of halo, to love him, but not to adore him or idolize him, to come to him—as to all great music—with the ears, the goodwill, the attentiveness, the heart, and, I hope, with the human experience to awaken him.

—M.S.

On the Trail of W. A. Mozart

Vincent Novello called Mozart "the Shakespeare of music." No phrase so grand or telling exists to describe Novello himself, and though to call him the Leonardo of musicians might suggest the breadth of interest and experience he brought to his profession, he would have dismissed that label as grandiose or stupid. At any rate, composers need people like Novello. He was an organist, a choirmaster, a conductor, an editor, a publisher. He dedicated himself to preserving and spreading the word about music he cared for. He had good taste and even better judgment, and the music he championed grew healthy and strong, into long and distinguished life.

Novello's own life was distinguished—and long. He was born in London in 1781, ten years before Mozart's death and about a month before Cornwallis surrendered at Yorktown, and he died in Nice in 1861, about three months after the fall of Fort Sumter. The son of an Italian immigrant who set up shop as a baker, he was a man of character, one who believed in art's power to improve the human race, and during his time he applied steady purpose and clear thought to the conscientious service of music, with results like these: editions of Handel's and Haydn's oratorios; four-hand arrangements of excerpts from operas by Mozart and Spohr; the publication of five volumes of the sacred music of Henry Purcell, including four anthems and an Evening Service that Novello had copied by hand in one day from unpublished manuscripts at York Minster, manuscripts that a year later were destroyed by fire; the editing and publication of *The Fitzwilliam Music,* a five-volume collection of seventeenth-century Italian church music; the presentation with his choir of the Masses of Mozart and Haydn; and, perhaps his greatest achievement, the publication (at his expense) of inexpensive editions of Mozart's and Haydn's choral works in vocal score, with piano or organ accompaniments he had arranged himself, and with separate vocal and orchestral parts. This music had never been available in such form in England, and when the Novello editions made it available, choral societies began to be founded throughout the country.

Novello's children, too, continued in the tradition their father had established. Daughter Clara became a famed soprano and sang in the first performance of Rossini's *Stabat Mater.* Son Alfred founded what would become the music-publishing house of Novello & Co., which would go on to publish such composers as Elgar and Holst. Musician, advocate, and patriarch, Vincent Novello somehow also found the time to become a knowledgeable admirer of poetry, painting, and architecture, and he was a lively conversationalist who was part of a circle that included Leigh Hunt, Charles and Mary Lamb, Keats, Shelley, and, later, Mendelssohn. The inexhaustible Novello found many ways to serve the art he loved so completely, and he understood better than most the hollowness of any attempt to serve by only standing and waiting.

And so in 1829, when Novello learned that the widowed sister of his revered Mozart was lying on a sickbed in Salzburg—blind, seriously ill, and seriously in need of money—his instinct was not to wring his hands, but to act. He approached fellow musicians to raise a fund for this woman who, in the days when she had been known by her nickname, Nannerl, had presented concerts across Europe with her brother Wolfgang, two little prodigies on the road. Now, at the age of seventy-eight, she was called Frau Hofrath Maria Anna von Berchtold zu Sonnenburg, a name that implied wealth but did nothing to guarantee it. To help Frau Sonnenburg, Novello collected money from fifteen subscribers. His own contribution, £10, and an equal sum from J. A. Stumpff (who had been a friend of Beethoven's), were the largest amounts in the total, which came to £63—not so insignificant a sum: The British pound in the early nineteenth century was probably worth about fifteen to twenty current U.S. dollars.

Funds in hand, Vincent Novello understood that he also had an opportunity by the collar. He had, in effect, a perfect pretext to call on those who had actually been on Sacred Ground, in the presence of the Great Man. Mozart had been dead for almost forty years. If any impressions were to be gathered from those who had known him, the time to gather them was now. Novello had questions to ask, and his anticipation of the answers must have been as pulse-quickening as love. Vincent and his wife, Mary Sabilla Novello, set out to deliver their gift to Frau Sonnenburg personally. Their departure from London was probably on 24 June 1829. They would stop in Vienna, of course, as would anyone with even a passing interest in music, and they would stop in Paris, to see to their eleven-year-old Clara's installation in Alexandre Choron's Institution Royale de Musique Religieuse, where she would learn to shade and color the lovely soprano voice that was to entrance Rossini. But their major destination was never in question. It was Salzburg, a place that for them held the evocative power of a Lourdes or a Fatima. It was the air of Salzburg that had first filled the Great Man's lungs; and, when he was old enough to have his first encounter with a keyboard, it was the air of Salzburg that had resounded with the first notes those small fingers had struck. In Salzburg they would find Madame Sonnenburg, and there they would find another Presence as well—the composer's widow, Constanze. For a wealth of intimate detail, she would be as good as going to the source. Through Calais, through Antwerp, through Cologne, through Mannheim, the days of travel began early and ended late.

How do we know all this? The Novellos kept diaries, extensive accounts of their travels. Yet their chronicle of this visit to Salzburg, a visit planned in part as a way of glimpsing a genius through eyes that had seen him, was all but lost. Only in 1944 were the Novellos' diaries discovered. In 1955, editors Nerina Medici and Rosemary Hughes published them as *A Mozart Pilgrimage* (in a volume that appeared under the Novello imprint). In this way, the Novellos' work was preserved, and to these four—the travelers and their editors—we owe shadings and details that add dimension to our portrait of Mozart.

The Novellos departed from Munich on 13 July, at six o'clock in the morning. Eighteen hours later, at midnight, Vincent made this cheery entry in his diary: "After one of the most delightful rides I ever enjoyed through one of the finest days I ever saw, concluding with a bright Moonlight Night, we arrived at the object of our Pilgrimage—Salzburg the Birthplace of Mozart."

What happened next seemed at first anticlimactic. Vincent's nerves were not the kind to create obstacles where he saw none. He decided simply to pay a visit to Madame Sonnenburg. Early the next morning, he was strolling the narrow streets that led to her house. He was disappointed when he arrived, for the lady was too ill to receive him. With this revision of his morning itinerary, he returned to his hotel to share the bad news with Mary. What he did not know was that, even as he was grumbling about the foiled plans, Madame Sonnenburg was sending a message to Mozart's widow, telling her about the visitors. When Vincent answered the knock at the door, he was handed a note from Constanze. Would the Novellos care to visit her that afternoon? You can imagine what followed—coat-dusting, boot-brushing, tie-knotting: a scene pungent with the scent of Crabtree & Evelyn. At two o'clock a servant girl arrived to conduct them to her mistress's door. There, waiting for them in a room on the first floor, was Constanze. With her was her youngest son, Franz Xaver Wolfgang—called simply Wolfgang—who had been about five months old when his father died, and who by coincidence happened to be in Salzburg for a visit. Constanze was sixty-six now, and a widow two times over—her second husband, the Danish diplomat Georg Nikolaus von Nissen, had died three years before. The young Wolfgang was thirty-eight.

"I felt during the whole interview as if his spirit were with us," writes Mary, and there is no mistaking to whom the "his" in that sentence refers. "When I first entered I was so overcome with various emotions that I could do nothing but weep and embrace her. She seemed also affected and said repeatedly in French 'oh quelle bonheur pour moi, de voir les enthousiastes pour mon Mozart.'" It was in French, their common language, that their conversations continued.

Vincent and Mary wanted to fill in the outlines. What was *he* like? What were his work habits? They queried Constanze with reverence—not the most useful attitude for an interviewer to assume, as Larry King or Geraldo Rivera will tell you. But to the questions they asked, the Novellos received answers. They recorded these dutifully. They wrote down everything, all in the spirit of those who refuse to wash the hands that have touched the star. And when Vincent notes that Mozart was "particularly fond of fish, especially trout," we have a hint of what will show up on the Novellos' dinner table that first night back in England.

"QUESTION. Which were the greatest favorites with him of his *own* compositions?"

"V[incent] N[ovello]. She said he was fond of 'Don Giovanni,' 'Figaro' and perhaps most of all 'Idomeneo,' as he had some delightful associations with the time and circumstances under which it was composed.

"There were three of his Sinfonias which he liked nearly equally and preferred to all the others. She could not tell me in what keys, but as well as I could make out they were the ones in G minor, that in E flat, and the 'Jupiter' in C." [Corresponding to the keys, in the order in which Novello lists them, these are the final three symphonies, nos. 40, 39, and 41.]

"QUESTION. Whether he was in the habit of playing and singing much, . . . or whether he generally played *extempore* when alone. . . ?"

"V.N. He did not play much in private, but would occasionally extemporise when he was sitting alone with her. . . . [He did not] like playing to strangers [in private], except he knew them to be *good judges*, when he would exert himself to the utmost for their gratification." . . .

"QUESTION. In composing, whether he sat at the instrument and tried over different passages as they occurred to him, or whether he deferred writing down any piece until he had completely constructed and finished it in his own mind, and then *scored* it at once?" . . .

"V.N. He seldom went to the Instrument when he composed. . . . In composing, he would get up and walk about the Room quite abstracted from everything that was going on about him. He would then come and sit down by her, tell her to give him his inkstand and paper . . . then [he] went on writing by her side while she talked to him, without the conversation at all impeding his occupation." . . .

"QUESTION. Whether his general disposition was lively and playful—or melancholy—whether he could draw, or paint well—or possessed any particular talent for any other art or pursuit than his own science." . . .

"M[ary] N[ovello]. She told us that he drew a little and was fond of all the arts, that he had indeed a talent for all the arts—that he was always in good humor, rarely melancholy . . . , indeed he was an angel she exclaimed, and is one now—there was no affectation about this, but said quite simply."

The Novellos learned that the best likeness of Mozart was, in his widow's opinion, the unfinished portrait by his brother-in-law, Josef Lange; that he "frequently sat up composing until 2 and rose at 4, an exertion which assisted to destroy him"; that "his death was at last sudden." Mary relates Constanze's account: ". . . But a few moments before he had spoken so gaily, and in a few moments after he was dead—she could not believe it, but threw herself on the bed and sought to catch the fever of which he died, but it was not to be."

They were satisfied with what they were learning, pleased with the rarefied air of the Salzburg shrine. Constanze took to this gentle couple who had traveled so far to render a kindness, and after the few days they spent together she was ready to bestow upon them certain relics: a lock of the composer's hair, part of a letter addressed to Mozart by his father, and "a small portion of the little Hairbrush with which he arranged his Hair every Morning. . . ." She also parted with something more substantial than commonplace objects rendered magical by the role they had played in Mozart's life: she presented Vincent with a manuscript, that of "*Al desio*" (K.577), an aria composed for the 1789 Vienna revival of *Figaro*, a more brilliant substitute for *Deh vieni, non tardar*.

The Novellos were pleased, too, in their eventual meeting with Madame Sonnenburg. Nannerl received them graciously. She lay there on her sickbed, Vincent seated to one side of her and Mary to the other, each of them holding one of her hands as they chatted. In her room stood "the Instrument on which she had often played Duetts with her Brother. . . . You may be sure," Vincent tells us, "that I touched the keys . . . with great interest." Three months later Nannerl would be dead. In her memory, Vincent would direct a performance of her brother's Requiem in London's Portuguese Embassy Chapel, where he had served as organist for twenty-five years. But here in the present, Mozart's sister was as touched as Constanze had been by the Novellos' graciousness and generosity. She gave Vincent a portrait of Mozart, a token of her esteem for this virtual stranger who loved her brother's work.

Novello noted the tenderness and affection with which the composer's son Wolfgang treated his Aunt Nannerl, and he was impressed with the young Mozart's manner and bearing. But it is also in relation to him that Vincent records the only melancholy passages in his journal of pilgrimage: "He is (*unfortunately*, I think) a Professor of Music"—meaning a musician—"and seems to be impressed with the idea, that everything he can possibly do will be so greatly inferior to what was accomplished by the wonderful genius of his illustrious father, that he feels disinclined to write much, or to publish what he produces." And again: "[He] says so much is expected of him from the circumstance of his name that it has become a burthen to him." The comparison was inevitable, and though that vilified lesser master, Antonio Salieri—who was in fact one of the young Mozart's teachers—predicted that he would have a career "not inferior to that of his celebrated father," Wolfgang was haunted by a past he had never been part of. The catalogue of his works is small, and he spent most of his fifty-three years as a teacher and a sometime concert pianist. (His brother Karl Thomas took a wiser route and chose not to compete with his father's memory. He became a civil servant in the Austrian kingdom of Lombardo-Venetia and lived to seventy-four.)

Interviews and social hours with Mozart's wife, sister, son: in what they had set out to accomplish, the Novellos had been spectacularly successful. Granted, hero worship and the Romantic spirit—which by 1829 permeated the air of Europe—had blurred their sight and kept them from probing the complexities of their idol. In Vienna, Mozart's friend the Abbé Stadler hinted to Vincent about a more human Great Man, one who "would not take pains in giving lessons to any Ladies but those he was in love with," one who "did not show the great genius in his conversation." But these were suggestions that Novello chose not to pursue. Instead, he would create his own evidence for characteristics he wanted his Mozart to possess, as when he maintained that Mozart could not have written the kind of music he did "If he had not been an enthusiastic admirer of nature." Who knows what Mozart, so cosmopolitan in his upbringing and sophisticated in his musical artifice, would have made of that? But a belief in nature's inspirational power—a belief in the untutored genius—all this was part of the Romantic *Zeitgeist*. Consider Vincent as he contemplates the cathedral at Strasbourg: "I should much like to hear a funeral service performed in this noble church at midnight." He had the Romantic imagination in full force. How could he help but see what he wanted to see in "the Shakespeare of music"?

None of this matters when we glimpse Vincent and Mary strolling down a path in Salzburg, Constanze between them, her arms entwined in theirs. It is a touching portrait, and a reminder that art is made by humans, not gods. Whatever the shortcomings under which the Novellos labored as they pursued their ideal—and who doesn't work under similar shortcomings, in any era?— whatever their shortcomings, the Novellos were too wise to try to answer questions about the interplay of art and life. Theirs was a tangible pleasure: they had been a hit with the people who mattered to them. Constanze, speaking to them one last time, assured them that their visit to Salzburg "had been one of the most gratifying compliments that had been paid for several years, both to herself and to the memory of 'her Mozart.'" And speaking to her diary, Constanze gave the Novellos their private place in her memories. "Very attractive man," she wrote of Vincent; and of Mary, "altogether charming wife." And of both: "good people." Good people, and servants of music. We owe Vincent Novello thanks for many things, not the least of which is his documentation, incomplete though it may be, of moments in a great artist's life, a documentation that helps us follow, as he did, the trail of W. A. Mozart.

—*L.R.*

What They Saw

hen Michael Tilson Thomas and the San Francisco Symphony announced a June 2003 festival built on the theme of *Wagner, Weill, and the Weimar Republic*, I did not get it. What path could there be from Wagner to the composers who worked in Germany between the end of World War I and the power grab that put Hitler in charge of a nation too willing to nurse its grudges? The answer came from a source I could not have imagined: my father.

My father was born in a small German city in 1897, when the optimism of one century was slowly being displaced by the pessimism of a new century. I suppose Germans, at least German politicians and military men, were still optimistic enough. Scarcely thirty years had passed since Prussia had crushed France into submission and gathered the German states into a nation. Feeling for the *Vaterland* was strong—the *Vaterland*, and the great German destiny as enshrined in the heroic myths that Richard Wagner had launched into the world with music of unprecedented and unparalleled power. All this glory had a darker side. For as the nineteenth century ended, Field Marshall Alfred von Schlieffen sat brooding over his plan to achieve another quick victory over France, this one a decisive blow to be engineered by sweeping through Belgium, encircling Paris, and destroying the French army within forty-two days. The great military historian John Keegan, looking back in 1999 in his book *The First World War* (Knopf), described the scheme that Schlieffen eventually produced—a blueprint for the first weeks of World War I—as, arguably, "the most important official document of the last hundred years, for what it caused to ensue on the field of battle, the hopes it inspired, the hopes it dashed, were to have consequences that persist to this day." Schlieffen was already starting to formulate his plan in 1897, essentially writing the death certificate for many who were just being born and many yet to be born and who would not be as lucky as my father was—lucky to come back from the trenches of France. All this is simply one more reason that Germany in the wake of the Great War became a byword for disillusionment and cynicism, and also for a *carpe diem* hunger for life and good times. Weimar Germany—the realities it came from, the dreams on which it foundered, and the nightmare in which it ended—is an object lesson in the tolls of war, greed, and desperation, but it also proves what great art can be born when great artists confront such things.

Growing up in a household headed by a bandleader-and-music-teacher father, my own father was surrounded by a fair number of second-rate marches and waltzes but also by Beethoven and Weber and Flotow and Meyerbeer. He gravitated especially to opera, and in that genre, Wagner ruled. By the time I was born, my father had not heard any opera in years, yet certain works seem to have anchored themselves in his memory and imagination. One was *The Flying Dutchman*—which he never referred to by its English title, but always as *Der fliegende Holländer*. "*Der fliegende Holländer!*" he would cry out at moments when the recollection of the music leaped out of hiding and into his mind. "*Matrosen Chor!*"—meaning the Sailors' Chorus, that great outpouring of sound and fury toward the opera's conclusion. Then he would begin whistling the music with which that chorus ends, complete with grace notes: "*Nachschläge!*" It was an odd musical education that I had, odder than his own. But years later, when I first heard the Sailors' Chorus performed, I understood why this music had made such an impression on my father.

The Flying Dutchman seems part of the cultural consciousness of every music-loving German of his long-past generation. He heard the work only once. He had purchased a standing-room ticket at the opera house in Braunschweig, where he was serving his apprenticeship. This must have been around 1912. He would have been fifteen, and *Dutchman* would not yet have been a century old—the work had been premiered sixty-nine years earlier and had received its final revisions only some forty years previously. The opera kept my father and his friend, a fellow apprentice, out late that night, after their boss—who was also their landlord—had locked the doors. As they made their way back through narrow streets flanked by gingerbread facades like those silhouetted against the moonlit sky in Murnau's *Nosferatu*, they were preparing their excuse. But when the light inside came on and the door opened, the *Lehrmeister* cut to the chase. If these two had been to see *The Flying Dutchman*, could they please tell him the story of the opera? They obliged. Satisfied that his charges had been occupied with innocent pleasures, *der Chef* let them in without his customary verbal or physical abuse.

Think of it. This music is so potent that it could sink into the mind of a fifteen-year-old and exert its power for the remaining seventy-six years of his life. It has taken its hold on others, too. If Weber's *Der Freischütz* marked the coming of Romanticism to the opera house, *The Flying Dutchman* marked a whole new way of uniting music and drama. In *Dutchman*, Wagner dispensed with set pieces and vocal pyrotechnics for their own sake. The play was the thing, and the music was the thing that carried the play.

The play was also a good story, a story to which anyone with a shred of Romantic sensibility could relate, a story of ghosts, damnation, and love that has the power to redeem. In 1843, when *Dutchman* was premiered, people believed in these things—not the ghosts, perhaps, but love and its redemptive possibilities. People still believed in those things in 1912, although by then the modern world had begun to make its incursions. The Prussian chancellor Bismarck had picked a fight with Austria in 1866 and with France in 1871. The other German states, looking to Prussia for guidance and protection, aligned themselves with that power, and the German nation was born. Germany: Before Bismarck, it had been an idea. Now it was a country. Not surprisingly, that great Teutonic saga, Wagner's *Der Ring des Nibelungen*, was introduced in this period of burgeoning German nationalism—the entire cycle was first produced in August 1876, and those who experienced what Wagner had created in those four operas might have been forgiven for believing that there really was something mystical and divinely inspired in German art. Not only Germans embraced such grandiose notions in the nineteenth century. Americans saw Manifest Destiny—a term first used by journalist John L. O'Sullivan in 1845— when they looked westward, and it was in 1869, right around the time that Bismarck was laying his plans to consolidate the German states, that the Union Pacific and Central Pacific railroads met at Promontory Point, Utah, and the last spike was driven into the tracks that spanned the North American continent.

In any talk of destinies, whether national or personal, there is an element of the mystical, of what psychologists call "magical thinking"—grandiosity, the poetic and the irrational. The Romantic manifesto places high value on intuition, the spiritual, the dark power of the unconscious that will lead us to enlightened bliss. (See *Dutchman*: Why, but for her Romantic soul, would Senta be so drawn to the mysterious doomed sea captain rather than to Erik, who is dependable, straightforward, and made of mortal flesh?)

In the later years of the nineteenth century, and as the new century began to take shape, Romanticism assumed new forms. Freud began his explorations of the mind, and in painting such as Kokoschka's and music such as Mahler's and Schoenberg's the tendency toward the mystical, the individual consciousness, and the irrational begins to incline so far from "realistic" moorings that the ties to the concrete world threaten to sever. Sometimes we think of the period immediately after World War I as the great age of Modernism in art and music, and it was, but the Modernist spirit was born much earlier. Schoenberg's *Herzgewächse*, a wild post-Wagnerian leap into the unknown, was premiered in 1928, but it had been composed in 1911.

How does such Romanticism, or ultra-Romanticism, find its place in an increasingly bourgeois world, where tastes are dominated by an expanding middle class? Here the ideas of national destiny and Romantic ideals become confused. As Peter Gay writes in his study *Weimar Culture: The Outsider as Insider* (published in 1968 by Harper & Row, and also the source of my subsequent references in this essay to Gay's work), "In August 1914 the Western world had experienced a war psychosis: the war seemed a release from boredom, an invitation to heroism, a remedy for decadence. But it was in Germany that this psychosis reached heights of absurdity. The overaged, the adolescent, the unfit, volunteered with pure joy, and went to death filled with their mission. The war offered"—and here Gay quotes Thomas Mann—"'purification, liberation, and enormous hope'; it 'set the hearts of poets aflame' with a sense of relief that 'a peaceful world had collapsed,' a world of which 'one was so tired, so dreadfully tired.'"

That a cataclysm on the scale of World War I should have happened, when it happened, may strike us as incomprehensible today. Tracing the events that led to the outbreak of hostilities is fairly simple (see John Keegan's *The First World War* for a chilling exposition), but one wants to find causes other than treaties, alliances, and bruised honor for a conflict that took millions of lives and whose repercussions were so profound. Destiny, Romanticism—all those great abstractions that are transformed by Wagner's music into pulsing, gleaming resonance that bypasses reason and goes straight for the gut: they could still enflame young men (and old) fed up with the commonplace. Shortly after August 1914, a few years after he saw *The Flying Dutchman* in Braunschweig, my father attempted to enlist in the Kaiser's army. He had had it with his baker's apprenticeship and saw military service as the way to a better life—as the way, at any rate, to a more adventurous life. He was only seventeen but lied about his age and was inducted, only to be discharged when somehow the truth came out. Of course, he was back in the recruitment office soon after his next birthday. This would have been in March 1915. He saw plenty of action in France, though it was probably not the kind of adventure he'd bargained for. To the end of his long life, he had occasional nighttime episodes that began with low moans and crescendoed in horrible screams. He never remembered what all the noise had been about the next morning, and in those days I had never heard the term "post-traumatic stress disorder."

When the war ended, he was released along with so many others into a broken society. The Kaiser had been forced to abdicate. Worker unrest in various cities seemed based on the Bolshevik model that had toppled Tsar Nicholas II. In Weimar, city of Bach and Goethe and Schiller and Liszt, a new government was formed, the first constitutional republic in Germany's short history. It was a government plagued with problems from the beginning. It satisfied neither left nor right, suffered takeover attempts by the Spartacists—communists bent on establishing a Soviet-style government—and had to rely on the remnants of the defeated German army to maintain order. And all that happened before May 1919, when the terms of the Versailles Treaty were announced, wresting Alsace and Lorraine from Germany and returning those territories to France, wresting away parts of the nation's eastern provinces, demanding that Germany admit full responsibility for starting the war, and imposing punishing reparations payments. Within a year a right-wing splinter group attempted to take control of the government in Berlin, and soon after, in the industrial Ruhr District, a Red Army formed and was brutally suppressed. Perhaps the nadir came when, in 1923, after Germany defaulted on its reparations payment, French and Belgian troops invaded the Ruhr. German workers there responded with passive resistance and went on strike. But the shutdown of factories was not an action that aided a faltering economy.

The formula for demoralization was so clear you could almost call it elegant: disillusionment over the war, disenchantment with those who had led the country into that conflict, and now rage at those who had (it was believed) betrayed the nation by accepting the terms of Versailles. Not that Germany had been in a position to negotiate at Versailles. When its delegates arrived in Paris in late April 1919, they were met with contempt and presented with peace terms that were *faits accomplis*. It was around this time, in 1920, that the Austrian novelist Joseph Roth published the first of the newspaper columns in which he shared his sad and cynical observations of contemporary Berlin, columns recently translated by Michael Hofmann and collected in a volume titled *What I Saw* (published by W.W. Norton & Company in 2003). "Sometimes, in a fit of incurable melancholy," Roth reported, "I go into one of the standard Berlin nightclubs, not to cheer myself up, . . . but to take malicious pleasure at the phenomenon of so much industrialized merriment." It was into a world like this that Berg's operas *Wozzeck* and *Lulu* were introduced, dramas whose heroes and heroines were not ghosts like the Dutchman or gods like Wotan but soldiers and sluts. The novel *All Quiet on the Western Front*, which appeared in 1929, is as succinct and powerful as any statement of how dreams of glory died in the trenches.

With the strikes in the Ruhr District, a major part of the country's economy came to a standstill. The treasury suffered, but reparations had to be paid and striking workers looked after. The government responded by printing more money, about the worst solution imaginable to an economic quagmire. Foreign investors, worried about Germany's financial condition, withdrew. The quagmire turned into a crisis of hyperinflation, with prices rising faster than money could be printed. My father told stories of handing over 3 million marks for a cigarette—cigarettes could be bought by the piece—and about how he was paid daily because the currency was so unstable. "By October 1923," Peter Gay writes, "not millions, or billions, but trillions of marks were needed to buy a loaf of bread or mail a letter." That November, Adolf Hitler's right-wing National Socialists staged their abortive attempt in Munich to seize control of the government. But Nazis—Romantics intoxicated with that old sense of German destiny and willing to be vicious in its pursuit—were still thought of as a fringe group, filled with what my mother (who grew up in the Weimar years, though she left for America in 1927, at seventeen) always called *der deutsche Fimmel*: Germans' crazy obsession with being German.

Peter Gay has described the Weimar Republic as representing the ideals of rationalism in opposition to the Romantic-Wagnerian glorification of the irrational. In that Weimar-rational spirit, a new chancellor, Gustav Stresemann, helped Germany shake hyperinflation. He negotiated a deal whereby American gold would back a new currency. He also worked with American banker and vice-president-to-be (in the Coolidge administration) Charles Dawes to devise a more realistic schedule of reparation payments—a plan that included withdrawal of Allied troops from the Ruhr and that would bring Dawes the Nobel Peace Prize. The Dawes Plan went into effect in September 1924. Foreign investors returned, and the economy began to stabilize.

My father had decided not to wait for this. Determined to find a better life, he booked passage for the United States in 1925. One of his last images of his homeland came in Hamburg, the night before he was to board the ship for New York. He had been intrigued by a marquee outside a nightclub, promising that the show inside would give patrons a look at *Hamburg bei Nacht, wie es weint und lacht*—Hamburg at Night: Its Tears and Its Laughter—a come-on based on Hamburg's reputation for illicit pleasures. My father bought a ticket and took his place at a bar table in a room full of smoke and other adventurers. An entire wall was draped with heavy fabric, and as the lights dimmed a tuxedoed waiter with slicked-back hair gathered a fold of curtain at one end and drew it back to the other. The curtain had covered a large window, and beyond that window now was the city, or at least part of it: buildings and docks silhouetted against a darkening sky. That was it. Hamburg at Night. This kind of show seemed to sum up a society of promises only partially kept, in which the parties to contracts had radically different understandings of the terms to which they had agreed. In a world like this, you had to be your own person. My father understood that message, and he got out.

Some might think he left a little too soon. For the years that followed in Germany were the ones that people remember as a sort of artistic paradise. They were the years of Marlene Dietrich and Emil Jannings, of Kurt Weill and

Lotte Lenya and Bertolt Brecht (*The Threepenny Opera* opened in 1928), of cabaret and experiments in cinema and music and theater. In this rejuvenated economy, Berlin and Munich were the focal points of a kind of anything-goes cornucopia of sensual and sexual liberation, out to seize the day. In October 1925 the Locarno Treaty had been signed between France, Great Britain, Belgium, Italy, and Germany. The next year Germany had entered the League of Nations. It was back in the international community. Jews like Victor Klemperer, who in his two-volume diary *I Will Bear Witness* documents the maddening humiliations he and his wife were subjected to by the Nazis, still identified themselves during the Weimar years first as *Germans*, and they were proud of their service to the fatherland in the Great War. It was about as open a society as Germany had seen, and it seemed as though the wretched mistake that had been World War I could be righted if one could only have fun, make love, drink fancy cocktails, hear the latest music, see the latest theater, and read the latest books.

"The name '*Weimar Republic*,'" writes Michael Hofmann in his introduction to Roth's *What I Saw*, "has a whiff of fragility, of scandal, of doom about it. It denotes a tiny period of German history, the years from 1918 to 1933; an interval of tremulous republican government, between monarchy and dictatorship, between one catastrophic war and the approach of another; but most of all a period that was fast and febrile and fun, and . . . became practically synonymous with the Jazz Age or the Roaring Twenties." Composers such as Ernst Toch and Paul Hindemith tried to incorporate popular song and jazz into their concert music. And in fact the music of those years reflects the society: To think of the Weimar years is to think of music that is bitter, ironic, determinedly "modern," frequently sad, often funny, and perhaps even touched by nihilism.

But the Weimar years were over almost before they began, and musical exploration, always such a potent force in the country, came to a halt. The Nazis banned composers such as Toch and Schoenberg not simply because they were Jewish but because their music was somehow "degenerate"—and you didn't have to be Jewish to earn that label, only quick-witted and questioning, and a perceived subversive; it was applied even to Hindemith, "pure" German though he was. After the war, German composers had catch-up work to do, rediscovering their voices and learning about techniques and styles with which they had had little contact for more than a decade.

The Nazis: Where did they come from, and how did the Weimar Republic finally die, that strange experiment in popular government following the rule of an emperor and leading to the terror of a dictator? By 1930, the whole world was feeling the effect of the Wall Street crash of 1929. The United States demanded that Germany begin repaying the loans that the U.S. government had made. German companies went bankrupt. Unemployment, which had doubled between 1928 and 1929, more than doubled again between 1929 and

1930, to 3 million. By January 1932, more than 6 million Germans were unemployed. The Nazi Party that had seemed so lunatic throughout the 1920s and had almost gone bankrupt itself in 1928 now seemed to offer some hope of a better world, playing on those old feelings of Romantic destiny, and on the hurt feelings of Versailles. It is often said that Wagner contributed to Nazi ideology. True, he was anti-Semitic and seemingly proud of it, putting some of his ugliest thoughts on the subject into an essay called "*Das Judentum in Musik.*" Yet Wagner's anti-Semitism is confined to his prose, which even at its most benign has a lot less appeal than his music. That music—that glorious music— does not in itself legitimize anti-Semitism, but to the extent that it romanticizes and glamorizes nationalism, those inclined to xenophobia could embrace it. Outsiders beware. Group identity can be dangerous when the group you identify with is any subset of the human race. Certainly Hitler was cynical enough to use anything at his disposal to get what he wanted. Wagner's music was one of those things.

Another was the Treaty of Versailles. Recently, historian Margaret MacMillan in *Paris 1919* has reexamined the conventional wisdom that the Treaty led ultimately to World War II. She reminds us of how right-wing nationalists such as the Nazis kept a sense of German grievances fresh but proposes that "Hitler did not wage war because of the Treaty of Versailles, although he found its existence a godsend for his propaganda." This still does not dismiss the question of whether the Versailles Treaty helped spark another war. The framers of Versailles could not have foreseen the Wall Street crash, but had they displayed more imagination and exercised more tact, they might have stolen some of Hitler's ammunition. But Hitler made his ammunition on the spot and as he chose. He engineered his appointment as Chancellor in January 1933. Two months later, the Reichstag—the German Parliament building in Berlin—was destroyed by fire. Presumably the blaze had been set by a Dutch communist, but it has been speculated that a Nazi cadre was responsible. For now Hitler had what he wanted: the specter of national catastrophe, a country on the verge of communist takeover. He declared a national emergency and suspended civil liberties. With that, for all purposes, he became dictator. The Weimar Republic was dead.

The world was about to enter a very bad phase. Joseph Roth had moved to Paris as soon as Hitler came to power. (Kurt Weill had moved to Paris, too, and his *Seven Deadly Sins* was composed and premiered there.) Writing from the French capital in 1933, Roth spoke of Nazi book-burnings, pointing out that the Weimar Republic's last president, Hindenburg, once "openly admitted that *he had never read a book in his life.*" Roth bemoans this anti-intellectual bent but believes it has long been present—its roots are in that sense of destiny, in Wagnerian Romanticism, in *der deutsche Fimmel*—and he finds everyone responsible. "It was this icon"—Hindenburg—"that the workers, Social

Democrats, journalists, artists, and Jews worshipped during the war, and that the German people (workers, Jews, journalists, artists, Social Democrats, and the rest of them) then re-elected president. Is a people that elects as its president an icon that has never read a book all that far away from burning books itself?"

From Wagner to the Weimar Republic, Romanticism to Modernism, is not so long a trip. As a parable of where Romantic illusion can lead, this span of years and the music it produced offers much for reflection. The conclusions you could draw would be unbearably depressing if the music, from Wagner to Weimar, were not so compelling. "It was the cultural task of the Weimar Republic," writes Peter Gay, "to restore the broken ties" of its people "both to the usable past and to the congenial foreign environment."

Nations may try to identify parts of the past as usable or not; but what of a personal past? What parts of that are usable? The ones that continue to give us pleasure, like a suddenly remembered chorus from *The Flying Dutchman*? Or the ones that continue to haunt our dreams? A personal past always intersects with history, just as the composers of the Weimar years restored Germans' sense of cultural ties to the world, looking to a great heritage that went back to Wagner and further. The spirit they communicated found an audience in the world beyond Germany, an audience perhaps more receptive than in Germany itself. That spirit, forged in the awful battles that opened a new century, expressed a people's hopes and a nation's character no less than did Wagner, if more realistically. The greatest of the Weimar composers championed an honesty for which their own country was not fully prepared. Other battles would have to ready that ground.

—L.R.

A Short Life of J. S. Bach

> In the two hundred years since [Bach's] death each rising
> generation has seen him differently; his creations have
> been analyzed and criticized, performed and deformed,
> used and abused; books and pamphlets, paintings and
> plaster busts have made him a common household
> article; in short he has finally been transformed into a
> statue. It seems to me that having this statue constantly
> before our eyes has impaired our view of the true stature
> of Bach, both of the man and of his work.
>
> —Paul Hindemith

The voice is Paul Hindemith's, the occasion the city of Hamburg's Bach
commemoration of 1950, and the tone woven through the words like
a ground bass is one that tells us to beware. But the statue Hindemith
speaks of doesn't bend or move to music, hewn as it is from a psychological
granite or marble—our conceptions and preconceptions of Bach. Who was
Johann Sebastian Bach? "This genius," says Albert Schweitzer, "was not an
individual but a collective soul." In other words, a statue. Bach the man remains
a puzzle—both because we know so little of his personal life and because we
feel entitled to know more. The correspondence he left behind is mostly official
business—recommendations for students or organ builders, requests for work,
hagglings over salary. It is as difficult to draw a sense of the man from such
documents as it would be to piece together a life from the scraps of paper that
litter your desk, or mine. Absent from Bach's writing is any mention of his own
inner workings—how he must have felt, for example, after the death of Maria
Barbara, to whom he had been married for twelve years and who had borne

their six children. Absent is any mention of how he reacted to the comings and goings of friends, or the seasons, or night and day. To appreciate how private—or perhaps simply undemonstrative—Bach must have been, we need only compare the notes and letters he left behind with the kinds of letters Mozart wrote, by turns playful, intimate, and grousing, or with that great document of spiritual torment and *angst*, Beethoven's Heiligenstadt Testament. It is the difference between eras, between ways of perceiving the world and how you fit into it, but also simply a reflection of one man's natural reserve.

Our ideas of The Artist have been conditioned largely by figures such as Beethoven, romantic culture heroes who fashion their work from the details of their lives, who invite us to share in the spectacle of their loves and frustrations. Our demand for the biographical facts or fictions surrounding, say, Berlioz or Tchaikovsky isn't so different from the demand satisfied by the *National Enquirer* and its siblings. We expect to be on familiar terms with our artists, and we expect our artists to be celebrities. Bach would have been surprised to learn that his audience was interested in the "story" of his life. And he would have been appalled. For he was a worker—a pro: a musician and composer, with lower-case "m" and "c." Art may have been his vocation, but it was also his livelihood. To say that he wrote to eat may be a grossly simple way of saying why he composed, but it is not a gross distortion. Throughout his life he held six respectable and responsible positions—now as organist, now as court composer, now as city music director— in places scattered across east-central Germany, a small parcel of territory where he was born and within whose boundaries he remained, though he was willing to move to where the work was. From what we can deduce, he could write by inspiration or on demand. One of the miracles is that the quality of his music is as consistently high as the quantity is great.

Still the question is unavoidable, because we are, after all, creatures of our own time: What was Bach like? And the question becomes more nagging when we look at that portrait of 1746 by Elias Gottlieb Haussmann (the eighteenth-century equivalent of a photograph sent with the announcement of an executive promotion). Here is the master—wigged and well-fed, but with a look in his eyes and a pursing of the lips so suggestive and so undefinable that he becomes more enigmatic than ever. In his right hand he holds a slip of paper bearing the six-part canon (BWV 1076), his membership submission to the Society of Musical Sciences. Here is a picture that encompasses the two Bachs—the "Bach" that is an edifice of musical literature and the "Bach" who is one of us. Schweitzer may maintain that Bach is "a collective soul," but to lose sight of Bach the man is to do ourselves a disservice, allowing ourselves to be overwhelmed by Bach, the music. To the extent that he can speak, we must let him. Hearing Bach's voice became suddenly easier in 1945, when Hans T. David and Arthur Mendel published *The Bach Reader*, a collection of letters and papers from the composer's life. The documentary biography that follows is culled from *The New Bach Reader*, a 1998 revision by Christoph Wolff of

David and Mendel's work. I have added commentary (in italics) in an attempt to create a narrative. In this story, the voice is Bach's, joined by the voices of people who knew him.

From the church records of Eisenach, where Johann Sebastian Bach was born on 21 March 1685, the entry of a baptism:

Monday, March 23, 1685. To Mr. Johann Ambrosius Baach, Town Musician . . . , a son, g[odfathers] Sebastian Nagel, Town Musician at Gotha, and Johann Georg Koch, Ducal Forester of this place. Name: Joh. Sebastian.

Bach's mother died in 1694; after his father's death the following year, Johann Sebastian joined the household of his brother, Johann Christoph, who gave him musical instruction. By 1703 J. S. was organist at the New Church in Arnstadt. It was here, on 4 August 1705, that his sharp tongue led him into the first of many disagreements with lesser talents. The source of conflict was a student musician at the church, J. H. Geyersbach. David and Mendel offer a reconstruction from Church records.

[On August 5, 1705,] Johann Sebastian Bach . . . appeared [before the Consistory] and stated that, as he walked home yesterday, fairly late at night, . . . six students were sitting on the "Langenstein" (Long Stone), and as he passed the town hall, the student Geyersbach went after him with a stick, calling him to account: Why had he [Bach] made abusive remarks about him? He [Bach] answered that he had made no abusive remarks about him, and that no one could prove it, for he had gone his way very quietly. Geyersbach retorted that while he [Bach] might not have maligned him, he had maligned his bassoon at some time, and whoever insulted his belongings insulted him as well; he had carried on like a dirty dog's etc., etc. And he [Geyersbach] had at once struck out at him. Since he had not been prepared for this, he had been about to draw his dagger, but Geyersbach had fallen into his arms, and the two of them tumbled about until the rest of the students . . . had rushed toward them and separated them. . . . He had said to Geyersbach, to his face, that he would straighten this out tomorrow, and it would not be becoming to him and his honor to duel with him [Geyersbach].

As it turned out, Geyersbach's attack was not unprovoked, and on 19 August, the Consistory reprimanded Bach.

He might very well have refrained from calling Geyersbach a *Zippel Fagotist* [a "nanny-goat bassoonist"]; such gibes lead in the end to unpleasantness of this kind, especially since he had a reputation for not getting along with the students and of claiming that he was engaged only for simple chorale music, and not for concerted pieces, which was wrong, for he must help out in all music making.

Ille: He would not refuse, if only there were a *Director musices.*

Nos: Men must live among *imperfecta;* he must get along with the students, and they must not make one another's lives miserable.

In 1707 Bach became organist at Mühlhausen, in the Church of Saint Blasius. He decided to leave after only a year. When he approached the patrons, parishioners, and Church council to request his dismissal, he mentioned in passing some of the conditions and goals he considered professionally important.

[H]owever simple my manner of living, I can live but poorly, considering the house rent and other most necessary expenses.

Now, God has brought it to pass that an unexpected change should offer itself to me, in which I see the possibility of a more adequate living and the achievement of my goal of a well-regulated church music without further vexation, since I have received the gracious admission of His Serene Highness of Saxe-Weimar into his Court Capelle and Chamber Music.

Accordingly, I have felt I must bring my intention in this matter, with obedient respect, to the notice of my Most Gracious Patrons, and at the same time beg them to content themselves for the time being with the modest services I have rendered to the Church and to furnish me at the earliest moment with a gracious dismissal.

Bach was court musician at Weimar for nine years. When he left, his parting with his employer, the Duke Wilhelm Ernst, was anything but gracious. For Bach had received an offer to become Capellmeister at the court of Cöthen, and he wanted desperately to break his ties with the Duke. We do not know what Bach did or said to evoke Wilhelm Ernst's extraordinary response, but we may speculate from this entry in the reports of the Secretary of the Weimar court:

On November 6, 1717, the quondam concertmaster and organist Bach was confined to the County Judge's place of detention for too stubbornly forcing the issue of his dismissal and finally on December 2 was freed from arrest with notice of his unfavorable discharge.

Bach spent six years at Cöthen, the first few of which, as David and Mendel wrote in their original edition of The Bach Reader, *"must have been the happiest in [his] life." Prince Leopold loved music and was a friend. For him, Bach composed the Brandenburg Concertos. The Prince, however, married a woman who had little feeling for music, and this apparently caused his highness's own interest to wane. Again Bach looked elsewhere for work. What he found was the position in which he would spend the rest of his life—Cantor of Saint Thomas's Church and School in Leipzig, a post that brought with it the position of City Music Director, a higher salary, and free schooling for his children. Christoph Wolff points out (in the New Grove Bach Family) that the Leipzig position "was one of the most notable positions in German musical life," for it had been "associated with a wealth of tradition since the sixteenth century." It was, in short, the kind of position that a man of forty-eight—a ripe age in 1723—would see as the consolidation of a career. Whatever Bach's high expectations may have been, he soon found he had become a member of a bureaucracy, and he ran into constant disagreements with the City Council, made up of men more concerned with protocol and propriety than with the demands and urgencies of art. Consider this excerpt from the Council proceedings of 3 April 1724, regarding a performance of the* Saint John Passion.

Mr. Johann Sebastian Bach, Cantor of St. Thomas's School, was notified of the decision previously made by the Honored and Learned Council that the Passion Music for Good Friday should be given alternately in St. Nicholas's and St. Thomas's. But since the title of [the libretto to] the music sent around this year revealed that it was to take place again in St. Thomas's, and since the Superintendent of St. Nicholas's had requested of the Honored and Learned Council that this time the above-mentioned Passion music should be given in St. Nicholas's, therefore, the Cantor should for his part act accordingly.

Hic: He would comply with the same, but pointed out that the booklet was already printed, that there was no room available, and that the harpsichord needed some repair, all of which, however, could be attended to at little cost; but he requested at any rate that a little additional room be provided in the choir loft, so that he could place the persons needed for the music, and that the harpsichord be repaired.

Senatus: The Cantor should, at the expense of the Honored and Most Wise Council, have an announcement printed stating that the music was to take place this time in St. Nicholas's, have the necessary arrangements in the choir loft made, with the aid of the sexton, and have the harpsichord repaired.

Six years later the Leipzig Council admonished Bach for neglecting his teaching duties. In the minutes of 2 August 1730:

[I]t should be remembered that when the Cantor came hither he received a dispensation concerning the teaching; . . . [but the Cantor] did not conduct himself as he should (without the foreknowledge of the burgomaster in office [he] sent a choir student to the country; went away without obtaining leave), for which he must be reproached and admonished; at present it must be considered whether the [third and fourth] classes should not be provided with a different person; Magister Kriegel was said to be a good man, and a decision would have to be made about it.

Court Councilor Lange: Everything was true that had been mentioned against the Cantor, and he could be admonished and the place filled with Magister Kriegel.

Court Councilor Steger: Not only did the Cantor do nothing, but he was not even willing to give an explanation of that fact; he did not hold the singing class, and there were other complaints in addition; a change would be necessary, a break would have to come some time, and he would acquiesce in the making of other arrangements.

Diocesan Councilor Born: Adhered to the above votes.

Dr. Hölzel: Likewise.

Commissioner Dr. Falckner: Likewise.

Commissioner Kregel: Likewise.

Syndic Job: Likewise, since the Cantor was *incorrigible.*

Commissioner Sieber: Likewise.

Commissioner Winckler: Likewise.

Commissioner Hohmann: Likewise.

I [the clerk]:—Likewise.

Hereupon it was resolved to restrict the Cantor's [incidental] income.

Bach became so frustrated at Leipzig that he decided to seek another position, as he disclosed in a letter dated 28 October 1730 and addressed to Georg Erdmann, a childhood companion, now the "Imperial Russian Resident Agent in Danzig":

Most Honored Sir,

Your Honor will have the goodness to excuse an old and faithful servant for taking the liberty of disturbing you with the present letter. It must be nearly four years since Your Honor favored me with a kind answer to the letter I sent you; I remember that at that time you graciously asked me to give you some news of what had happened to me, and I humbly take this opportunity of providing you with the same. You know the course of my life from my youth up until the change in my fortunes that took me to Cöthen as Capellmeister. There I had a gracious Prince, who both loved and knew music, and in his service I intended to spend the rest of my life. It must happen, however, that the said *Serenissimus* should marry a Princess of Berenburg, and that then the impression should arise that the musical interests of the said Prince had become somewhat lukewarm, especially as the new Princess seemed to be unmusical; and it pleased God that I should be called hither to be *Director Musices* and Cantor at St. Thomas's School. Though at first, indeed, it did not seem at all proper to me to change my position of Capellmeister for that of Cantor. Wherefore, then, I postponed my decision for a quarter of a year; but this post was described to me in such favorable terms that finally (particularly since my sons seemed inclined toward [university] studies) I cast my lot, in the name of the Lord, and made the journey to Leipzig, took my examination, and then made the change of position. Here, by God's will, I am still in service. But since (1) I find that the post is by no means so lucrative as it was described to me; (2) I have failed to obtain many of the fees pertaining to the office; (3) the place is very expensive; and (4) the authorities are odd and little interested in music, so that I must live amid almost continual vexation, envy, and persecution; accordingly I shall be forced, with God's help, to seek my fortune elsewhere. Should Your Honor know or find a suitable post in your city for an old and faithful servant, I beg you most humbly to put in a most gracious word of recommendation for me—I shall not fail to do my best to give satisfaction and justify your most gracious intercession in my behalf. My present post amounts to about 700 thaler, and when there are rather more funerals than usual, the fees rise in proportion; but when a healthy wind blows, they fall accordingly, as for example last year, when I lost fees that would ordinarily come in from funerals to an amount of more than 100 thaler. In Thuringia I could get along better on 400 thaler than here with twice that many, because of the excessively high cost of living. . . .

I shall almost transgress the bounds of courtesy if I burden Your Honor any further, and I therefore hasten to close, remaining with most devoted respect my whole life long

Your Honor's most obedient and devoted servant

Joh. Sebast. Bach

Erdmann never came through. By 1739, the feud between Bach and the Council appears to have become institutionalized. Both parties accept the fact that their personalities will never mesh. In the Leipzig Council Archives, 17 March 1739:

Upon a Noble and Most Wise Council's order I have gone to Mr. Bach here and have pointed out to the same that the music he intends to perform on the coming Good Friday is to be omitted until regular permission for the same is received. Whereupon he answered: it had always been done so; he did not care, for he got nothing out of it anyway, and it was only a burden; he would notify the Superintendent that it had been forbidden him; if an objection were made on account of the text, [he remarked that] it had already been performed several times. This I have accordingly wished to communicate to a Noble and Most Wise Council.

Andreas Gottlieb Bienengräber

Clerk

With my own hand

Thus the Bach who could close a letter with the assurance that he was his Honor's "devoted servant" could also speak plainly, and his bluntness was not reserved just for the Leipzig Council. In a note of 2 November 1748, Bach thanked cousin Johann Elias for a cask of wine, several quarts of his kinsman's best—and then asked that no more gifts like this be sent.

Although my honored Cousin kindly offers to oblige with more of the *liqueur*, I must decline his offer on account of the excessive expenses here. For since the carriage charges cost 16 groschen, the delivery man 2 groschen, the customs inspector 2 groschen, the inland duty 5 groschen, 3 pfennig, and the general duty 3 groschen, my honored Cousin can judge for himself that each quart cost me almost 5 groschen, which for a present is really too expensive.

If Bach could be crotchety, it was not because he was one of those geniuses whose accomplishments go unnoticed in their lifetimes. He was a major figure in the German musical world, as attested in this report, from a Berlin newspaper of 11 May 1747, of the genesis of the Musical Offering.

One hears from Potsdam that last Sunday [7 May] the famous Capellmeister from Leipzig, Mr. Bach, arrived with the intention to have the pleasure of hearing the excellent Royal music at that place. In the evening, at about the time when the regular chamber music in the Royal apartments usually begins, His Majesty was informed that Capellmeister Bach had arrived at Potsdam and was waiting . . . to listen to the music. His August Self immediately gave orders that Bach be admitted, and went, at his entrance, to the so-called *Forte* and *Piano*, condescending also to play, in His Most August Person and without any preparation, a theme—for the Capellmeister Bach, which he should execute in a fugue. This was done so happily by the aforementioned Capellmeister that not only was His Majesty pleased to show his satisfaction thereat, but also all those present were seized with astonishment. Mr. Bach has found the subject propounded to him so exceedingly beautiful that he intends to set it down on paper as a regular fugue and have it engraved on copper. On Monday, the famous man let himself be heard on the organ in the Church of the Holy Spirit at Potsdam and earned general acclaim from the audience attending in great number.

But this was late in Bach's career. In March 1750 the English eye specialist John Taylor attempted to restore the composer's failing sight by an operation. It helped only partially, and Taylor repeated the surgery in April. This, too, was unsuccessful, and it left Bach so weakened that his health declined steadily. He died after a stroke on 28 July 1750. On 3 August the Spenersche Zeitung *of Berlin carried this report:*

Last Tuesday, that is, the 28th instant, the famous musician Mr. Joh. Seb. Bach, Royal Polish and Electoral Saxon Court Composer, Capellmeister of the Princely

Court of Saxe-Weissenfels and of Anhalt-Cöthen, *Director Chori Musici* and Cantor of St. Thomas here, [died] in the 66th year of his age, from the unhappy consequences of the very unsuccessful eye operation by a well-known English oculist. The loss of this uncommonly able man is greatly mourned by all true connoisseurs of music.

* * *

An uncommonly able man greatly mourned. Let the closing voice once again be Hindemith's. In Bach, Hindemith says, "we see a man who, in spite of a life spent in petit bourgeois doings and surroundings, has built up a completely independent world of artistic creation. . . . Any musician, even the most gifted, takes a place second to Bach's at the start."

—L.R.

Stravinsky's Ear-stretching, Joy-giving Legacy

The first time I heard Stravinsky's name was when I was eleven or twelve and saw *Fantasia*, the original, good 1940 version. (I say more about that in "How I Fell in Love with Music," beginning on page 3.) I had no context, no awareness of what else he had composed or what it sounded like, and of course no idea that what Stokowski served up in that film was far removed from *The Rite of Spring* as Stravinsky had written it. I was both excited and puzzled by this music, which was so unlike any I had ever heard before. I spoke about it to my mother, who, like a lot of intellectual and artistic types, disapproved of *Fantasia* without having seen it, but she did recall that some time in the 1920s Furtwängler and the Berlin Philharmonic had brought the *Firebird* Suite to Breslau, where my parents lived, and how adventurous that had made them feel. My own first encounter with Stravinsky's music in the dingy Cosmopolitan Theater in Cambridge, England, was the start of a lifelong love affair.

By a pleasing chance, just as I was about to start on the first version of this piece a few years ago, an old opera program fell out of a score. It was from a performance in Rome of *Boulevard Solitude*, a reworking of the Manon Lescaut story by the then very young Hans Werner Henze. The date on the program was 7 April 1954, forty-five years to the day before its surprise reappearance. I was then in Italy on a Fulbright fellowship, far more interested in the new music of Luigi Dallapiccola, Bruno Maderna, Luigi Nono, Goffredo Petrassi, and Giacinto Scelsi than in that of Bartolino da Padova, the fourteenth-century *Kleinmeister* (*sehr klein*) about whom I was supposed to be writing a doctoral dissertation.

For some reason *Boulevard Solitude* scandalized the first-night audience, but as we learned, first through rumors that circulated in the house during the evening, then in more detail in the next morning's papers, the real scandal had occurred in the lobby: Igor Stravinsky, in town for a concert with the Rome Radio Orchestra, had been refused admission. The Rome Opera had a strict rule that any man sitting in the orchestra or in a box had to wear black tie, and Stravinsky had shown up in a plain dark suit. Reporting this silly event, the music critic of one of the Roman newspapers asked: "For *Petrushka*, might the Maestro not have been forgiven the dinner jacket, or the black tie for the *Symphony of Psalms?*"

Indeed. And recalling that writer's question now, I go to Robert Craft's *Stravinsky: Chronicle of a Friendship* and reread the account of his and Vera Stravinsky's visit to the composer's grave on the funeral isle of San Michele just off Venice, three weeks after his death in April 1971. "And again," writes Craft, "we follow the path to the Orthodox section, where lilacs and oleander are in bloom, and it is full springtime except for the man who created a spring of his own that of all mortally begotten versions will give Nature its longest run for everlasting joy. . . . It is impossible to believe that the man whose immortal celebration of the resurrection of nature, and all his other continuations of the highest humanizing art of man, lies beneath that mound of earth."

Thirty-four years have passed since that death and that funeral—a full generation—and for students, even for the younger members of our orchestras, Igor Stravinsky is already a remote classic, almost as remote and almost as classic as Brahms (who died only thirty-one years before I was born). What a feeling of emptiness Stravinsky's death left! He was nearly eighty-nine, and it was no secret that he was exceedingly frail, that he had not composed since 1966, the year he completed the *Requiem Canticles* and *The Owl and the Pussy-cat*, and that he had conducted for the last time (the *Pulcinella* Suite in Toronto in May 1967). On that occasion Craft noted in his diary "the special warmth of the audience, whose applause had distinctly said, 'This is the last time we see Igor Stravinsky.'"

But still, what a jolt it was, the news of his death, a death about which I learned in such a strange way. Wearing my *Boston Globe* music critic hat, I was accompanying a European tour of the Boston Symphony. At one point I jumped ship for a few days to visit a friend who was a singer at the Düsseldorf Opera. While I was waiting for a performance of *Eugene Onegin* to begin, an opera in which Fyodor Stravinsky, the composer's father, had been a famous Gremin, my neighbor turned to me and asked, "Where do you suppose Stravinsky will be buried?" It seemed a strange opening gambit for a conversation, and only gradually did the reason for the question become clear to me. It was 6 April 1971, and Stravinsky had died in New York that day. I still remember the surreal experience of sitting in that theater, the sounds of Tchaikovsky filling the room, but those of *Petrushka*, *The Rite of Spring*, *The Soldier's Tale*, *The Wedding*, *Persephone*, *Oedipus Rex*, *Apollo*, the two symphonies from the 1940s, the Mass, *Orpheus*, *Agon*, *Threni*, and I don't know what else playing in my head as a counterpoint both *funèbre* and happy. It filled me with such happiness that this wonderful music existed, that I had been allowed to hear it and even sing some of it, that I had even been granted the extra magic of here and there, most often on the podium, once at JFK airport, once for a handshake at a reception in Rome, seeing the tiny man who had invented these amazing sounds, who indeed liked to think of himself as an inventor rather than a composer, who had created worlds, who had changed the face of music.

And I wondered, now what? Again I turn to Robert Craft's diary in which he quotes some of the messages that arrived after Stravinsky's death: "'This is the first time since Guillaume de Machaut that the world is without a great composer.' Claudio Arrau cables from London: 'Now he joins the immortals where in any case he has already been for fifty years.' But perhaps the most nearly perfect of them all, from Luciano Berio, simply says, '*Adieu père Igor et merci.*'" It is tempting to bristle at the message about Machaut. Some wonderful composers were left alive in April 1971, but every one of them, even Messiaen, would have acknowledged that Stravinsky was in another league.

I loved typing that sentence that had both the *Requiem Canticles* and *The Owl and the Pussy-cat* in it, the one a hieratic act of mourning for a woman he did not know and at the same time a memorial for friends who died during its composition—Edgard Varèse, Alberto Giacometti, and Evelyn Waugh—the other, one of countless messages of love, musical and otherwise, to Vera Stravinsky, who had come into his life in 1921 and whom he married in 1940, a year after the death of his first wife. The pairing of the Mass for the Dead and Edward Lear might seem incongruous, but each composition—or invention— is completely characteristic, personal, authentic, and in each the whole artist is involved, and the whole man. And how beautifully those two works, the canticle and the little song for soprano and piano, begin to give us some idea of Stravinsky's range.

Both are a long way from *The Firebird* and *Petrushka*, even from *The Rite of Spring*. Few composers traveled so far in a lifetime. There was a fan who told Stravinsky how much she loved *The Firebird*, *Petrushka*, and even *The Rite of Spring*, then wailed, "But why did you stop?" To which Stravinsky replied, "Why did *you* stop?" That admirer of the early ballets was not alone. In my teens— this must have been in reading I did on my own; in college I don't think Stravinsky was even mentioned in Music 101—I was instructed that Stravinsky had indeed "stopped" after *The Rite of Spring* in 1913, that he had run dry and taken refuge in mannerism and masquerade.

In recent years I had thought that with so much post-*Rite* Stravinsky having become central repertoire this canard had died, but it seems there is still some life in that tough old duck. Browsing in a bookstore, I took a look at *The Picasso Papers* by Rosalind Krauss, one of our most provocative art critics. Like Stravinsky, Picasso has been accused of having no center, of being like one of those dressmakers' wire forms, decorated by one costume and disguise after another, and much of Krauss's book appeared to be accusatorial in just that spirit. I wondered whether I would find Stravinsky in *The Picasso Papers*, and sure enough, there he was, described as writing in his so-called neoclassical works, a label that would account for a large number of important works from *Pulcinella* in 1920 to *The Rake's Progress* in 1951, "borrowed music of the pastiche," which Krauss goes on to characterize as "fake modernism, which is nothing but a betrayal of real modernist procedures." She actually bases her severe judgment not on her own listening to Stravinsky's music but on the strictures of Theodor Wiesengrund Adorno, a passionately polemical Stravinsky-hater—and Schoenberg booster—at a time, one that now seems remote indeed, when those two composers were perceived, by themselves among others, as representing irreconcilable opposites.

Of course we find pastiche in Stravinsky. *Pulcinella* is a delightful example, one in which he changed the rules about the relationship to another composer's works. It is a reworking of eighteenth-century pieces all believed at the time to be by Pergolesi, undertaken as an exuberant declaration of "how I would have proceeded if I had come up with these themes." Stravinsky, moreover, was absolutely right when he observed that *Pulcinella* was Pergolesi's best piece. In 1928, for a dance score, *The Fairy's Kiss*, Stravinsky enjoyed himself with similar reinventions of mostly obscure Tchaikovsky, a composer he loved deeply. Still later he added new strands of counterpoint to Bach's last organ work, the Canonic Variations on *Von Himmel hoch* ("with the Master's permission," says the score in German), and fashioned exquisite pulcinellizations of madrigals and sacred pieces by that sixteenth-century maverick, Carlo Gesualdo. And let us not forget that brilliant one-minute firework, the *Greeting Prelude* for the eightieth birthday of Pierre Monteux, who had conducted the first performances of *Petrushka* and *The Rite of Spring*. That spirited salute is a bouquet of canons on guess what tune.

Stravinsky always found the absorption of preexisting material stimulating. It also got him into trouble from time to time. Not only had he erroneously assumed that *Happy Birthday* was a folk song in the public domain, but years earlier he had, under the same mistaken assumption, put into *Petrushka* a song he had heard a barrel-organ play outside his window. When, in 1944, he led the Boston Symphony in his new orchestration and harmonization of "The Star-Spangled Banner," he found himself in violation of a Massachusetts law forbidding "tampering with national property." He was arrested, and his Boston

Police Department mug shot is surely one of the oddest among the thousands of images of this extraordinarily photogenic man.

The strangest case of Stravinsky's tampering with national property, as it turns out, is *The Rite of Spring,* a work that left as huge and indelible a mark on twentieth-century music as the Beethoven Ninth and *Tristan* had on that of the nineteenth century. *The Rite of Spring*—and isn't it remarkable how that phrase and variants of it have entered the English language?—stands as a symbol of musical modernism and its rhythms can still jolt you. It is also full of tunes: there is plenty to hum and whistle as you leave the hall. Stravinsky declared that, while what the bassoon plays at the beginning of the work is a folk song, all the other melodies were his own. Not so. Most of them come from published collections of folk music, including ones assembled by his teacher Rimsky-Korsakov. It was the musicologist Richard Taruskin who blew Stravinsky's cover, and his researches culminated in a double tome, *Stravinsky and the Russian Traditions,* that is one of the most exciting books on music to have come out in the last half-century, and for reasons that go far beyond the issue of the composer's prevarications.

Through much of his life, in countless interviews, but more weightily in his ghost-written *Chronicles of My Life* and the famous, also ghost-written, Harvard lectures titled *The Poetics of Music,* Stravinsky followed a strong urge to explain, justify, and ever more to invent and reinvent himself. One thinks of Wagner, a composer with an even greater penchant for explanation, justification, invention, and reinvention, and one, moreover, who did it without ghostwriters. Stravinsky on Stravinsky can be as unreliable as Wagner on Wagner.

Whatever Stravinsky did and whatever he pretended in his long life as an inventor and explorer, it allowed him to turn out masterpiece after masterpiece in incredible profusion and with incredible confidence and joy. To have been his contemporary was a joyous privilege. My awareness of him as a living composer who was still writing began with my first radio hearing of the 1940 Symphony in C, an experience as puzzling in its way as *The Rite* had been in *Fantasia* because to my inexperienced ear the Symphony seemed to sound nothing like *The Rite.*

My first actual sight of Stravinsky was at Carnegie Hall during my freshman year at Princeton. It was January 1946, and the occasion was the first performance of the Symphony in Three Movements, with Stravinsky conducting the New York Philharmonic, for whom he had written it. The new 1945 version of the *Firebird* Suite was on the program and, I believe, *Scènes de Ballet.* The last time I saw him was in the summer of 1962 at one of those Lewisohn Stadium concerts that were for so many years such a precious and beloved source of summer refreshment for New Yorkers. That concert followed what was by then a familiar pattern: Robert Craft led most of the program (it included *The Rite of Spring*), and then Stravinsky came out to conclude the evening, most often and on that occasion with the 1919 *Firebird* Suite (which, he said, he had conducted well over a thousand times, but that another thousand would not suffice to erase the memory of the terror the first had caused him).

In those sixteen and a half years Stravinsky's standing had changed entirely. I still remember how excited I was in 1946 at the thought of seeing him in the flesh—I could hardly have been more fevered with anticipation had it been Beethoven or Brahms—and how shocked I was to observe that the Philharmonic's subscription audience didn't seem to give much of a damn and that the applause for the new symphony was pretty perfunctory. It was no better, or maybe even worse, at a Carnegie Hall concert by the Boston Symphony a few years later when he conducted what in my years of working at program-planning for symphony orchestras I used to call a suicide program, one without a guaranteed hit. I believe then we had the Concerto in D for Strings, the Piano Concerto (the soloist was Stravinsky's son Soulima, and if you ever wanted to see genetics at work . . .), and the new ballet score *Orpheus*.

In the 1940s Stravinsky was at the nadir of his reputation. The legend of his having long ago run dry had taken hold. Then, very late in the game he became transmuted into Grand Old Man. The publication in 1957 of his first book of conversations with Robert Craft had something to do with that, and so did a few television documentaries. One exception to the astounding lack of interest in Stravinsky in the 1940s and 1950s, or even respect for him, was the ballet audience. They—we, I should say—always loved him, and when he appeared in the pit at the mosque that had so bizarrely become the New York City Center to conduct the final number at one of the New York City Ballet's Stravinsky evenings, there was an instant sense of festivity, and the cheering was loud and long. Another happy memory: attending rehearsals for that wonderful company's first production of *Agon*, with choreography of course by George Balanchine. Leon Barzin, the company's music director, conducted, but Stravinsky was a watchful and swift-moving presence in the auditorium. At one point he wanted a more emphatic *portamento* from the violas and, with a wicked smile, he leaned over the edge of the orchestra pit and said, "Like Ormandy."

What was Stravinsky like as a conductor? He certainly understood how the pieces went (he rarely conducted music other than his own). He did not underline what did not need underlining and even when he took interpretive risks—I recall an unforgettable *Symphony of Psalms* at Saint Thomas's Church in New York with a finale vastly slower than what the score indicates—the result never came across as eccentric, self-indulgent, or, in that very dangerous page of the *Psalms*, sentimental. His best performances had an exhilarating toughness and ruggedness. Famously, he fussed a lot about wanting no "interpretation," just get the notes and the rhythms right. If, however, you go to the pieces he recorded more than once, and the Symphony in Three

Movements is a good example, you quickly hear that he was anything other than an unyielding, unchanging, mechanical conductor of his own music.

Like Schoenberg and Copland, Stravinsky had one of the twentieth century's great composer faces. He was imperturbably elegant when he walked onto the stage, and even in his last years, when he used a cane and had become tinier than ever, he was a courtly host to his audience. When he turned to face the orchestra he hunched over, sank his head into the score as though the notes even of *Firebird* were startling news to him, and conducted with symmetrical motions of both arms. No question, his technique was limited, and he knew it. There is a rehearsal tape where at a transition with a difficult meter change he coolly tells the orchestra, "I'm sorry, I cannot help you here." With no other conductor was it so hard to figure out how what you *heard* was somehow the result of the awkward and constricted performance you *saw*. Still, especially in his later years, his presence could impart magic to an occasion. There was that special crash of applause when he appeared in the door, and those evenings were events.

Robert Shaw liked to remind us that creation did not stop after the Sixth Day and that the power to create is one of the great gifts granted us as human beings. Igor Stravinsky's immense, light-shedding, ear-stretching, joy-giving legacy was perhaps the most potent evidence in the sad twentieth century of the human creative gift.

—M.S.

III.
THE RECENT SCENE

A Visit with Lou Harrison

hat's an awfully damn East Coast thing to say!" That scornful remark was addressed to me by the composer and writer Charles Shere. I no longer remember what terrible thing I had said that elicited Shere's words. I do remember that he spoke them at Tanglewood in the summer of 1974 at a workshop on music criticism and that it came as a shock to me that there could be an "East Coast thing to say" or, by obvious inference, a "West Coast thing." I was the *Boston Globe*'s music critic then, and we on the East Coast thought of our "thing" as central and normative, and of everything else as eccentric and peripheral.

To Michael Tilson Thomas, music director of the San Francisco Symphony since 1995, one of the most significant things about that orchestra is that it is *in* San Francisco, "on the Pacific and facing Asia, [and thus] geographically and sociologically the right place to be for the twenty-first century." One of MTT's initial plans for the San Francisco Symphony was to celebrate the orchestra's Pacificness, so to speak. That is one reason for special attention paid to Lou Harrison, a figure so lively and forward-looking that the word "senior" sat oddly upon him, although, at almost eighty, he can be said to have earned it.

Lou Harrison is very much a West Coast phenomenon. To visit him, as I did in the summer of 1995, at the house in Aptos where he lived with his partner, the instrument-builder William Colvig, was first of all to be reminded why some people love to live in California. (Bill Colvig died in 2000 at the age of

82; Harrison, busy to the last, died in February 2003 while on the road.) In his directions to the house, Harrison told me to look for "a jazzy-looking roof"—and it does indeed present a striking ballet of planes and angles—and for the tallest chimney in sight. The house is on what he called the third story above sea level, with just the sort of spectacular view of the Pacific that this suggests, but Lou immediately added that the way the world is going it might well be the second story before long. When I visited in August, he and Bill Colvig had not yet seen *Waterworld,* the Kevin Costner film about a future plagued with the effects of global warming, but it was definitely on the agenda.

I want to return to that scene in 1995. Like his music, Lou seems so much a part of the present. Before we settle in the lush garden to talk, Lou and Bill offer a quick tour of the house, where the beautiful, the practical, and the enchantingly kitschy cohabit harmoniously and happily. Just to the left of the main entrance is the subtly lit gamelan room—its official name is the Ives Room—its ample floor area covered with bronze, iron, wood, and bamboo instruments, all built by Bill. A group of students and practitioners of all ages, most associated with the University of California at Santa Cruz, and including Lou himself, meets there regularly to study and practice. But this is California at its best, an open world, and so the gamelan shares space with a clavichord, several reed organs, and a beautifully carved, brown 1871 Steinway grand piano that was the favorite West Coast instrument of the Australian composer and pianist Percy Grainger (1882–1961), a forward-looking figure whose disinclination to believe that wonderful music happened only in Europe and was produced only by white men made him highly *simpatico* to Lou. One of the most conspicuous objects in the room, and surely the most startling, is a life-size cutout of Patrick Stewart as Captain Picard. It is not that Lou and Bill are Trekkies; rather, the actor has been assigned this central position in honor of his role in the new Paul Rudnick/Christopher Ashley movie *Jeffrey,* which focuses on gay relationships in the shadow of AIDS.

In the garden, Lou shows me a fine growth of English roses, these being raised not only for their looks but to ensure a supply of rose hips for rose-hip tea and jam. Off in the background is a cutout of a comfortably 1940s-looking automobile by the sculptor Mark Bulwinkle. Lou points to the open-mouthed figure in the back seat: "That's me, telling Bill how to drive." He laughs, as he does often. His face, white-bearded, is open and serious, the eyes almost alarmingly scrutinous, but when he is amused and goes into his laugh mode, it happens without warning or modulation, the jaw drops like that of an old-fashioned nutcracker, and the whole structure is realigned in a smile of totally enveloping warmth.

I ask Lou about the East Coast/West Coast Atlantic/Pacific thing. His immediate response is that one of the salient differences is the interest on the part of West Coast composers in new instruments and new tunings—new to traditional European-based music, that is: "None of us can resist making or incorporating new instruments." Just the three pieces that appear on San Francisco Symphony programs this season include ranch triangles, sleighbells, big bells made from large, gassed-out oxygen tanks that are struck with baseball bats, sweet bell tree, the deep, bossed gong of the Javanese gamelan, spoons, tackpiano, iron pipes, brake drums, elephant bells, and tongued teponaztli (a Mexican slit drum); the Varied Trio played on the orchestra's chamber music series last season called for tuned rice bowls and bakers' pans. Among his allies in this kind of exploring of colors and textures, Lou mentions Henry Cowell, one of the great California pioneers in the first half of the twentieth century and one of own his chief mentors, Janice Giteck, Morgan Powell, and of course Harry Partch, one of the boldest of all the explorers, inventor of many new instruments (among them seventy-two-string kitharas, boos, cloud-chamber bowls, and blow-boys), and the proponent of a forty-three-note scale.

Lou Harrison was born in Portland, Oregon, in 1917, but he was raised in San Francisco, where his family moved when he was nine. His father was the second Harrison in whom his mother had a romantic interest, and his business was "automobiles and stuff," and he was for a time the proprietor of one of those grand palaces on Van Ness Avenue in San Francisco. He was not a musician himself, but he got great pleasure from music, his favorite performer being the banjo virtuoso Eddie Peabody. Lou's mother had "one of those romantic Victorian inheritances," which came in handy on those occasions when her husband wandered into financially uncertain waters, such as the establishment of a factory for the production of Chinese jugs. She was a good pianist and her sister Lounette was a fine violinist. The son and heir, for some reason expected to be a daughter, was to have been named for Aunt Lounette, "but when they discovered I had ornaments they cut off the 'nette.'"

In San Francisco, Lou studied Gregorian chant at Mission Dolores, went to dancing class where he and his brother dutifully learned to maneuver their way through waltzes, schottisches, and polkas, and listened with curiosity and delight to whatever music came out of the Chinese and Japanese communities. It was a varied diet that led naturally to a life in which, along with being a prolific composer, Lou has at different times been a florist, record clerk, poet, dancer ("when I was in shape acceptable"), music and dance critic, music copyist, and playwright. Versatility and flexibility have always been among his outstanding attributes, and now there seem to be no barriers of geography and history that stand between Lou Harrison and the world's music.

In 1934, Lou became a student of Henry Cowell, which was probably the single most critical decision of his musical life, and although the formal teacher-pupil relationship went on for only one year, the deep friendship endured until Cowell's death in 1965. He remembers with special gratitude a course on what later came to be called "world music" that Cowell taught for the extension division of the University of California at San Francisco. (Having fallen on hard times in 1940, Cowell worked for a time as secretary to Percy Grainger, and it was through the good offices of Cowell's widow that the Grainger Steinway came to its present home in the gamelan room at Aptos.)

At Cowell's suggestion, Lou went to Los Angeles to work with Schoenberg. It is hard to imagine two composers more different than Arnold Schoenberg and Lou Harrison, but Schoenberg was not the rigid sort of a musician he is often made out to be—he had, for example, invited Cowell to play for his composition class in Berlin in the 1920s—and the relationship, though brief, was thoroughly cordial. Lou remembers Schoenberg fondly: "He was very open and he took *you* seriously." The class was set up as a kind of Platonic symposium, "though we didn't drink. Schoenberg constantly moved me, and all his students, in the direction of simplicity—bring out *only the salient*; and when he dismissed me, he urged me above all to study Mozart." Lou notes extraordinary similarities between what he was taught about orchestration by Schoenberg and later by Virgil Thomson, another pair of composers who could hardly be more different. Among his fellow students, Lou particularly remembers the teenage Dika Newlin, who went on to write one of the first important books in English about Schoenberg, and the photographer Harold Halma, "author of the famous picture of Truman Capote *en odalisque*."

After Los Angeles, Cowell, as Lou puts it, "spread me around." He got him jobs, the first of them as accompanist for Tina Flade's modern dance classes at Mills College; during this association he became expert in Labanotation for dance. It was also during this period that he had his first contact with the San Francisco Symphony: Pierre Monteux conducted his Prelude to *The Trojan Women* of Euripides (from incidental music written for a production at Mills), not on a subscription concert, but on one of the popular Standard Hour broadcasts. "He also encouraged what became my *Elegiac Symphony*" (begun in 1941, completed in 1975). Monteux regretted not feeling able to do more for the gifted and original young composer: "If this were Paris . . . " he sighed.

In the 1940s, Lou Harrison had his East Coast period. Again through Cowell, he had met Virgil Thomson, that fascinating amalgam of Kansas City and the 7th Arrondissement, who had moved back to America after many years in Europe to become the *Herald-Tribune*'s music critic. Not only did Thomson himself, on his best nights, spark true glory years in the history of music criticism in America, but he engaged younger writers who also added to the luster of the *Tribune*'s arts pages. Lou was one of these, as were Paul Bowles, Elliott Carter, Edwin Denby, Arthur Berger, B. H. Haggin, John Cage, William Flanagan, and Peggy Glanville-Hicks. At the same time, Lou contributed to that invaluable journal *Modern Music*, served as editor for New Music Editions, and conducted. It was he who, in 1947, led the first complete performance of a symphony by Charles Ives—No. 3, a work then thirty-eight years old. It was at that memorable concert in the tiny Carnegie Recital Hall (now Weill Hall) that I first laid eyes on Lou Harrison; the next time was in Rome in 1954 when, at an in part dauntingly severe new-music festival, the twenty-seven-year-old Leontyne Price sang his enchanting *Rapunzel*. The Ives connection continued: Lou became one of the musicians involved in preparing Ives's often chaotic manuscripts for publication and performance, and himself became one of the heirs of the Ives estate, something that allowed him to do much quiet good in the music world. It also made possible the establishment of the gamelan in his house, and hence the naming of the room where it is housed for the great American composer.

Another vitally essential mentor—along with Cowell, John Cage (to whom he was also bound in close friendship), Thomson, and the Korean musician Lee Hye-Ku—has been his own Javanese gamelan teacher, Pak Chokro. Lou says of him: "There's nothing you could hope to surprise him with. Like Henry Cowell, he's all for mixing it up and having a good time." That double encomium says it all.

When I visited Lou Harrison in August, it was in the middle of the amazing Cabrillo Festival, one devoted primarily to twentieth-century music and commanding an audience of unsurpassed loyalty and enthusiasm. Cabrillo, too, is one of Lou's gifts to the music world. He founded the festival at Cabrillo College in Aptos in 1963 together with the bassoonist, conductor, and scholar Robert Hughes and Ted Teows of the Cabrillo College faculty. At Cabrillo, Lou Harrison is royalty. The applause was immense when he and Bill Colvig walked onto the stage of the Santa Cruz Civic Auditorium to be the narrators for a performance of Lou's dance score *The Marriage at the Eiffel Tower*, and when the two sat in the audience, there was an unceasing stream of visitors and friends who came to greet them.

Lou Harrison loved it when people cared about his music, and he made no bones about that. At the same time, he noted ruefully that the beautiful house at the top of Aptos had virtually become a business office where the telephone answering machine and the fax were constantly engaged. He and Bill harbored plans for the purchase of a real hideaway. One of his current projects was taking weekly classes in American Sign Language. That was something he had gotten into because of a dear friend who was profoundly deaf, but Lou commented that one of the things he most treasured about this course of learning was that it guaranteed him five hours of silence each week.

Invitations to concerts, schools, conferences, and symposia came in constantly, and so did requests for new compositions. At the head of the list was one from the choreographer and dancer Mark Morris. Lou remarked that he had recently bought a set of CDs of the Beethoven string quartets. He shook his head, laughed the Lou Harrison laugh, and said, "Maybe I'll actually have time to listen to one or two before I die." Busoni said that only he who looks ahead is truly happy. I saw that in action at the hilltop in Aptos.

—M.S.

George Perle:
Composing a Way of Life

Had you been the kind of clairvoyant who utters pronouncements over children as they trade the womb for daylight, you could not have predicted that the child born in Bayonne, New Jersey, on 6 May 1915, and named George Perle, would grow up making music: making it in the most literal way, by putting notes down on paper, but also by discerning its inner grammar, the structural principles it demanded since the breakdown of the tonal language that Western composers had spoken for the last two hundred years. The deep currents of the music, the soul-piercing insights of the discoveries—they have been the adventure of a lifetime for this son of Russian immigrants, a man whose father was a housepainter and whose mother was a housewife; a man who could not, but for the kind of brain that makes its own destiny, be doing what he is doing today.

George Perle's adventure began in Chicago, where the family had moved shortly after George was born. From the early gauze of memory he recalls the first sound in his ears, Yiddish; short winter afternoons when he would wait with his mother in the front yard for the mail, for news from Russia—where an influenza epidemic and political turmoil made relatives more uncertain than ever of what the next day would hold. From abroad, too, came a newly arrived older cousin, Esther, who was to live with the family and for whom George's father had saved enough to buy a piano. One day, when George was six, Esther played the F-minor Étude from Chopin's *Trois Nouvelles Études*. It is the first piece of music he recalls hearing, and almost seventy years later, he wrote that the experience "was so intense, so startling, as to induce a traumatic change of consciousness." He also knew—immediately—that he wanted to compose.

It is October 1990, shortly after publication of Perle's fourth book, *The Listening Composer*, and soon after he had begun the second season of his three-year appointment as the San Francisco Symphony's composer-in-residence. He is sitting now in his studio on the eleventh floor of Opera Plaza in San Francisco, three blocks north of Davies Symphony Hall. He and his wife, pianist Shirley Rhoads, have just moved here from across town—their full-time residence is in New York City, where Perle has been based for thirty years—and this room is still waiting for a piano and a few more chairs. A desk is covered with sheets of music—he is orchestrating his Sinfonietta II, due for its world premiere by the San Francisco Symphony in February. A Macintosh computer, the great eliminator of drudgery that he uses for tasks as various as writing books and summoning complete arrays of chord relationships, drones an incantation to technology, its screen glowing ocean-gray. A potted white anthurium is in the corner next to the balcony doors, overlooking Van Ness Avenue and a cityscape formed by the Bank of America building, a recently opened Marriott hotel that has appalled local architecture critics, and other symbols with which corporate America has defined the urban skyline. George Perle is a long way from that day in 1921 when the Chopin entered his mind, but the memory is as vivid as the sound of his own music.

"Nobody told me what composition was. I just knew that that was my connection with music, not sitting there playing the piano." He has the voice of a tough guy, rough-grained, and the accent is equal parts Chicago and New York. The delivery is unhesitating, the words well-chosen. "I didn't know where this music came from. Yet when I heard that first piece I identified with the *source* of the music, and not with my cousin's playing."

The "source of that music" was the person who conceived it and translated the conception to the page. "I didn't know what that meant. I realized it only little by little." And without any help from Esther, who never understood what her young pupil was about, and whose teaching days ended because of what George's father learned when he sat in on a lesson: that his son's mistakes were answered by a wooden ruler cracking across his knuckles. "She felt that all the music worth knowing had already been written. I was stupefied by my lack of communication with her."

And frustrated. But childhood can be a frustrating proposition in any case, and he also remembers more typical aspirations—days when he imagined himself sliding down the fire-pole and clinging to Hook and Ladder No. 1 as it leaned into a turn. Always, though, he knew that any dream but composing was bound to remain fantasy. And then one day—he thinks he was about seven—he scribbled a few bars he wanted to present as a gift to a teacher at school. He showed his mother what he had written. She had no idea what it was, but her response, he believes, made all the difference, and has ever since. It was simply this: "George, that's wonderful!"

"I could go to my mother. She had complete faith in whatever I wanted to do. She had this idea that the most important thing in the world was your inner life. I can't remember once when she asked me how much money I made. Isn't that extraordinary? (It was always my father's first question!) I didn't realize until much later—when I ran into people who didn't know what they wanted to do, or who were scared of it or something—what a special piece of luck I'd had in having a mother like this, and the extent to which that early experience conditioned all the rest of my life, right up to this moment."

He is talking about self-confidence, something he has had more than one occasion to fall back on. Because for most of his life, George Perle has been trying to do something that only one other composer in the twentieth century— Arnold Schoenberg—tried to do: lay down a system of composition that would bring a common language back to music. If this is your aspiration, you are bound to run into two kinds of people among your colleagues, those who will hail you as a master, and those who will brand you as conceited (at best) or a lunatic (at worst). George Perle has been called everything between those extremes.

In 1937, Perle first saw the score of Alban Berg's *Lyric Suite*. He picked it up himself. No one would have encouraged him to look at this music, for interest in the work of Schoenberg, Berg, and Webern was in eclipse. The encounter with the *Lyric Suite* had two consequences. One is easy to describe. It led him to studies of Berg's music, studies of such completeness and depth that he has become recognized as the world's leading authority on the composer. The other consequence is more complicated. The *Lyric Suite* led Perle into the work of the Second Viennese School, and then almost immediately into an understanding that Schoenberg's theories of atonality required modification. That modification has been the Polar Star of Perle's professional life, influencing everything he does, a goal that he has approached gradually at times, more quickly at others. He has given his formulated concepts a name that sounds at first like a contradiction in terms but which in fact holds the key to his search for unity and comprehensiveness, his attempt to reshape the strands of a fragmented art into the strong and comely whole it once was: "Twelve-tone Tonality." This is a still-evolving system of compositional rules and guidelines Perle has *deduced* over the years: by writing music, certainly, but also by analyzing the work of Schoenberg, Berg, Webern, Bartók, Stravinsky, Scriabin, Debussy: all in an attempt to give composers today the kinds of tools available to the great tonal composers—Bach, Mozart, Haydn, Beethoven, Schubert, Brahms—an attempt to embrace the history of the art in an all-encompassing way and to compose a music that does not break with, but rather continues the great tradition of Western music that grew out of the Renaissance. By 1941, Perle had begun to organize his ideas about twelve-tone tonality: The System, he calls it.

"In the tonal system, you have very basic structural principles. You can say about two different pieces that they're in the same key. You can ask if a note is a leading tone, a passing tone, a structural tone. These are the things that define tonality. But already in the nineteenth century, we encounter details—in Chopin, in Liszt, for example—that call the structural basis of tonality into question. And not to recognize that we have a twelve-tone scale is to pretend that the history of music since Schubert never happened. But I think music should be able to do what it has always done. I think it should be coherent. I think it should have cadences and phrases. A lot of contemporary music is like finger-painting—an impressionistic thing that makes no serious sense to me. I think people have forgotten what music is supposed to do.

"For me, the tonal language is something miraculous. It has structure and coherence. It is a *language*. I felt from the beginning that it was of unbelievable interest that you could take a chord and follow it with another chord, and that there was a way to do this and make a progression—they weren't just two chords next to each other. You could make choices in going from the first chord to the second. Each one said something different—don't ask me what. But I knew that going from a C-major chord to an A-minor chord was not the same thing as going from a C-major chord to an F-major chord. And *anybody* can hear this! You don't need to be a musician. I don't want simply to eliminate all this and go around finger-painting. I think I have a language—deducible from everything that has happened in music."

Though Schoenberg is one of Perle's heroes ("I think he was a very great man"), Perle believes Schoenberg's work was unfinished. "He was looking for a language. And he made a step toward it in the twelve-tone system. But he didn't go far enough. When the internal combustion engine was invented, they stuck it in a carriage. And it took a while before they figured out that it needed a different suspension system, different wheels, that it didn't have to look like a buggy. Schoenberg's twelve-tone system was like that. He took a terribly bold step. But his system had to be modified again. And somebody had to come in from the outside to do it."

Perle is speaking from experience. His own system of twelve-tone tonality underwent what he calls an "explosive" development when a former student, Paul Lansky, approached it from the outside and posed questions whose effect was to help Perle complete various puzzles whose solutions had eluded him for years. Perle's new understanding of his own system led to his second book, *Twelve-tone Tonality*. It also led to his understanding other music in a new way. He now perceived connections between Bartók and Schoenberg—connections "infinitely more important than the stylistic features that separated them"—and his own work, and he arrived at a broad conception of twelve-tone music that went well beyond Schoenberg's system, even encompassing Debussy, Scriabin, and Stravinsky, going back to developments as early as some that appear in Rimsky-Korsakov's *Coq d'or* Suite. "The System" today is very different from what it was in 1941. "And when it gets along further it may look very different from the way it looks now. It is just the beginning of a language. But for me, it provides a total structure with which I can think." This language, he believes, is also what makes his music accessible to an audience of musical sophisticates and novices alike.

"I don't think directly about an audience when I'm composing. I hear what I'm doing and decide whether what I'm writing is effective and exciting. But I decide for myself. I think it has always been like this. When Beethoven started his Fifth Symphony da-da-da-DA, nobody had ever done that before. It had a certain impact on him. He was his own audience. Everyone else eventually *becomes* the audience.

"There's this mystique that there's an elite of specialists for whom contemporary music is written. I don't write up or down to anybody. I'm just doing what composers have always done. Some people have written about me as though I were a composer of inaccessible music." No doubt they were jumping to conclusions, extrapolating from the difficulty of Perle's first book, *Serial Composition and Atonality*—those subjects cannot be written about in an easy way—that an explicator of such stuff must himself write a tuneless, uncrackable code. "But my experience has been that people who *listen* to my music are amazed by how accessible they find it."

When Perle's String Quartet No. 8, *Windows of Order,* had its premiere in New York in 1989, a critic for one of that city's major papers, a man who loathes twelve-tone music, raved about the new piece—despite the fact, he suggested, that it had been written according to some sort of system. "Why didn't he consider the possibility that the music makes sense *because* of what I'm doing? Which is the case. I have a language that permits progression, and cadences, and keys. I can think in a systematic way about music. That's what you can do when you have a language—as with Mozart, Brahms, Palestrina, Schubert.

"I can do what a tonal composer can do. I can look at what I have and say, 'I can do this again in another mode. I can do something to each of these intervals that will transform it in an ordered way, and then I can transpose it so that I'll be in another key as well as in another mode. And if I go through so many progressions, I'll get back to where I was at the beginning.'" He grows increasingly impassioned. "Now, that is not *any* different from what Beethoven did when he composed, or Mozart, or Chopin. *They had a system.* Having a system doesn't mean you're composing according to some abstract formula. It means just the opposite. I can go to my music and tell you what the connection is between the chord that ends one movement and the chord that ends another. And Beethoven could have told you the same about his music. Any tonal composer could have told you. Composers today have *forgotten* about those things. The composers at the beginning of the twentieth century—Debussy and Stravinsky and Scriabin, Schoenberg, Berg, and Webern, even Hindemith: *They knew what music was supposed to be like.* And they took these things seriously, and they came up with answers."

His own search for answers has often led him to reassess earlier works as he looks back on them from ever-new vantage points of further development. He has withdrawn much music that no longer satisfies him. "But a composer can make mistakes about such things." When pianist Michael Boriskin asked him for some of his music for a recording of American piano works he was planning— it turned into an all-Perle collection—Perle came across two pieces he had withdrawn, the Suite in C (of 1970) and the Fantasy-Variations (of 1971). "I didn't understand them any more. Well, Michael learned them and they're wonderful. The development that had happened in my work had been so great that I didn't even know how to analyze the difference between those pieces and what I was currently doing. I learned that that didn't take anything away from their integrity."

Another piano work, the *Pantomime, Interlude, and Fugue*, which he wrote in 1937, had its premiere forty years after it was composed. This early piece, which reveals Perle's kinship with those who put a premium on wit, composers like Haydn and Prokofiev, was introduced to the world by—and thanks to the persuasive powers of—Shirley Rhoads, his wife since 1981 and a close friend since 1946. Herself a fine and perceptive musician, she is one of the few people whose judgment and criticisms he trusts completely, and she is also the only one allowed to hear works in progress.

Perle admits that his belief in The System has to some extent isolated him, though it may be an exaggeration to call someone an outsider after he has won the Pulitzer Prize, two Guggenheim Fellowships, and a MacArthur Foundation "genius award," and who has had his music played and recorded by major orchestras, chamber ensembles, and soloists. He writes good music, and audiences genuinely like his work. One need only listen to a piece such as the Sinfonietta I to hear that this was not written in the antiseptic environment of the academy. It is unafraid to laugh, or make jokes. (Footnote: We owe the Sinfonietta I to Shirley, whose horror at learning that her husband had thrown out what she called "that beautiful stuff you started the other day" made him retrieve the discarded pages and continue work on the piece.) The Sinfonietta I is the real thing. It ought to be. Music is more than George Perle's job. It is a love and a passion, a sweetly caring mistress who has recompensed his attentions by granting him what seems to be the secret of endless youth. To see George Perle at seventy-five, and to hear him speak, is to feel yourself in the presence of a man half his age. He talks about music old and new with equal enthusiasm. He reveres Berg of course, but also Stravinsky. "Beethoven I never listen to when I'm composing—it's too intimidating." He laughs. "You listen to Beethoven if you want to stop writing music.

"Haydn is a composer's composer. He takes such pleasure in what music can do, and the fun you can have in the way you modulate, in having a couple of extra bars where you don't expect them, in false recapitulations. He just enjoys doing these things. It's not a question of any message. It's a way of taking pleasure in being alive."

Being alive, after all, is what composing is all about, the ideas welling up from a source as mysterious as creation. George Perle keeps odd hours, rising at four in the morning to begin work, catching up on rest with naps throughout the day. The genesis of his musical ideas is a secret even from himself, though he recalls what sparked some of them. He went to sleep one night in 1981 after reading about the imposition of martial law in Poland. He awoke thinking first of the Solidarity movement, then made a mental leap to Chopin, then heard the first phrase of what would become the second of his Six New Etudes. He leaped out of bed, went to the piano, and wrote six bars of music. Later that morning he continued and reached the end of the first page. Then he got stuck. For five years he stayed stuck with this piece while he began and completed others. One day, as suddenly as the Etude had come into being, the block to its continuation vanished, and it was finished.

Perle is a constant worker. In the months just after our conversation, he completed the Sinfonietta II and the First Piano Concerto within weeks of each other. He was planning other music—a second piano concerto, an overture for large orchestra for Carnegie Hall's centennial season, a symphony for the New York Philharmonic. He was revising books and writing articles. In the forefront of his mind was The System. It is in the forefront of his mind now. The System: that attempt to put the entire realm of music on a firm theoretical and structural basis, to do for composers what one of his literary idols, Henry James, did for writers when, as Leon Edel says, he "put the house of fiction in order." If Perle has not achieved out-and-out popularity—and he would be the first to tell you that he is not trying to win a popularity contest—one reason is that he disdains simple answers and easy solutions. There again, he is like James— who was also somewhat of an outsider in his time, though those who knew better also recognized the staggering importance of his work to those who write fiction. And, like James, Perle believes in himself, through and through.

"I never asked myself how many other people were doing what I was doing. I just made my own judgment, and I never questioned it. Even if it meant people weren't interested in my music. I never thought about that. Of course I felt bad about the fact that I wasn't getting performances and that other people were more successful than I was. But I did what I was supposed to do. And I've often thought: Maybe it all has been because, after one of my cousin Esther's piano lessons, I went to my mother and she made me feel that, if I wanted to write music, that was just fine. I think it must have just settled with me at that point. And it's been there ever since."

—L.R.

A Quintet for American Music

Writing a program note on William Schuman's Violin Concerto for some concerts in November 1992, I had, for the first time, to include the date of his death, 15 February 1992. That brought to mind other recent losses—Virgil Thomson, Leonard Bernstein, Aaron Copland, John Cage. They were all more than just composers. All were possessed by a lust, through some form of teaching, to change the face of American music, and they all left a mark. And they were, all five—this is dangerous because so hard to define—so essentially American.

Thomson, born in 1896, was the oldest and the first to go (on 30 September 1989). He spent long and crucial years in Europe, which made him a curious mixture of worldly Parisian and Kansas City organist. I am sure it annoyed him, as it would any composer, that he was better known as a writer about music than as someone who invented music. He certainly thought of himself as a composer first.

He was confident with and about words: "I like my book better than yours," he wrote to Copland, comparing his own *The State of Music* with Copland's *What to Listen for in Music.* He was our best critic, no contest; in literary skill he was up there with Berlioz and Shaw. For him, clarity was the key to impact, and impact was everything. When he taught criticism classes, he never dealt with musical questions, concentrating instead on good habits of precision and proper usage. None who survived his classes has ever written "prestigious" again (unless of course the subject was juggling or legerdemain).

When I started out at Princeton as a college freshman, one of my first acts was to subscribe to the *New York Herald-Tribune*, whose music critic Thomson had been since 1940. (He stayed until 1954.) How I knew to do that I no longer remember for certain, but it probably came about because B. H. Haggin, then the critic of *The Nation* and someone I read hungrily, had said good things about him. At the still missed and lamented *Trib* Thomson was a desperately needed antidote to the pompous and often tin-eared Olin Downes at the *Times*.

Thomson was vivid in praise, deft in blame. He could hit home with a sudden dart of colloquialism—"The Martinů Symphony is a beaut"—or set Ernest Ansermet before our eyes in metaphor at once charming and exact: "In appearance a simple professor, touched up perhaps toward both Agamemnon and the King of Clubs, he is at once a sage, a captain, and a prince. With wisdom, firmness, and grace he rules his domain." But the review of a Heifetz recital was headed "Silk-Underwear Music," and he described how a concert by the duo-pianists Luboshutz and Nemenoff included the "masquerade . . . [representing] a world-famous two-piano team being nice about modern music . . . false notes being thrown in to show that the piece probably wasn't worth learning completely."

Did he make sense? Not always. He spun theories that were too loosely rooted in the soil of real life. He rode hobbyhorses to exhaustion—for example, about French music and French performance style. He was not shy about using his power at the *Herald-Tribune* to the advantage of his situation as composer. He was a notorious sleeper at concerts. Samuel Barber, present at a conversation between Thomson and Eugene Ormandy, wrote that "the amount of musical politics shamelessly exchanged between these two made one tremble for the American musical world." Most of the time, we gladly put up with all that for the sake of the best of his perception and wit, and Thomson's writings—collected reviews, published correspondence, his autobiography—will long yield pleasure.

In person, he was a teller of treasurable tales, often[1] followed by the carefully enunciated admonition: "Of course, if you use this I shall sue you for *One Hun Dred Thou Sand DOLLARS*." His voice was like the best butter, but with something gritty and dangerous ground into it. Speaking of butter, I think of Virgil often because it was he who taught me that when scrambling eggs you should put half your quota of salt into the mixture before cooking and half on top just before eating: the distinction between salt inside and outside is real and worth preserving.

And Virgil Thomson the composer? Looking at the six-column work list *in Grove*, I am appalled at my ignorance. Some strong impressions remain. If the critic and musical politician was Thomson the Parisian, the composer was mostly Thomson from Kansas City, Missouri. His prescription for how to be an American

---

[1]I had written "not infrequently" but immediately heard Virgil's admonishing voice.

composer was straightforward: be an American and write whatever kind of music you like.

His own music was open, simple. Hymns had formed his language. Perhaps it was naïve, perhaps not. *The Seine at Night* and *Wheat Fields at Noon* are evocative pictures. The *Stabat mater* on a text by his friend Max Jacob, taken to a concentration camp as a homosexual and a Jew, is a sweet *tombeau*. Above all, his two Gertrude Stein operas, *Four Saints in Three Acts* and *The Mother of Us All* (whose heroine is Susan B. Anthony), are, for me, with those of John Adams, the most enjoyable American operas—and among the most touching, the most amusing, the most personal of any. There, too, as in the best of his prose, he taught us clarity.

Bernstein died on 14 October 1990. At seventy-two, though ravaged by cigarettes and Scotch, he was young. Composer, conductor, pianist, writer, teacher, endlessly inquisitive, energetic, bold, reckless, impulsive, he could have made a full-time career just out of being a mensch.

It happened that I arrived in America as a boy of fifteen just two weeks after Bernstein had made his sensational New York Philharmonic debut, substituting for Bruno Walter without rehearsal on a coast-to-coast broadcast. Very hung over, too, he later confessed. Because of that success, he was given an extra assignment, to conduct the "Star-Spangled Banner" and Bloch's *Three Jewish Poems* as a prelude to the Mahler Second, to be conducted by Artur Rodzinski, the Philharmonic's music director. I was taken to that concert by a relative who knew Bernstein a bit. Aunt Annie also led me backstage afterward, and so he was not only the first conductor I heard in my new country but also the first Famous Person I ever met. I remember his run to the Carnegie Hall podium, as though he wanted to start conducting before he even got there, and I remember as well his whirling, punching, singing as he conducted. Afterward there was this short and pencil-thin man with big ears, chain-smoking, hugging everyone within reach. Me in my new suit he checked out, asked something about piano lessons, encouraged me to keep listening. "We need you," he said, "we need you." I left, a fan.

The last time I saw him was backstage at Davies Symphony Hall in San Francisco after he had conducted a transcendent Mahler Ninth with the Israel Philharmonic, still chain-smoking, still somehow engulfing. (Rather indiscriminate French-kissing now supplemented the hugs.) The years between had brought affectionate encounters, especially while my son Adam was dating one of his daughters—"We're *machetaynes* now," he exclaimed when he spotted me on the grounds at Tanglewood—and also rough ones, when I expressed my dislike for his *Kaddish* Symphony and his Norton lectures at Harvard. Then, the first time he encountered me as the Boston Symphony's program note writer rather than a reviewer, he said: "You have always been such a bitch to me, but now it turns out you love music."

He grew to be a larger-than-life phenomenon in every way. Someone who had grown up with him told me that as boys they had once talked about what they wanted out of life. His friend said "I want to fuck every woman in the world." Bernstein replied: "I want everybody in the world to love me." Years later, the friend observed: "I get further and further away but Lennie gets closer and closer."

He was the ultimate example of a musician baffled by the challenge of being more than just a composer, and he couldn't help spreading his energies into conducting, playing the piano, writing about music, doing television and radio, sounding off on politics any more than Niagara can help doing what it does. His tumultuous energy was a force not to be contained. And most of what he got into he did brilliantly much, perhaps even most, of the time. Because all his other desires and talents were tugging at him, he did not always—perhaps not even often—compose at a level commensurate with his gift. He knew that. It pained him, just as it pained him to be thought of not as a "real" composer but as a conductor who composed, and even though he knowingly invited adoration on the podium. It comforted him slightly that his beloved Mahler had felt similarly misunderstood. His prodigality frustrated him; he never seemed a man at peace.

He made an incredible difference. He loved music and felt its balm and its pain deeply. More than anyone I have known, he had the gift for communicating his love. (Like a politician, he could also misrepresent things just amazingly, as I mention in my essay on Schumann.) His Young People's Concerts changed lives. His best conducting could create an almost disconcerting sense of being in the composer's presence. I think especially of Haydn, Beethoven, Mahler. That I often wanted to quarrel with the details made no difference.

As for Bernstein's own music, perhaps, with his own commanding presence gone, we might become freer to attend to it and explore it. And the composer who gave us the *Jeremiah* Symphony, the Masque in *The Age of Anxiety*, the Serenade, the delights of "America" and "Somewhere" in *West Side Story*, and *Songfest* will be worth getting to know better.

Copland died not many days after Bernstein, on 2 December 1990. He was ninety, had stopped composing at seventy, and, a sad victim of Alzheimer's, had hardly been seen in public since he turned eighty. The pianist Paul Jacobs told me about visiting Copland, then in his early seventies, and first seeing him through the window, seated at the piano, just staring.

There is a sound that haunts me. When Copland recorded *Appalachian Spring*, Columbia issued a rehearsal record along with the finished product. It is the usual thing, in more or less equal parts illuminating, amusing, routine. At one point Copland's voice floats across the music in remembrance: "Miss Graham is dancing."

Less spectacular and sexy as a personality than his old friend Bernstein, he was no less versatile. He composed for Carnegie Hall and Hollywood, conducted, played the piano, wrote about music with blessedly demystifying clarity, taught, did television shows, encouraged the young. He defined what we have agreed to recognize as a distinctively "open" American sound (even though it first appears in Roger Sessions's First Symphony). More than anyone, he symbolized the possibility of being a serious composer in his country and his century. He was a composer first, and everything else was subordinate to his primary calling. He enjoyed acclaim, but for him it was not the staff of life.

He was quick, responsive, unfussed, generous. When I was the *Boston Globe*'s music critic, I wanted to surprise Walter Piston, who lived just outside Boston, with a bouquet of greetings in the Sunday paper on his eightieth birthday. I asked several composers for a brief paragraph. Most eventually came through, though not without a lot of preliminary grandstanding about how busy they were. Copland's response, handwritten, came by return mail.

He was, likewise, always and indefatigably generous to younger and sometimes struggling colleagues. Schuman and Bernstein were two of them. When I lived in New York thirty and more years ago, I went to many concerts where music by young and unknown composers was played. These were evenings in dismal venues, with never an audience whose numbers went into three figures. Sometimes the concerts were rewarding, sometimes not. Often, just before the lights went down, Copland, with that unforgettably sculpted head, exuberant stride, and a smile composed in equal parts of benevolence and mischief, would walk in. One of those times, Milton Babbitt, another great man loyal to the young, looked up and said: "Aaron has really kept the faith."

Virgil Thomson's book, *American Music since 1910,* includes a photo of five composers in Thomson's living room. The host, seated, is commanding, self-pleased, wearing just a touch of smile. Behind him stands Samuel Barber, eyes cast down. Copland, leaning on the piano, observes him coolly. Gian Carlo Menotti looks up at Barber, his longtime lover. And off to one side—he might be in a different picture, even in a different room—sits William Schuman.

He looks rather as though, like that character in Molière, he is wondering—but about himself—"What the devil is he doing in that galley?" Like Thomson, Copland, and Menotti, Schuman was endlessly and usefully busy attending to matters other than composition—teaching, publishing, administering, adjudicating, power brokering. Had you found yourself sitting beside him on a plane, you would at once have "fixed" him as a prosperous businessman. His knowledgeable talk about baseball and politics would not have disabused you.

Like most American composers, Schuman got into college teaching because he had to make a living. The vigorous Sarah Lawrence professor was a natural candidate to be the new president at Juilliard; there his aim was quiet and at least reasonably courteous revolution. He changed the teaching of theory in ways that made waves all over the country. He went after that ever-elusive goal of lightening the trade-school atmosphere and turning conservatory students into Complete Musicians. He decided the school needed a resident string quartet to represent professionalism to the students and Juilliard to the world, and, not so incidentally, to bring twentieth-century music, particularly twentieth-century American music, to the head table.

Schuman turned the Juilliard presidency into a major power base. He saw the possibility, for the good of the arts and for the good of those who would get a cut of the pie, of binding Juilliard, the New York Philharmonic, the Metropolitan Opera, the New York City Ballet, the New York City Opera, and other organizations into an alliance which, one hoped, would not be too uneasy. He was a man with a sense of possibilities *and* a sense of realities. Inevitably, he became the first ruler of the empire created by the new alliance, the Lincoln Center for the Performing Arts. To borrow a phrase from the philosopher Ernst Bloch, he loved power and the tools of power. He understood the tools too. His power was different from the power of Thomson (local and laser-sharp), Bernstein (engulfing *eros*), and Copland (all in the magic of his music), but it was real power and, for many years, immense.

All that time, Schuman composed some of our best music, music of hard-edged, deeply felt Romanticism. It can be muscle-bound and loudmouth, but the best of it is tender, rich, fiercely athletic, funny, imposingly rhetorical, always forthright. Barber told him how much he envied his ability to write and control that gigantic crescendo in the Third Symphony. His stuff could be wildly optimistic, and he enjoyed that mood, but his emotional range also encompassed the marvelous Symphony No. 6, which is, with the Sessions Seventh, the darkest American one we have.

He was scrupulous about congratulating colleagues on their new works, pleasing them because his comments were so attentive and specific. (No other composer wrote letters on such creamy paper.) And, not to be taken for granted in his world, Bill Schuman could laugh about himself. He loved the story of the woman in Macon, Georgia, who told him how much she had enjoyed his Violin Concerto "even though it was atonal." With characteristic and exquisite courtesy he pointed out that none of his music was atonal, that it was always centered on a key. His new admirer set him straight. "Mr. Schuman," she said, "in Macon your music is atonal."

The last time I saw him was in Carnegie Hall when Edo de Waart was to conduct Schuman's Symphony for Strings with the Minnesota Orchestra. I was on the orchestra's staff then and was asked to sit with Schuman, look after him, see that he got backstage at the end, and so on. Beethoven's Second

Piano Concerto was on the program as well. Schuman looked over the program, nodded, turned to me, and said: "I think I'll take a bow after the Beethoven. I'll get a bigger hand."

John Cage, who died on 12 August 1992, is the odd man out here. Sadness shot through me in a way that, I admit, surprised me when I saw the news of his death. I was with my sons, rock musicians both, when the news came, and I was struck by the intensity with which they were affected.

Cage presented the paradox of an important musician who really did not write interesting music. His work and his words called into question nearly everything Thomson, Bernstein, Copland, and Schuman stood for (though among the many accomplishments of his seventy-nine energy-charged years was the co-authorship of a book on Thomson—praised by its subject for the care of its analyses and the accuracy of its work-list). He had very little to do with the world of symphony orchestras, and the little was unhappy more often than not.

His most famous piece is one that contains, in the conventional sense, no music at all. 4'33" consists of that amount of silence. Or "silence." David Tudor sat at a piano. That was it. Our shufflings and coughs and whispers were the piece, they and the noises inside our heads as we searched for sense. There was a phenomenal virtuoso doing what—in some sense—any of us could have done. "In some sense" is important because it would not be in the least interesting to have a nonpianist not playing a piano. Cage waked us right up. What are we doing here? What are our expectations? What do we or are we expected to bring? 4'33" was self-destroying. Once an audience knew what was coming—or not coming—it was no longer a viable piece. That was typical Cage— in the age of the infinitely reproducible art work (to borrow Walter Benjamin's phrase) to offer something that defied repetition. Not surprisingly, his questions got drowned in cheap mockery, dismissal, and ultimately "business as usual."

Cage's impact was in the questions he asked or caused others to ask. *Silence* is a book worth knowing. As charmingly anarchic as a Warner Brothers cartoon, he was a brilliant man whose mind had been formed by such inventors as Schoenberg, Robert Rauschenberg, Marcel Duchamp, Jasper Johns, and Merce Cunningham as well as by his profound knowledge of the writings of Thoreau and Joyce. He was an expert mycologist, a superb cook, a skilled worker in wood and metal.

He was a real American authority-defying rebel, but in his celebration of the Bicentennial, *Renga with Apartment House 1776*, with its Protestant, Sephardic, Native American, and African American voices, he was completely the old-fashioned, idealistic American.

Once, in Buffalo, I heard Cage give a lecture in which David Tudor manipulated the sound electronically, distorting and chasing it through speakers that lined the four walls, so that one could not understand a word. Inevitably, someone asked him why, since presumably he had something interesting to say, he had made it impossible for us to hear it. Cage's smile, then and always, was beatific: "It is to prepare you for your daily life."

In Boston at the New England Conservatory, Cage and I did a pre-concert conversation preceding the Friday matinee of his sweetly poetic *Renga with Apartment House*. Before moving on to Symphony Hall for the concert, we stood talking on Huntington Avenue. I forget why, but I remarked on something on the other side of the street. At the very moment Cage looked up to follow my pointing finger, a Bekins truck thundered by, blocking the view. He laughed aloud with delight. It was, once again and perfectly, the World According to Cage.

He taught us to hear and to see. That much he had in common with Thomson, Copland, Bernstein, Schuman. To hear their music and to read their writing is to know these men best, and to meet any one of them that way is to be brought face to face with more than the work of a single individual. For each pointed in the direction of something larger—music itself, and then life.

—M.S.

Three American Composers
in Pursuit of the White Whale

When we want to find out if a film or book that has caught our interest is worth seeing or reading, one of our first questions is "What is it *about?*" We don't ask that of music we've never heard. We've been taught that music is abstract, and to ask what it *means* is as naïve as trying to figure out the point of a white-on-white canvas. But three important works that span the twentieth century and that take us into the twenty-first point in directions beyond the music itself—each is "about" something. Perhaps we could focus on other works as well, yet these deal with monumental issues that in their own ways touch us all. Charles Ives's Fourth Symphony is a quest for nothing less than the meaning of life. John Corigliano's Symphony No. 1 is a tribute to those who have died of AIDS. John Adams's *On the Transmigration of Souls* is a response to the terrorist attacks of 11 September 2001. Perhaps it's coincidental, but each of these works is by an American.

It's not that American music has a monopoly on public utterance. In fact, the best example of music that makes political statements, still maintaining its artistic integrity, is that of Dmitri Shostakovich; and the Austrian dramatist Franz Grillparzer once told Beethoven that if the Imperial censors could understand music the way they understood words, Beethoven would be in jail. Still, we like to believe it is typically American to let one's voice be heard. Think of writers such as Melville and Whitman, Stephen Crane responding to the Civil War and John Steinbeck to the plight of migrant farmers, about composers like Roy Harris and Aaron Copland, who wrote major works spawned by the Great Depression and World War II.

Admittedly, the greatest artists everywhere have shouldered the task of helping whole societies make sense of the things that shape destiny. "Social responsibility" is a pretty dreary way of describing what stokes the forge of creation, but you get the idea. Abraham Lincoln, Susan B. Anthony, and Martin Luther King, Jr., wanted to change the world; artists want to change the way we see it. They too are reformers. What does all this have to do with Charles Ives, John Corigliano, and John Adams, and how can we say that they are particularly American in their musical outlook?

The composer and critic Virgil Thomson said that the definition of American music was simple: It was music written by Americans. That's a good line, but it tells us nothing. Concert music *has* a national character—though this does not necessarily mean it incorporates folk songs or popular tunes. Ives, Corigliano, and Adams help define a peculiarly American abundance. Their music—and the work of each of them sounds very different from that of the others—is vastly different from the music of, say, the American composers Samuel Barber or Charles Wuorinen. Barber's Adagio for Strings could—almost—have been written in the nineteenth century; Wuorinen comes from the post-tonal tradition that traces its genesis to Schoenberg, who in turn maintained that his development of the twelve-tone system expanded and extended the tradition of Beethoven and Brahms. Yet audiences at large have never responded to Schoenberg the way they respond to Beethoven and Brahms, nor do they respond to Wuorinen the way they respond to Ives, Corigliano, and Adams, composers who write in a tradition that grows from a fundamental tenet of this country: the tradition of the melting pot, of diversity, *E pluribus unum*— one out of many: the elemental force symbolized most profoundly in Melville's White Whale. Born of this society, their work has a strength multiplied by the many strands of its heritage.

Every one of us is the product of a heritage—we are all literally "eclectic" and the sources of our human education are many. As surely as the three composers we're viewing here, Barber and Wuorinen have strong and individual voices. But rightly or wrongly, we tend to lump Barber with the Romantics and Wuorinen with the serialists. Neither Ives, Corigliano, nor Adams are open to such classification.

Ives in fact made eclecticism his trademark, juxtaposing the sublime and the ridiculous, the serious and the comic. An amateur marching band plays at full blast outside the church where the choir raises its voice in a stately hymn. Talking about his technique, he once wrote: "This may not be a nice way to write music, but it's one way!—and who knows the only real nice way?"

John Corigliano objects to the description of his music as eclectic, though he incorporates various styles and strategies into his work, and when he characterizes his music, it's clear he is describing an eclectic approach. Nevertheless, as he told Allan Kozinn in a 1991 *Gramophone* interview, "the problem with eclecticism is that it comes with a responsibility, which is to make the combination of styles and techniques seem inevitable. How do you make them seem inevitable? Through structure and architecture. I truly believe that in any of my pieces, I can show you why any world that I inhabit is a necessary part of the work."

John Adams, as Richard Stayton wrote in the *Los Angeles Times Magazine* in 1991, has refused to remain consistent. This "frustrates critics, who alternately define Adams as neo-Romantic, neo-Expressionist, postmodernist or antimodernist." When Adams first began to be noticed, in the early 1980s, he was indeed classified—as a minimalist—and his name was included in conversations about Terry Riley, Steve Reich, and Philip Glass. But while his early work is characterized by repetitive melodic cells and slowly changing harmonies, anyone who has heard *Harmonielehre* (1985), the operas *Nixon in China* (1987) and *The Death of Klinghoffer* (1991), the symphony (Adams doesn't use that word) *Naïve and Sentimental Music* (1999), or the multimedia oratorio *El Niño* (2000) knows that Adams has developed in a way that is anything but minimal. He can spin out long and impassioned melodies and make an orchestra shine with rich and brilliant sound, or pummel the ear with densely interlocked textures. "What I think is the most wonderful aspect of American culture," he has said, "is that we are a culture with very few dividing lines. I grew up in a household where Benny Goodman and Mozart were not separated."

If their willingness to confront the White Whale of their heritage is a sure sign that these composers produce uniquely American work, another sign is their need to write music that, as Daniel Barenboim said before conducting the world premiere of Corigliano's Symphony No. 1 in 1990, "is not disassociated from our society but reflects our everyday life and the problems we face as human beings." Of course the best music—from Bach to Beethoven to Stravinsky and Carter—always speaks in some way to "the problems we face as human beings," even if you can't say specifically what Beethoven's Opus 131 String Quartet or Carter's Variations for Orchestra are "about." But Ives, Corigliano, and Adams, in publicly stating the "subject matter" of their music, follow in the tradition of the great American novelist-poet-composer social commentators.

This needs elaboration. As Tchaikovsky said, Beethoven's Fifth Symphony has a program, whether Beethoven owned up to it or not. Some program music, like Berlioz's *Symphonie fantastique* or Richard Strauss's *Till Eulenspiegel's Merry Pranks*, has an external program, and it describes a literal scenario. Other music has an internal program. Apparently abstract, it can only be re-created with the listener's active participation. Like a drama in the theater, its action is initiated, rises to a climax, and subsides. But what about the actors? The secret of dramas such as the Beethoven Fifth or the Brahms First—or the Ives Fourth, the Corigliano First, the Adams *Transmigration*—is that we, the listeners, are the actors. By responding to the music's urgings and following it as we wait expectantly for vacuums to be filled and energies to be dispersed, we engage ourselves with the music, simultaneously assigning and discerning its meaning.

In his Symphony No. 1, John Corigliano has written a work that stands as a monument to those who have died of AIDS. Would we know that simply by listening? The answer has to be no, though asked to characterize the first movement after even a casual listening, you would probably describe the state of mind set forth here as "enraged." Fair enough. Our experience leads us to associate loud music in the minor mode with anger. In fact this movement is subtitled "Of Rage and Remembrance." But what are we to make of it when the loud music subsides and an offstage piano introduces an Albéniz tango? The effect of this—it is a very Ivesian move—is eerie, and when the violins softly begin to sketch the outline of the tango melody, the effect is sad, overwhelmingly sad. Corigliano has said that what he wanted to evoke "is what it feels like to lose someone you care about to a terminal illness, whether it be cancer or AIDS or whatever—the injustice of it, the rage. And then you have these nostalgic remembrances of the person."

The composer's inspiration for the symphony came one day in 1988, when he saw the AIDS Memorial Quilt in Washington, D.C.—that gigantic fabric in which the names of almost 10,000 people who had died of AIDS were woven. (By 2005 the number of names in the Quilt was almost 83,000—representing, according to The NAMES Project Foundation, approximately 17.5 percent of all AIDS deaths in the United States alone.) "It was one of the most powerful and moving human statements I have ever seen. It made me want to memorialize in music those friends that I have lost—to touch concertgoers the same way that I was touched." Corigliano nonetheless maintains that he wants "the human part of it to be part of the subtext, but I don't want it to be the only thing with which people identify this piece. I wanted this to be an abstract work, because I think that abstract music can touch the deepest and most basic emotions." It invites us to become actors in the drama. Yet what are our lines?

There are no lines as such. As Corigliano suggests, to tie music to specific scenes or ideas is to rob it of its evocative powers. In liner notes for a recording of his Symphony No. 2 of 2000, Corigliano is determinedly anti-programmatic, beyond stating a subject of the work: "chosen loss," the loss of parting. Yet to experience this symphony is to be convinced that some underlying scenario is present, so suggestive is the music, so deeply serious, searching, dark, lamenting, anguished, compassionate: a beautiful nightmare that, ultimately, we have to accept on its own terms without attempting to dramatize (or melodramatize) the content and so diminish it. Good music, like good poetry, never means whatever the listener (or the reader) wants it to mean; it communicates its points in an odd and almost paradoxical way, by allowing us enough room to bring our own experience and intelligence to it as we receive its sounds and structures, and through some not-yet-understood but undeniably real process our minds interpret the physical and sensual impact that registers in our bodies. Music not tied to a specific program becomes music for all who hear it, not just for the one who conceived it. Gustav Mahler, who offered detailed programs for his first three symphonies and then withdrew them, understood this when he said that no music is worth anything if it needs a program to be understood. Yet Mahler, like Corigliano, knew that even music with no specific program has points to make. It has points to make because it is *about* something—and though the first movement of Beethoven's *Eroica* Symphony may not be *about* Napoleon, neither is it, as Toscanini said, simply *about* Allegro con brio.

Back to Corigliano. The "program" of his Symphony No. 1 does not over-shadow it. The second movement is, technically, a scherzo; programmatically, it is a crazed tarantella that is a memorial to a friend driven insane by AIDS dementia. You can appreciate the somber slow movement as a long and mournful threnody; it isn't necessary to know that it is built on a theme Corigliano and a cellist friend, now dead, improvised almost thirty years before—a theme Corigliano recalled only through his accidental discovery of a tape recording they had made in 1962. Technically, the fourth movement, the epilogue, recapitulates the work's various themes; programmatically, it weaves together the themes—the names—of Corigliano's lost friends in a quilt-like texture.

By contrast, as Elliott Carter has said, "Ives's music is, for the most part, very programmatic." You might expect programs in the music of a man who wrote pieces with titles like *The Unanswered Question* and *Central Park in the Dark*. But how do you discern the meaning of a piece called Symphony No. 4? This work, says the conductor James Sinclair, "is the quintessential collection of all of Ives's inventions, all of the chances he was willing to take . . . all of the desire . . . to reach people in a deeper way": to invite listeners in, to act.

Ives himself described "the aesthetic program of the work [as] that of the searching questions of 'What?' and 'Why?' which the spirit of man asks of life. This is particularly the sense of the Prelude. The three succeeding movements are the diverse answers in which existence replies."

We know we are in larger-than-musical territory from the outset, when in a hush the chorus sings a hymn: "Watchman, tell us of the night / What the signs of promise are." In purely musical terms, this introduction establishes a mood shattered by what comes next, something Ives called "not a scherzo in an accepted sense of the word, but rather a comedy." This is the kind of everything-including-the-kitchen-sink music that gained Ives notoriety. He quotes dozens of tunes—"Camptown Races," "Turkey in the Straw," "Jesus, Lover of My Soul," "Columbia, the Gem of the Ocean"—all played in wild cacophony punctuated by odd *pianissimos* that have the effect almost of silence. The program here, says Ives, is similar to the story of Hawthorne's "Celestial Railroad," in which a train line to the Celestial City of Bunyan's *Pilgrim's Progress* has rendered obsolete the roughness of spiritual quest, though some faithful pilgrims still choose to walk the dangerous path, to the great amusement of the train's passengers.

Ives's third movement is a sumptuous fugue on two hymns, and, in programmatic terms, "an expression of the reaction of life into formalism and ritualism." In the concluding movement, built on the hymn "Nearer, My God, to Thee," program and pure music are inseparable. Over and over we hear the tune. In the mind's ear, the listener—the actor—hears the words: "Nearer, My God, to Thee." They become anguished, strained, and at one point you will swear that you hear the word "Nearer" repeated, over and over. In this spiritual pilgrimage, the art and the emotion are one. You don't have to be a practicing Christian to be moved by the *Saint Matthew Passion* or Beethoven's *Missa solemnis*, and you need not believe in an afterlife to be moved by Ives's vision.

Entering the heart of his audience is also fundamental to John Adams's artistic agenda. "My music is emotionally committed," Adams says. He describes *Harmonielehre*, for example, as being "about revelation and healing. Music is a means of getting myself and my listener in touch with our deepest selves." Adams is a master of drama in music, a man who in the opera *Nixon in China* made something almost mystical from a brief sequence of repeated tones to underscore the lyricism of Chou En-lai's great visionary aria on the future and life's potential; and who filled Nixon's response with short quick phrases and pounding rhythms, capturing the kind of tension and inner discomfort the thirty-seventh president exuded. Already in *Nixon* we heard intimations of a languorous, almost impressionistic sound that even Adams's detractors admitted came to blossom in his next opera, *The Death of Klinghoffer*, which has as its subject the 1985 murder of an elderly Jewish invalid by the Palestinian hijackers of the cruise ship *Achille Lauro*, and which is a plea for human understanding among all sides in a Middle East whose people have been poisoned by hatred.

Poisoned environments—natural as well as spiritual and political—concern Adams, and someone who uses the evening news as subject matter for his art is clearly intent on making a statement beyond that art's boundaries. *El Dorado* is purely orchestral. The title doesn't refer to the automobile, the Cadillac Eldorado, though that might come to mind as a symbol of a uniquely American brand of conspicuous consumption. Adams's subject is gridlock, the emotional gridlock that has become identified with the United States of the Reagan years, though the title *El Dorado* also conjures an image of the realm of gold that

Coronado and his conquistadors sought, and it's easy to imagine the Berkeley-based Adams writing a lament for the peaceful inhabitants of an *Ur*-California ravaged by those European intruders. In *El Dorado*, Adams says he is "exorcising my feelings about our maniacal concerns for material gains in the '80s. But the first movement is the most terrifying, most violent music I've done yet"—he said this in 1991—"and I'm sure it was my own response to the [First] Gulf War, which also needed to come out." Always, though, the responses he talks about are couched in purely musical terms (as when he refers to "those crashing E minor chords" that open *Harmonielehre*). In *El Dorado*, as at the conclusion of *Harmonielehre*, Adams also taps into his minimalist heritage, playing different musical cells against each other in a crest of sound that creates a sense almost of levitation, a genuine physical high. Eight years after *El Dorado* came *Naïve and Sentimental Music*. Here Adams fuses the ideals of minimalism and Romanticism, and his understanding of how those styles can intersect yields music of huge, pulsating energy. Adams calls this work self-referential, and though it includes no specific quotations from his earlier music, it can strike a listener as his *Heldenleben*.

Michael Steinberg has written that "Adams . . . believes in his harmonic style as a human necessity and is willing to risk taking the controversial position that our response to tonal harmony is not so much cultural as genetic. 'Something tremendously powerful was lost when composers moved away from tonal harmony and regular pulses [Adams says]. . . . Among other things the audience was lost.'"

In listening to Adams, the audience has won. Because for an entire legion of concertgoers, he has reaffirmed the continuing vitality of concert music.

Besides writing music of enormous appeal, Adams always treats music as something men and women need to help them make it through the world as it is today. His is a music, as I said, often based on the headlines, and he has been criticized for that—and for his interpretation of the news. *Nixon* and *Klinghoffer* show us how much music can say about the way modern history has unfolded. Adams continues on this path in his 2005 opera *Doctor Atomic*, whose subject is J. Robert Oppenheimer and the Manhattan Project. But it was in 2002 that Adams took on what may have been the most daunting of the projects in which he responds to contemporary life.

In *El Niño*, the multimedia "Nativity oratorio" introduced late in 2000 and created in conjunction with director Peter Sellars, Adams invented a hopeful piece suggesting the possibilities of human love and potential, something to herald the fresh slate of a new millennium. With *On the Transmigration of Souls*, Adams produced something genuinely of the twenty-first century, something tied to the century's first epochal event, the destruction of the World Trade Center on 11 September 2001. Five months after the terrorist attacks, the New York Philharmonic announced that it had commissioned Adams to write music commemorating that day. The week before the Philharmonic revealed the commissioned composer's identity, Justin Davidson, writing for the Web site Andante.com, expressed his reservations about music to memorialize such horrific events. "The odds, it seems to me, are low that the music will be up to the occasion—that a composer, asked to interpret in tones a calamity mere months after it has happened, will have the clarity and the inner urge to write just the piece we need." What he dreaded most, he continued, was "the possibility that the composer will resort to Shostakovichian scene-setting."

What was "the piece we need"? For Adams, living across the country in California and feeling frustrated by his inability to offer something immediate to the relief efforts in New York, the commission was first of all "an opportunity," as he told Kerry Frumkin in a radio interview after the first performance of *Transmigration* on 19 September 2002, "to use my abilities—what I have to give—in a way that could contribute." The commission was for a choral work. Adams found his texts in unexpected places: in snatches of phone calls to loved ones from those caught in the planes and buildings that day; in the recitation of victims' names; in "Portraits of Grief," those eloquent tributes to the victims that ran daily in the *New York Times* for almost a year after the events. Incorporating sources from the external world: it is a move worthy of Ives. Adams in fact went on after *Transmigration* to compose a piece whose title, *My Father Knew Charles Ives*, pays tribute to his great forebear. And for musical guidance in *Transmigration*, Adams looked to Ives and *The Unanswered Question*. "This whole event," he told Frumkin, "and the loss of all these lives so suddenly was—and is—an unanswered question." In *Transmigration* Adams embeds references to the Ives work—hear the muted strings under the repeated utterance of the beautiful and ghostly words, "I see water and buildings." "I think of [*The Unanswered Question*] as a kind of guardian angel for the piece," Adams says. "It's there, hovering about it."

Nor did Adams attempt any onomatopoeia in this music, which is essentially quiet and contemplative. "If pressed," the composer told a New York Philharmonic interviewer, "I'd probably call the piece a memory space. It's a place where you can go and be alone with your thoughts and emotions. The link to a particular historical event—in this case to 9/11—is there if you want to contemplate it. But I hope that the piece will summon human experience that goes beyond this particular event." The story—the program—is part of the music, but there's more. Perhaps it was that *more* that a longtime concertgoer meant when, immediately after the first performance, he told an interviewer for the New York radio station WQXR-FM that this music was the most moving thing he had ever heard in a concert hall.

Adams had set out to write a work, as he has suggested, for those left behind. In *On the Transmigration of Souls* he sought to capture something of the calm majesty one feels on entering a great cathedral. "When you walk into Chartres

Cathedral, for example, you experience an immediate sense of something otherworldly. You feel you are in the presence of many souls, generations upon generations of them, and you sense their collected energy. . . . " Was he attempting to heal wounds? In answering this, Adams spoke both of art's limitations and of music's power:

> It's not my intention to attempt "healing" in this piece. The event will always be there in memory, and the lives of those who suffered will forever remain burdened by the violence and the pain. Time might make the emotions and the grief gradually less acute, but nothing, least of all a work of art, is going to heal a wound of this sort. Instead, the best I can hope for is to create something that has both the serenity and the kind of *gravitas* that those old cathedrals possess.

> We modern people have learned all too well how to keep our emotions in check, and we know how to mask them with humor or irony. Music has a singular capacity to unlock those controls and bring us face to face with our raw, uncensored, unattenuated feelings. This is why during times when we are grieving or in need of being in touch with the core of our beings we seek out those pieces that speak to us with that sense of *gravitas* and serenity.

Gravitas and serenity are but two of the pathways through which John Adams has led listeners to the place where they become actors in music that satisfies deep needs: the need to live dramas of life and death, good and evil, love, hatred, injustice, salvation: the need for beauty.

All good composers want to lead their listeners to that place. And the work of Schoenberg, Carter, Sessions, Wuorinen—music that is not as easy to enter as that of Ives, Corigliano, and Adams—is not about to vanish. Their music satisfies similar needs, admittedly in different ways and sometimes, but not necessarily, for different listeners. Art may serve political purposes, but art is not a political system. And unlike politicians, composers, though their means may vary, are all after the same thing.

What is so thrillingly American about Ives, Corigliano, and Adams—this trio whose work reminds us constantly that they have sighted the White Whale—may finally be found not so much in the characteristics of their music as in the fact that it has thrived in native soil alongside the very different music composed throughout most of the last century, adding more panels to the tapestry and giving us—in the best sense of American capitalism—an ever broader range of choices. Here, in this country that is such a cornucopia of cultures and styles and ideals—*E pluribus unum*—is a richness of musical experience that encompasses and confirms both diversity and heritage.

—*L.R.*

A Century Set to Music

The idea first came to me a few years ago when I was coaching a student group in Shostakovich's harrowing String Quartet No. 8, the idea of summoning one of the twentieth century's eloquent artists to bear witness about what that—mostly dreadful—time was like. I imagined myself in some future century, seeking knowledge and understanding of what the poet Muriel Rukeyser once called "the first century of world wars." Art can impart such knowledge. Picasso's *Guernica* will send devastating news to our descendants. Thomas Mann's *Doktor Faustus* has its story to tell, and so do the writings of Franz Kafka, Albert Camus, and Heinrich Böll. Music can speak, too. I made a list, not of the twentieth century's most important or most beautiful pieces, not even of my favorite pieces, though I do feel close to most of them. I was after something else. I was looking for composers to bear witness. My list is completely personal. It is also ever in flux, some of its items perhaps claiming longevity, while others are subject to shifting currents and moods. I first put the list together one weekend in August 1999, looked at it again in October 2002, and once more in May 2005. In August 1998, it would not have been the same, and were I to venture another go at it in August 2006, it would almost surely be different again.

1909: Gustav Mahler: *Das Lied von der Erde*
(The Song of the Earth)

The poems that Mahler chose for this great "song-symphony" encompass a range of feelings from nihilism to deep, heart-unsettling delight in the earth's manifold beauties. The glimmer of hope in the last lines is engulfed by some of the most heartbreaking music ever written. Mahler believed in the prophetic power of artists, and *Das Lied von der Erde* is a hymn in advance to the twentieth century as one of unquenchable *Weltschmerz*.

1909: Arnold Schoenberg: Five Pieces for Orchestra

In a masterwork that helped change the face of music, the composer of this century's most fiercely intense music enshrines the nightmare aspect of our time as well as its yearning for what we try to believe was a sweeter past.

1911: Edward Elgar: Symphony No. 2

The war that was still three years away would sweep away much of the world Elgar cherished. This glorious, impassioned symphony, suffused with melancholy, is another prophecy in music, one that told the London audience, which hated the piece—they heard and understood better than they knew—that the glory years of late Victorian and Edwardian England were not forever.

1913: Igor Stravinsky: *Le Sacre du Printemps* (The Rite of Spring)

This exuberantly inventive explosion of energy and color is music's most famous monument of modernism. It, too, changed the face of music, and no single composition has been so much imitated. At Stravinsky's funeral in April 1971, Robert Craft reflected that it was "full springtime except for the man who created a spring of his own that of all mortally begotten versions will give Nature its longest run for everlasting joy." Music to hear with a smile!

1913: Claude Debussy: *Jeux* (Games)

If Schoenberg and Stravinsky were the fathers of musical modernism, then Mahler and Debussy were its forefathers. None of their scores points more provocatively into the future than Debussy's music for the ballet *Jeux*, introduced just a week after *Le Sacre*. The music is exploring, allusive, erotically charged.

1911–1914 (?): Charles Ives: *Three Places in New England*

Ives represents the coming of age of American music, its emancipation from European models. Our great pioneer of modernism was, all his life, lost in nostalgia for a pre–Civil War America not yet transmuted from a rural society to an urban one. Here he yokes opposites—the thoroughly "modern" collage in the second of the three places, Putnam's Camp, and, especially in his evocation of the Housatonic at Stockbridge, a longing for an idealized, rapidly disappearing past as well as his own vanished youth. Such a paradox is characteristic of twentieth-century *Zeitgeist*.

1915: Charles Ives: *From Hanover Square North, at the End of a Tragic Day, the Voice of the People Again Rose* (From Orchestral Set No. 2)

The Tragic Day was 7 May 1915, the day the British liner *Lusitania* was sunk by a German submarine off the coast of Ireland. Of 1,959 persons on board, 1,198 perished. This was one of the first in a series of events that eventually led to the entry of the United States into the war. In this astounding and visionary piece, Ives depicts his experience of waiting for the "El" to take him home from his office, with the crowd on the platform singing the hymn *In the Sweet Bye and Bye*, which a nearby organ grinder had begun to play. Strangers are pulled together in grief: it is like a rehearsal for 9/11.

1915: Alban Berg: Three Pieces for Orchestra

A powerfully imagined triptych by Schoenberg's phenomenally gifted student, looking back longingly at a world that no longer seems viable and at the same time descrying the disintegration to come.

1916: Carl Nielsen: Symphony No. 4, *The Inextinguishable*

When I began to think about this list, it was the dark pieces that came rushing to mind. But then I remembered Nielsen's celebration of "the elemental will to life," which to him was an "inextinguishable" principle. Victory is not easy, but the final arrival is truly *glorioso*, to use one of the Danish composer's favorite adjectives.

1922: Alban Berg: *Wozzeck*

An opera that depicts defeat, perhaps *the* opera that depicts defeat. It is the defeat of a common soldier, not by an enemy in war, but by the play of callousness, betrayal, and his own innocence, all that projected through some of the most compellingly imaginative music ever invented for the theater.

1923: Béla Bartók: *The Miraculous Mandarin*

Bartók wrote his most brilliant and fantastical score for a ballet with a seamy subject. The characters on stage are a gang of robbers and killers, the woman they use as bait to draw their victims, and a Chinese gentleman who for all his wounds will not die until he has achieved sexual release. It is the creepiest of twists on the thanatos-eros connection. At what was supposed to be its first performances *The Miraculous Mandarin* was banished from the stage of the Cologne Opera by the Mayor, none other than Konrad Adenauer. Here modernism and supposed immorality collide head-on with The State.

1924: Jean Sibelius: Symphony No. 7

Sibelius is an artist whose life work is of a piece, and his seven symphonies are the backbone of that life work. The crunch of instruments converging in the last bars of the intensely compacted Seventh Symphony unmistakably says The End. With more than thirty years of life left to him, Sibelius wrote just one more major work, the miraculous tone poem *Tapiola*, but the writing of symphonies was over. What was the despair that made Sibelius declare that it was enough, that the time for the symphony, that glorious survivor from the nineteenth century, was over? Was it private or was it the world he observed about him?

1934: Paul Hindemith: *Mathis der Maler* Symphony

This is music taken from an opera. Matthias Grünewald was a sixteenth-century painter caught in the political and religious conflicts of the Thirty Years' War. In his opera *Mathis der Maler* (*Mathis the Painter*) Hindemith asks: Should an artist engage in the struggle or attend to his art? Can "non-engaged" art be justified? Good questions for a German in the early Hitler years.

1934, 1943, 1947: Ralph Vaughan Williams: Symphonies 4–6

Nourished by his love of English folk song and Tudor church music, Vaughan Williams reminds us in his Fifth Symphony that horror can be transcended and death swallowed up in victory. This work is the central panel of a symphonic triptych. The fierce Fourth Symphony ventures further into modernism than anything else Vaughan Williams wrote; the Sixth, begun during World War II and completed two years after its conclusion, ends in bleakness. Vaughan Williams rejected topical interpretations of these two works, the Fourth as a commentary on Europe in turmoil, the Sixth as a picture of post-atomic devastation. But whatever RVW had or did not have in mind, whatever he perhaps had in mind but chose to conceal (except in the music itself), those two symphonies *are* dark, and the quiet beacon of the Fifth is the more moving by contrast.

1940: Olivier Messiaen: *Quartet for the End of Time*

The story is wonderful: a young French composer in a German military prison composes a huge and inspired piece for himself and three other musicians whom he meets there, and on a winter day in 1941 they play it for an audience of five thousand. What actually happened, while wonderful, is slightly less wonderful than that. Some of the Quartet had been composed before Messiaen ever got near Stalag VIII-A, and Messiaen, who rivaled Ronald Reagan when it came to believing his own legend, exaggerated the size of the audience by a factor of twenty or so. But what matters is the music, and this meditation on The Revelation of Saint John is one of the miracles in the history of chamber music— fiery, colorful, and in its slow movements serene beyond anything since the last quartets of Beethoven. It is a lesson in how to rise above circumstances.

1941: Michael Tippett: *A Child of Our Time*

This is a great humanist's far-seeing response to the pogroms in Germany in November 1938. Tippett was not interested in producing the musical equivalent of a documentary; rather, for him, this was an occasion for a searching look at the human condition. Incorporating influences as diverse as Handel's *Messiah*, African American spirituals, and Jungian imagery, he composed a powerful oratorio for soloists, chorus, and orchestra.

1943: Dmitri Shostakovich: Symphony No. 8

Unlike Vaughan Williams, Shostakovich had no compunction about writing topical music and admitting it; after all, the Soviet society in which he worked defined that as an artist's obligation. The Eighth Symphony mirrors a Russia in the midst of World War II—intensely emotional, heroic, elegiac, and with a quiet finale that is music of timidly awakening life.

1945: Benjamin Britten: *Peter Grimes*

A worthy successor to *Wozzeck*, with whose composer Britten always wished he could have studied. Here the setting is English and the situation civilian. It is a picture of how a "nice" community locked in self-righteousness can destroy a human being, helpless in the face of hatred of "otherness."

1947: Arnold Schoenberg: *A Survivor from Warsaw*

No one was better versed in the language of nightmare, no one could have more vividly told the story of a group of Jews being shipped to one of the extermination camps—*and* compressed it into a six-minute drama for speaker, chorus, and orchestra. *Survivor* comes with the brutally realistic trappings of a documentary, but the flow of time in the narrative is entirely unreal, a blurring that adds to the sense of nightmare.

1960: Krzysztof Penderecki:
Threnody for the Victims of Hiroshima

As pictorial as a tone poem, this documents one of the most horrifying moments in world history. Using only a string orchestra, but as strings had never been used before, Penderecki also works in utmost brevity. Terror. Screams.

1960: Dmitri Shostakovich: String Quartet No. 8

Composed "in memory of the victims of fascism and war," this quartet, full of self-quotations as the composer seems to relive experiences he has, to his amazement, survived, brings us music that is now brutally driving and frighteningly oppressive, now quiet and deeply inward. It is the most poignant music of mourning I know, not easy to confront for players or for listeners.

1962: Benjamin Britten: War Requiem

A powerful union of the Catholic Requiem Mass with writings by Wilfred Owen, the most eloquent of the English war poets. And, I admit, a work that except in a few of the Owen songs, has meant more to many others than it does to me.

1970: Roger Sessions: When Lilacs Last in the Dooryard Bloom'd

In this requiem for Martin Luther King, Jr., and Robert F. Kennedy, Sessions responds sensitively and with immense musical power to the Biblical majesty and musical fluidity of Whitman's poem, a requiem for Abraham Lincoln. Lilacs reaches beyond its immediate occasion to become a lament for a world knotted in tragedy, and it is also one of the century's great love letters to Nature.

1970: George Crumb: Ancient Voices of Children

A death-haunted piece, daughter of Mahler's Kindertotenlieder, for me the most evocative of Crumb's many settings of the poetry of Federico García Lorca. It was written for the extraordinary mezzo-soprano Jan de Gaetani, with a chamber ensemble that includes, along with conventional instruments, toy piano, mandolin, musical saw, and Tibetan prayer stones. Crumb, whose voice was one of the freshest on the scene in the third quarter of the last century, writes that the essence of the poetry "is concerned with the most primary things: death, love, the smell of the earth, the sounds of the wind and the sea." The music, or poetry-in-music, lets us experience it all.

1985: John Adams: Harmonielehre

Adams took his title (which one could translate as What Is Known about Harmony) from the great treatise on harmony and composition by one of

Modernism's Founding Fathers, Arnold Schoenberg. This vibrant work, though, is a major monument of the counter-revolution. Like Schoenberg, Adams means more by harmony than the study of chords. His *Harmonielehre* is a hymn to personal and human harmony, and it ends in an upsurge of hard-earned optimism. Very American it is, too. Hearing it in the almost immediate aftermath of 9/11, as I had the privilege of doing, in a marvelous performance by Markus Stenz and the Minnesota Orchestra, was one of the truly uplifting moments of a musical lifetime.

1987: John Tavener: *The Protecting Veil*

Serenity and stillness: *The Protecting Veil*, a series of meditations for cello and orchestra, is more steadily consonant than anything by Bach, Mozart, Beethoven, or Brahms, but Tavener has found a way of making those harmonies fresh, as though new-minted. His music does not invalidate the music of, say, Babbitt and Carter, but it presents an alternative that is alive and imbued with spirit.

—M.S.

IV.
MISSIONARIES

Making America Musical:
A Salute to Theodore Thomas

B ach's Two-Violin Concerto, Brahms's Hungarian Dances and *Academic Festival* Overture, the *Hexameron* by Liszt et al. and Liszt's orchestration of Schubert's *Wanderer* Fantasy, Mozart's Symphony No. 34, the Saint-Saëns *Organ* Symphony, the Sibelius Second, *The Blue Danube*, *Till Eulenspiegel* and *Ein Heldenleben*, Tchaikovsky's *Romeo and Juliet*, the Prelude to *Die Meistersinger*: every one of those pieces was introduced in America by Theodore Thomas, a name you have seen often if you look at the performance histories you sometimes find in symphony orchestras' program notes. A complete list of Thomas's American premieres would include and be less than one-tenth exhausted by Beethoven's *Great Fugue*; Berlioz's *Damnation of Faust*, *Harold in Italy*, and *Romeo and Juliet*; Brahms's Second Symphony and Haydn Variations; the Bruckner Seventh; *The Sorcerer's Apprentice*; Grieg's music for Ibsen's *Peer Gynt*; Handel's *Royal Fireworks* Music; Schubert's *Unfinished* Symphony; the *Nutcracker* Suite; and the Prelude and Love-Death from *Tristan*. And this list does not even include all the famous pieces.

Nor, remarkable though it is, does this catalogue by itself certify Theodore Thomas's greatness, although it is symbolic of what made him the most important performer in the history of concert music in America. A century after his death, the consequences of his life work are everywhere about us, in the prestige and ubiquity of symphony orchestras in our country; in the assumption that concert music is A Good Thing and an essential item on the cultural consumer-goods shopping list; in the concept of the Music Director, someone with power to hire and fire and to determine repertory and larger artistic policies; in the establishment of subscription sales, pops programs, and children's concerts; even in the matter of having the bow-strokes in each string section in an orchestra coordinated so as to go up and down together.

Theodore Christian Friedrich Thomas, the dedicated and prodigiously hard-working musician who left us this legacy, was born on 11 October 1835 at Esens in East Friesland by the North Sea. All his life, he remained deeply German in outlook. To some but hardly an extreme extent, his musical predilections would always reflect that, but in that matter he hardly differed from the most celebrated German and Austrian conductors of the late nineteenth and twentieth centuries, men such as von Bülow, Richter, Steinbach, Nikisch, Weingartner, Walter, Furtwängler, Knappertsbusch, Böhm, Sawallisch, Masur, and Thielemann. It did not keep Thomas, though, from being a responsible supporter of American composers, among them Chadwick, Foote, Loeffler, MacDowell, Paine, and Parker.

His father, a town musician in Esens, emigrated to New York with his large family in 1845. The nine-year-old Theodore was already an accomplished violinist, and he helped support the family by playing in theaters and for dancing masters. He had, by the way, no violin lessons, learning to get around the instrument by imitating his father. In fact, except for a few piano and cornet lessons and, much later, a little instruction in counterpoint, he had no formal training in music at all, nor did he attend school of any kind after coming to America as a boy. In 1848, father and son joined the Navy as bandsmen, becoming, respectively, first and second horn aboard the *Pennsylvania*, stationed at Portsmouth, Virginia. "Damn bad" was the son's later assessment of his own playing.

A year later, Thomas, now fourteen, made himself independent. He had some posters printed announcing a concert by "Master T.T." and headed south. He would get permission to use a hotel dining room, then go around town tacking up his posters. "When the time for the concert arrived, I would stand at the door of the hall and take the money until I concluded that my audience was about gathered, after which I would go to the front of the hall, unpack my violin, and begin the concert!" He was driven out of one Mississippi town because the authorities believed the fiddle to be the devil's instrument. When he stepped on his violin while camping in the woods, he repaired and re-glued the instrument at the nearest carpenter's shop and played a concert on it the next day. This resourceful boy is father to the conductor, manager, impresario, tour director, and fund-raiser who would soon begin to change America's musical life.

At fifteen, Theodore Thomas found himself back in New York. He meant to go to Europe to study but was snagged instead by an appointment as concertmaster at a newly established German theater. He played in many orchestras, in New York and on tour. His diet included a lot of opera, and what he heard from the great singers he worked with—among them Jenny Lind, Henriette Sontag, Giulia Grisi, Giovanni Mario, Raffaele Mirate, and Adelina Patti—gave him a lifelong ideal for phrasing and tone. In 1854, he was elected a member of the New York Philharmonic, then just beginning to become a respectable professional orchestra. With the pianist William Mason, he organized a series of chamber music concerts in New York, setting a new standard in America for the performance of that repertory. Thomas's lust for expanding American horizons is in evidence early. On their debut program, on 27 November 1855 at Dodsworth's Hall, he, Mason, and the cellist Carl Bergmann (later conductor of the New York Philharmonic) gave the first performance anywhere of Brahms's B-major Trio, op. 8!

His position as concertmaster of the Ullmann Opera brought him opportunities to lead the orchestra, and he became America's first real conductor—that is, an interpretive artist rather than just a time-beater. About 1860, Thomas realized that his apprenticeship was over and he began to see the direction his life must take. In her *Memoirs of Theodore Thomas*, his widow, Rose Fay Thomas, quotes him in words of characteristic simplicity: "In 1862 I concluded to devote my energies to the cultivation of the public taste for instrumental music. Our chamber concerts had created a spasmodic interest, our programmes were reprinted as models of their kind, even in Europe, and our performances had reached a high standard. As a concert violinist, I was at this time popular, and played much. But what this country needed most of all to make it musical was a good orchestra, and plenty of concerts within reach of the people. The [New York] Philharmonic Society, with a body of about sixty players and five yearly subscription concerts, was the only organized orchestra which represented orchestral literature in this large country."

It was obvious to Thomas that what the New York Philharmonic offered was insufficient in both quantity and quality. It wasn't good enough and it didn't reach enough people. Thomas got New York's best players together and began to give concerts of his own. The first of them, at Irving Hall on 13 May 1862, included the American premiere of Wagner's *Flying Dutchman* Overture.

Theodore Thomas was on his way. Over the course of the next ten years he became conductor of the Brooklyn Philharmonic, retaining that post almost continuously until 1891. He established his "Symphonic Soirées" on a regular basis, giving New York programs comparable to the best that might be heard in London, Paris, Vienna, or anywhere. He established a series of lighter summer concerts, leading 1,227 of them in eight years, most of them in the brand new Central Park. But the most important thing happened in 1869. That was when he took his orchestra of fifty-four on tour for the first time. Having given New York a first-class orchestral culture, he was ready to extend his missionary work to the rest of the country. One can say it simply: Baltimore, Boston, Chicago, Cincinnati, Cleveland, Detroit, Indianapolis, Philadelphia, Pittsburgh,

Rochester, San Francisco, Washington, and a dozen other cities have flourishing symphony orchestras today because they were tour stops for Theodore Thomas, over and over, and because he left a taste for the sound of Beethoven and Wagner, Mozart and Schumann, Berlioz and Brahms.

Thomas sketched this itinerary for that first tour: New York—New Haven—Hartford—Providence—Boston—Worcester—Springfield, Massachusetts—Albany—Schenectady—Utica—Syracuse—Rochester—Buffalo—Cleveland—Toledo—Detroit—Chicago—St. Louis—Indianapolis—Louisville—Cincinnati—Dayton—Springfield, Ohio—Columbus—Pittsburg (then still without its *h*)—Washington—Baltimore—Philadelphia—New York. It followed the railway; moreover, unlike someone planning an orchestra tour today, Thomas did not have to worry about the schedules of local orchestras: except in St. Louis, where one had been founded in 1860, there weren't any.

The Theodore Thomas Orchestra, as it was called, did not hit all those cities the first time around, but that list, with occasional expansions to such places as Kansas City, Milwaukee, Minneapolis, and Omaha, pretty well defines what came to be known as the Thomas Highway. He and his players traveled this Highway on an average of three times a year from 1869 until 1891. One year Thomas toured the South, another took him through New England to Montreal. In 1883 and 1885 he crossed the continent, once covering a whole series of Canadian cities and towns, the other time returning through Texas. In June 1883, he conducted a notable set of seven concerts in San Francisco, twenty-eight years before there was a San Francisco Symphony, including a Wagner night with three singers in selections from *Lohengrin, Tannhäuser, Walküre,* and *Götterdämmerung,* and a Beethoven night with the *Consecration of the House* Overture, the Fifth Symphony, the variations from the Septet, the first movement of the Piano Concerto No. 3, and vocal pieces, ending with the "Hallelujah!" Chorus from *Christ on the Mount of Olives.*

The point of Thomas's tours was summed up in an 1869 article in *Dwight's Journal of Music,* then the equal of any musical periodical in the world. This is what *Dwight's* said of the Thomas Orchestra's first concerts in Boston: "Boston has not heard such performances before. . . . We rejoice in the coming of this orchestra. It is just the kind of thing we, for years, have longed for in view of our own progress here. . . . We thank Mr. Thomas for setting palpably before us a higher ideal of orchestral execution. We shall demand better of our own in the future. They cannot witness this example without a newly kindled desire, followed by an effort to do likewise."

That was what it was all about. A good teacher works toward the point when he or she becomes unnecessary. In the same sense, the goal of the Thomas Orchestra tours was to become unnecessary as American cities established their own orchestras and concert series, though in some cities the daunting excellence of the visitors inhibited local enterprise for a few years. Boston, founding its Symphony Orchestra in 1881, was the first city fully to rise to the

Thomas Orchestra's challenge, and for all the satisfaction this gave Thomas, it was bitter for him to lose his best tour city and the one that offered him a singularly cultivated and prepared audience. Later he twice turned down offers to become the Boston Symphony's conductor. He finally disbanded the Thomas Orchestra in 1888, nine years after he had been named conductor of the New York Philharmonic. The missionary task of traveling on behalf of symphonic music was assumed after the turn of the century by the newly founded Minneapolis Symphony (now Minnesota Orchestra), which by the midpoint of the twentieth century had played more than three thousand concerts in over four hundred communities, most of which had no orchestras of their own.

Besides taking his orchestra on tour, Theodore Thomas did many other things, not all of them successful. He was Musical Director of the Centennial Exposition in Philadelphia in 1876, and as America's No. 1 Wagnerian offered a commission to *der Meister*. The cost was enormous, the reward—the undistinguished *Centennial March*—small. Thomas's involvement with the Centennial Exhibition was a fiscal disaster as well. Those crowds simply could not be persuaded to go to symphony concerts. Thomas found himself in debt to the point that the Philadelphia Sheriff seized and sold at auction his library of scores and orchestral parts, plus books, percussion instruments, podium, desk, and inkstand. Fortunately a friend in New York, Dr. Franz Zinzer, heard of the disaster in time to come to the rescue by buying the lot, renting it to Thomas for $100 a year, and after two years making it over to Mrs. Thomas as a gift.

Another disappointment was his directorship of the newly founded Cincinnati College of Music (now the College-Conservatory of the University of Cincinnati). He had hoped to establish a strong scholarship program for gifted young musicians, but his board was interested only in those students whose parents could pay the full tariff. A happier relationship with that city evolved when Thomas founded the Cincinnati May Festival, still going strong, and directed it until his death. He was Artistic Director of the American Opera Company, devoted to opera in English and opera without stars, but this proved another financial morass, and Thomas lost his shirt in that misadventure.

More happily, he was conductor of the New York Philharmonic from 1879 to 1891. In 1891, he founded the Chicago Orchestra, renamed the Theodore Thomas Orchestra in his memory, and now the Chicago Symphony Orchestra. He had, all things considered, chosen a tough road, but then, from the time he had landed in New York as a boy, he was used to hard work. Still, the financial struggle to make his various enterprises go was unremitting, and of course the tours themselves were exhausting. When he gave them up in order to settle in Chicago, he was, at fifty-six, a prematurely old man.[1]

---

[1] Another hero among nineteenth-century musical missionaries in America was the extraordinary Norwegian violinist Ole Bull, who, beginning in 1843 and continuing until his death in 1880, gave many hundreds of concerts all over this country. He was a greater musical genius than Theodore Thomas and a far more flamboyant personality, but he had none of Thomas's organizational skills.

Chicago was a splendid final chapter, whose culmination was Thomas's success at persuading the board to endow his orchestra permanently. "I would gladly go to hell if they gave me a permanent orchestra," he had exclaimed in 1889. He also talked the board into building him a proper hall. He conducted the inaugural concert at Theodore Thomas Orchestra Hall on 14 December 1904. The Salute to the Hall of Song from *Tannhäuser*, the Beethoven Fifth, *Death and Transfiguration*, and the "Hallelujah!" Chorus from Handel's *Messiah* were on the program. The Strauss tone poem proved a spookily prophetic choice, for this gala was Theodore Thomas's last concert. A cold progressed to pneumonia, and he died in the early morning of 4 January 1905.

I wish I had a clearer idea of what sort of music Theodore Thomas made. Unassuming on the podium, he regularly roused audiences to enthusiasm. Anton Rubinstein, Wieniawski, Nikisch, and Gericke were among the musicians who admired him. But neither newspaper reviews nor the comments of colleagues are specific enough to give a picture of his style. Some of what he did surely would not suit us: for example, his liberally thickened and reorchestrated Bach or his decision on one occasion in Chicago to drop the finale of Beethoven's Ninth from D to C so as to make it easier for the singers. But he constantly rethought such questions, just as he never stopped absorbing new scores or coming up with new ideas for the improvement of the musical state of the union.

He had difficulties and his life was not free of friction, but he was recognized and appreciated, valued and loved, during his life as well as after his death. Of all the things I have read about Thomas, the one that touched me most was a letter written to him on 26 October 1901 by the architect Daniel H. Burnham, the inspired designer of the Chicago Loop (including Orchestra Hall, Thomas's last dream) and of such masterpieces as New York's Flatiron Building and the Union Station in Washington, D.C. Burnham was in Washington with Frederick Law Olmsted, the landscape architect of New York's Central Park, Yosemite, and the Stanford University campus; Charles Follen McKim, architect of New York's Pennsylvania Station and the Boston Public Library; and Augustus Saint-Gaudens, America's greatest sculptor. "We have talked of you constantly," wrote Burnham, "and wish you were with us and you have come in and taken part almost as if present in body as well as in spirit. The Senate has appointed us to improve the park system. . . . Again has come the old joy of creating noble things [and] altogether we have risen where I never hoped to tread in this existence. And you have been with us and we all think of how much of our power to dream truly we owe to you, dear friend and comrade!"

It is noteworthy that Thomas's entire career took place in this country; he never played or conducted a single concert in Europe, though he was renowned and respected there. And when he was invited to conduct at the Paris Exposition of 1900, his indignation over the Dreyfus trial made it impossible for him to accept. He replied to the invitation with characteristic and terse dignity: "I regret sincerely that circumstances have so changed of late that I as an American, who love justice and liberty, am prevented from visiting the Metropolis of France next summer."

His is the story, of course, of how our musical life came to be what it is, but more largely it is a story of enterprise, resilience and good humor, infinite resourcefulness, a willingness to improvise, faith in education and improvement, belief in a land of unlimited possibilities. I see it also as a story of America at its best, and that makes it a special pleasure, at this dark moment in our history, to look at it and to retell it.

—M.S.

Sigmund Spaeth,
Someone You Should Know

Sigmund Spaeth. The name hardly seems real. Yet it was real enough between the 1920s and the early 1960s, four decades during which he wrote thirty-two books—good sellers, most of them—and hundreds of articles in newspapers and such magazines as *Esquire*, *The New Yorker*, and *The Saturday Evening Post*. He was friendly with George Gershwin and recalled the afternoon when he dropped in on the composer just as he was writing the last notes of *An American in Paris*. He turned pages for Richard Strauss on the stage of Philadelphia's Academy of Music while the great soprano Elisabeth Schumann sang the composer's lieder. He was a dinner companion to Albert Einstein, played chess with the violinist Mischa Elman, and appeared at the White House, twice, at the request of Franklin Roosevelt. As "The Tune Detective," he took to the stage at Radio City Music Hall. For years he was a regular on the Metropolitan Opera Quiz, the intermission feature of the Met's radio broadcasts. On television he appeared with Jack Benny, Steve Allen, Art Linkletter, Mike Wallace. He died in 1965, a year that continues to recede, as bygone years will do; but figures from the past sometimes seem even larger to us than they did to those who encountered them every day—Gershwin, perhaps, or FDR. You can't say that about Sigmund Spaeth. During his lifetime, he seemed to be everywhere you looked. Who knows him today?

Yet Sigmund Spaeth's life is more than an object lesson in the temporary nature of human glory. During his time, he was one of America's best-known music popularizers, and he is still one of the most tireless workers on music's behalf that this country has known. He was a believer. "Music for Everybody" was not simply the title of his syndicated newspaper column; it was the motto he lived by. But perhaps he believed too strongly. Perhaps his intensity, the source of so much of his appeal, eventually got the best of him, cutting him off toward the end from the truly populist ideal he cherished. For today Sigmund Spaeth is a cultural artifact, part of a past we will eventually and inevitably forget, since so much else is so much more important—the great music, for example, whose rhythms and harmonies shaped him, and which continues to extend its living influence into the present and into the future. Sigmund Spaeth's subject was greater than he was. He wouldn't have argued otherwise. He served music, but music also brought him celebrity that he enjoyed. In the end, as the world around him expanded and the pond he swam in grew, he just displaced less volume.

He was born in Philadelphia on 10 April 1885, the son of a Lutheran minister who had emigrated from Germany twenty years earlier. His father composed hymns, his mother played piano and organ, and she edited the *Church Book with Music* and wrote a book on Hans Sachs, hero of *Die Meistersinger*, which would become Sigmund's favorite opera. Sig, second youngest of seven children, grew up in a household where music was a given. Everyone, but for one older brother, sang and played piano or violin, which was not as remarkable in an upper-middle-class home of the late nineteenth century as it would be today. "It was always taken for granted in the Spaeth family that anyone at all could both sing and play on some instrument, by note or by ear," Sig wrote in the "Personal Reminiscences" with which he prefaced his *Fifty Years with Music*, a book published in 1959, by which time phonographs had taken the place of the family piano. "I cannot remember just when I learned to read music, for I assumed it was a perfectly normal process, like learning to speak and read one's own language." For the rest of his life, he would believe that "anyone at all" could sing or play music, and that conviction drove him in his campaign on music's behalf. He felt "that if you understood [music] a little better, like how the themes are put together, for example, that it would be more enjoyable," said his grand-niece, Patricia Spaeth, in 2002. "So that *you know what's going on*. Like some of us go to a football game and have no idea of what's going on, and it's really hard to enjoy it if you just see this ball going back and forth. It's the same way when you hear all these instruments going back and forth." A musician herself, Patricia Spaeth recalls Sig's visits when she was growing up in Southern California: the famous uncle from back East dropping in during his trips to Hollywood, cheering up her widowed mother and exercising his prerogative as an eminence, and a childless one at that, to assume a paternal role to the young girl and her brothers. Sig entertained the kids with corny jokes, but he also played piano duets with Pat, reliving those parlor musicales of his own childhood.

Sig attended Haverford College and did graduate work at Princeton, where he was concertmaster of a string orchestra conducted by Philip Mittell. Sig claims that Mittell had been a friend of Brahms's, but the name Mittell appears in no Brahms literature I have seen, and when I asked one of the composer's recent biographers if he had encountered it in his research, he drew a blank. None of this means that Mittell had no Brahms connection, but it does suggest that Sig—or perhaps Mittell—was overstating the relationship by using the word "friend." Throughout his college days Sig sang in glee clubs and arranged music for theatrical productions. He listened to concerts by the New York Philharmonic, which, he says, visited the Princeton campus under the direction of Gustav Mahler—though this information is also difficult to confirm. The New York Philharmonic has no documentation of having played at Princeton under Mahler, but its records from these years are incomplete. I am not out to prove that Sigmund Spaeth was deliberately misleading his readers, nor do two questionable assertions that can't be verified or conclusively disproved establish a pattern; yet it is hard not to feel that Sig was trying to deflect some glory in his direction. But other public figures, more famous than Sigmund Spaeth, have done worse, and his contentions here are pretty innocent.

Sig took his Ph.D. not in music but in English, German, and philosophy, and for a brief period after his graduation in 1909 he taught German at Princeton as a member of Woodrow Wilson's faculty. In 1912, after a few years teaching at a boys' school in North Carolina, where he also coached football, soccer, and swimming, he went to New York to work half time at the publishing house of G. Schirmer. Then he got his break—what he calls his "surprise appointment" as music critic on the *Evening Mail*. The staff included sports writer Grantland Rice, cartoonist Rube Goldberg, and reporter Ed Sullivan. The office boy, B. P. "Benny" Schulberg, would go on to become a motion picture magnate and to father a son named Budd, who achieved even greater celebrity as the author of *What Makes Sammy Run?* and screenplays for such films as *On the Waterfront* and *The Harder They Fall*. Only if you were made of granite would you not be shaped by company such as this.

Spaeth's next career move, after a stint covering sports for the *New York Times*, seems a retreat into calmer territory from the charged atmosphere at the *Evening Mail*, but it was really what pushed him into the front line. He took a position as educational director and promotion manager for the electric player piano called the Ampico. In his new capacity, he began speaking on music, and he made his first radio appearances. His public life had begun. In 1924 he published his first book, *The Common Sense of Music*, which he called "the first serious attempt to approach music in general from the layman's point of view and in everyday language, completely eliminating technical terms."

His goal was noble. It was to bring music to the people. His method was to demystify, to reduce complexities to simple forms. He would disassemble a

Haydn symphony, say, taking care to number the gears and valves and gaskets before spreading them out for examination, and then he put them back together again. He could come up with felicities of phrasing that spoke directly to his audience, such as this from "Symphonies for Business Men," an article written before the onset of the Great Depression and included in his 1929 collection *They Still Sing of Love*: "Form in music is very much the same as form in golf. Essentially it represents the power to secure the greatest results with the least waste of effort."

In the same piece, he expounds on aesthetics for Everyman. "'Why do men write symphonies?' asks the Practical Business Man. 'There is certainly no money in it.'" Granted, says Spaeth. But "the true creative artist always has the urge to do something in the grand manner, and this"—here comes the punch—"applies even to the books, the dramas and the epic poems of the world, many of which are a dead loss commercially." He continues with an object lesson in listening, rendering the abstract concrete by appealing to what his "Practical Business Man" already knows: "The best advice to the business man who would like to enjoy a symphony is that he should listen to it in the same way that he looks at a cathedral or a great picture or a group of statuary. With a book or a play, it is different, and rather easier. For a book or a play presents only one thing at a time, out of which a complete impression is gradually built up. . . . You cannot completely enjoy or appreciate a symphony in a single hearing any more than you can grasp the significance of a cathedral with a passing glance." What effect might his words have had on these practical commercial gents of the late 1920s, many of whom were just a few years away from becoming tragic figures, stepping into eternity from their office windows fifteen stories above Wall Street because a system they trusted had failed? Would any of the acquaintances they may have made through Spaeth—say, the recollected beauty of a passage from Mozart—have brought them back to safety?

Spaeth almost always had some genuine knowledge to impart, and almost always he began by imparting it in an engaging way, as he does in his tips for "businessmen." Yet once on to a good thing, he found it all but impossible to stop, like an evangelist who will not rest his case until the last member of his congregation steps forward to be saved. I have quoted from the first three paragraphs of "Symphonies for Business Men." The essay continues for ten more pages, and the variations Spaeth writes on his theme prove only that he was no Elgar or Brahms.

Yet he could cut to the chase. As early as 1929, in "What's the Matter with Music?" Spaeth addressed a question that has yet to be resolved. "The athletic coach in an American school or college would not dream of seriously urging his pupils to adopt a professional athletic career. . . . Yet the music teacher, with a smaller and less lucrative field than that of professional athletics, encourages any more-than-average talent to 'go in for a career.' As a result, the very ones who should be developing into good amateurs and therefore even better listeners, are struggling with the problems of professionalism, eventually becoming, at best, the tradespeople of their art." This is gutsy writing. It shows how much he cared.

The Spaeth method of demystifying reaches its culmination in one of his most ambitious projects, his 1936 *Great Symphonies: How to Recognize and Remember Them.* To my mind, this sums up his inconsistency as a writer and as a proselytizer, for it is perhaps also his biggest miscalculation. In *Great Symphonies,* Spaeth fits lyrics of his own to staples of the basic symphonic repertory. He was not the first to do this, and others have done it since, not always with as noble an intent as Sig's; but when a certain Mabelle Glenn of Kansas City asked him to prepare a set of mnemonic aids for a convention of music teachers in her home town, he was on his way to becoming the most celebrated of these unlikely collaborators. His Kansas City project gave him the idea for an entire book devoted to what he called "symphonic texts." He outlined his guiding principles: The texts "must be simple and direct enough to appeal to children, but not so silly as to offend intelligent adults." The point, again, is to render what might be intimidating a little less scary for new listeners. Once that is accomplished, he can go for the bull's-eye and get down to teaching musical form: "The composer does things with these tunes," he points out in his first chapter, "like a playwright or a novelist working with his characters, so every symphony really has a musical plot, in which each movement is like an act in a play." Throughout his book, Spaeth manages to convey lessons in musical structure. There is always a caveat, however, and in this case it is Spaeth's "lyrics." Even as you read this, he may be answering for them to Beethoven, Mozart, and Haydn. As generous as one wants to be, Spaeth's verses tend to range from the odd to the out-and-out bizarre. They have a sort of inspired goofiness about them, and they swell with unintended humor—the sorts of things with which graduate students in the liberal arts might entertain each other at parties after having had too much to drink, like reciting, from memory, the first twenty lines of *The Canterbury Tales* Prologue in Middle English.

All this said, I must share some of Spaeth's lyrics. Here is the opening of Mozart's Symphony No. 40, which only he and Robert Schumann seem to hear as happy music.

> *With a laugh and a smile like a sunbeam,*
> *And a face that is glad, with a fun-beam,*
> *We can start on our way very gaily,*
> *Singing tunes from a symphony daily;*
> *And if Mozart could but hear us,*

He would wave his hat and cheer us
Coming down the scale,
All hale and strong in song,
All hale and strong in song.

Here is what he does with the melody that opens the second movement of Beethoven's Fifth:

When the moon rises in the sky,
And all the stars of Heav'n are shining clear on high,
We fear no Fate,
No task too great,
We are masters!

And then this, for the great blaze of C major that opens the last movement:

Fall in line, and let your armor shine!
We have won, we have won,
And all the struggle with our enemy is done!

(Personally, I may never forgive him for that one. I first encountered these lines when I was in high school. To this day I have difficulty thinking of that great moment without Sigmund Spaeth's nutty verses banging around between the trumpets and the violins, threatening to turn the whole thing into a Looney Tune.)

Here is the opening of the "Merry Gathering of Country Folk" in Beethoven's *Pastoral* Symphony:

The peasants are dancing and prancing together,
The weather means nothing to them, ha, ha, ha!
Now swing your partner and don't let her go,
A dance in the country is never too slow!

More: The opening of Schumann's *Rhenish* Symphony:

Rhineland, lovely Rhineland,
Superfine land,
Full of beauty, song, and story,
Land of legend, land of glory!

My personal favorite is the opening of the Brahms Fourth:

> *Hello! Hello!*
> *What ho! What ho!*
> *Hello!*
> *What ho!*
> *Hello!*
> *What ho!*

This gives you an idea of what to expect from *Great Symphonies*. I think these verses are ridiculous, and I take pleasure in sharing them. But Sigmund Spaeth was not a ridiculous man—not even in his role as the "Tune Detective," in which he found surprising though usually not very meaningful correspondences between famous tunes. He points out, for example, the similarities between the Westminster Chimes of Big Ben and one of the tunes in the last movement of the Brahms First Symphony—the one played by muted horns over shimmering strings, just before the big chorale theme makes its first appearance in the trombones. The ability to spot things like this may strike you as a perverse sort of talent, yet Spaeth was often called on to testify in songwriters' plagiarism suits.

His writing could be stylish and elegant, or plodding. He wrote a lot, and one has the impression that he did not spend much time revising or agonizing over his words or his purpose. He knew he was right.

At the same time, he was a realist. In *Opportunities in Music*, published in 1950 by a firm called Vocational Guidance Manuals, he produced an entire volume on the various niches the music business offers, from performing artist to agent. And who can quibble with advice such as this:

> To those who honestly believe that they can win out as independent artists on a big scale one can only say, "Be absolutely sure that you have not merely an impressive talent but such extraordinary gifts as to amount to positive genius. Do not accept the flattering opinions of your friends and relatives as to your ability. Get yourself heard if possible by experienced and unprejudiced judges and by neutral audiences whose reactions are presumably sincere. Convince yourself that you have worked honestly and thoroughly, under competent teaching, and that you are fully equipped for a professional performance before asking anyone to pay to hear you. Make perfection your ideal, and do not be satisfied with anything 'good enough' even if it is indulgently accepted. When there is no longer any reasonable doubt as to your fitness for a professional career, get hold of the necessary capital somehow and begin the arduous campaign of 'winning friends and influencing people.'"

Sigmund Spaeth did not focus solely on concert music, nor was his emphasis merely on listening. He wanted people to *make* music. He loved barbershop quartets and thought their performance within virtually everyone's grasp—or every man's, at any rate. Barbershop quartets still exist, of course, and maybe I'm just revealing the limitations of my taste when I say that a little bit of "Sweet Adeline" in four-part harmony goes a long way. But I think that Spaeth's fondness for barbershop quartets really places him in another era, an era whose ideals were summed up by the 1950s, and which ended with JFK's assassination, Vietnam, and Watergate. Concert music survives such assaults on humanity. Barbershop quartets do not.

Today, much of Sigmund Spaeth's writing can be read as social documentary, not just as a document of musical taste and teaching. Just consider the esteem in which he was held by those who had forgotten that they were ever young. The stiffness of an entire generation is summed up when Eugene Ormandy, in a foreword to a 1952 reprint of *Great Symphonies*, says: "If every member of our concert audiences, plus the multitude of radio and record listeners, formed the habit of approaching great symphonies in this entertaining and informative manner, the enjoyment of the masterpieces of music would unquestionably be vastly increased, for the benefit of all concerned." The prose, sapped of heart and color, has all the eloquence of an Eisenhower speech, and in the smug assurance of this defender of the old guard we get a sudden flash of why, in just a few years, Elvis would be so adored, and of what, in a few more years, the 1960s would rebel against. Ormandy is not even honest in his introductory words. He claims that "these easy little jingles are actually forgotten once the music is firmly established in the memory, having served their obvious purpose." Perhaps—but only if you encounter them from Ormandy's perspective, which is the perspective of someone who has long known the music minus the words. For the rest of us, these easy little jingles, once they have hacked their way into brain cells, seem to replicate themselves like computer viruses.

Sig Spaeth stopped being a man of his time. In January 1963, two years before he died, in his preface to his last book, *The Importance of Music*, he sounds a bitter chord that had been absent in his previous work. "The opinions expressed are purely personal, as they should be, and if they create violent disagreement, or even significant controversy, so much the better. At least they are completely honest, and unfortunately complete honesty still seems difficult to achieve in the complex field of music, with all its prejudices, exaggerated enthusiasms as well as criticisms, its frequently false values and its continued vulnerability to the ancient handicaps of snobbery and hypocrisy."

Snob and hypocrite are not words to describe Sigmund Spaeth. But for all his dedication to the common man, to music for everyone, he failed to grasp something essential in music's nature. Call it spontaneity and improvisation. "It has long been a rule with popular singers to stay off the beat as much as possible, slowing up one phrase and hurrying another so as to keep up a running fight with the basic time marked by the instruments of percussion," he writes in a 1952 review of Peggy Lee's recording of Richard Rodgers's "Lover," a review that becomes a condemnation of song stylists—"one of the pet abominations of this reviewer." He continues: "Distortions of melodic line are also a fairly old story, with classic models in the 'breaks' and 'hot licks' of jazz." Then he assesses Peggy Lee's treatment of the Rodgers: "The fact that it is done with fiendish skill makes it all the more objectionable." Sigmund Spaeth did not get it. Sigmund Spaeth did not *realize* that he didn't get it.

He hated rock 'n' roll—*hated* it—and he believed it was his responsibility to say so. Perhaps it was just that change was coming too quickly for Sig, turning him into a proto–Patrick Buchanan. In 1957, he wrote this in his newspaper column: "Recent newspaper headlines have emphasized the fact that the illiterate gangsters of our younger generation are definitely influenced in their lawlessness by the parody of music known as 'Rock 'n' Roll.' Either it actually stirs them to savage orgies of sex and violence, or they use it as an excuse for the removal of all inhibitions and the complete disregard of the conventions of decency." Then he *really* lets go.

"In a theater not long ago an usher and several spectators were stabbed during a general riot of teen-agers. The picture which apparently aroused these violent emotions was something called *Jamboree*"—a B movie featuring Jerry Lee Lewis, Carl Perkins, Fats Domino, Slim Whitman, Frankie Avalon, Count Basie, Connie Francis, and Dick Clark, not names that come to mind when you think about performers who might inspire a riot. In *Jamboree*, Sig continues,

various reputable disc jockeys lent themselves to the exploitation of a series of Rock 'n' Roll specialties featuring imitators of Elvis Presley, whose leering, whining, moaning, and suggestive lyrics blandly offered a vicarious sexual experience.

If anyone missed the point of these filthy performances, a practically unique naivete would seem to be indicated. How this picture ever passed the censors is a mystery. Perhaps they are still unacquainted with the facts of life.

Aside from the illiteracy of this "music," it has proved itself definitely a menace to youthful morals and an incitement to juvenile delinquency. There is no point in soft-pedaling these facts any longer. The daily papers provide sufficient proof of their existence.

All this strikes us as so much wind today, but it is not the ranting of some old fuddy-duddy. These are the words of a man who felt the essence of his life being threatened. His great-niece Patricia, reflecting on this, thinks that Sig fell prey to "the feeling you tend to get when you're fifty or sixty, that the world is passing you by, and that suddenly there's all this incomprehensible stuff going on—music, modes of dress, modes of art. I'm not certain [Sig] was necessarily just negative, but he was saying *Don't forget* that these other people are still there. I think he had a feeling that maybe Mozart and Beethoven *weren't* going to survive without their champions."

As hard as Spaeth worked on behalf of the music he loved, he campaigned against music he abhorred. In the 1950s and 1960s, the *Encyclopaedia Britannica Book of the Year*, for which he wrote critiques of the previous twelve months' worth of popular music, gave him an annual forum for this. Here we read him decrying "the menace of 'rock 'n' roll'" that continued through 1959, the "curse of 'rock 'n' roll' [that] still hung heavily over most of the widely heard songs [of 1960, when] more than 90% of this material could be dismissed as unadulterated trash." He describes the rock 'n' roll of 1961 as "nauseous," and that year "even the titles appearing most frequently were singularly unattractive. Often they consisted of a single word—'Twist,' 'Kiddio,' 'Yogi,' 'Stay,' 'Sleep,' 'Hucklebuck,' 'Ruby,' 'Calcutta,' 'Wheels,' 'Runaway,' 'Apache,' and 'Cryin'.'"

The sheer intensity of his fury says much about the beast consuming him. Where did it lead? In a follow-up to the column in which he described the "general riot of teen-agers," Spaeth reveals some responses to his evaluation of rock. He quotes one teenager's letter "verbatim, without correcting . . . spelling or English": "Elvis Presley is the best singer in the U.S. as proved by a recent pole (*sic*). He sings wonderful and surley (*sic*) acts well. That something you couldn't do . . . you are a square."

"You are a square." It is a sad epitaph for a man so dedicated to populism, who even toward the end of his life could say, "Progressive educators now realize that the snobbery of the past was a serious mistake and kept millions from an honest enjoyment of music by making it a mystery and a matter of special privilege, talent and experience. 'Music for Everybody' has become a literal possibility." He wanted people to *enjoy* music. Imagine what he would think today, with Elvis an icon and five-CD collections of rock 'n' roll classics of the 1950s for sale on late-night TV. "I just couldn't seem to stop / Watching while other musical styles / Came stumbling to the top," wrote Patricia Spaeth's younger brother, Thaddeus Spae, in "Uncle Sig," a song he composed about his famous relative. "Psychedelic and surf came through," Spae's lyrics continue,

> *Heavy metal glitter and disco too*
> *Punk and funk and reggae, thrash and new wave*
> *Uncle Sig's whirling in his grave . . .*

Maybe Sig died in time, before he had to see the punk and funk coming through, and the pilgrimages to Graceland. But had he witnessed it, might he have come to some inner reconciliation, seeing at last that the world is big enough for rock 'n' roll *and* concert music, and maybe discovering—though this is probably too much to hope for—that a love of one does not preclude a love of the other? In an ideal world, he might have seen that the impulse to make music, whatever form the music takes, was the same for Bach and Chuck Berry. That we may not like all the music we hear, but that the reason music is bigger than any one of us is that it—all of it—is so much a part of us all. And that his work on music's behalf was good work, despite its shortcomings and occasional failures of vision. He lived, as Richard Rodgers said, "a productive and purposeful life." He died having earned the right to be satisfied with what he had done. I hope he was.

—*L.R.*

Isaac Stern—On Music and Life

I n 1987 Isaac Stern played the Brahms Violin Concerto with the Los Angeles Philharmonic, conducted by that orchestra's then favorite guest conductor, Kurt Sanderling. The opportunity to visit both these musicians was too good to miss, and wanting to ask Stern some questions about his early years in San Francisco, I called on him at the Beverly Hills house of his friend Richard Colburn, a generous patron of the arts with whom he was staying. I had hit, it turned out, on a topic especially dear to him. So here, from that sunny morning, is a bit of Stern on Stern.

"I love Tokyo, I love Paris, New York has been home for more than forty years, and I always enjoy being there," he said, relaxing after a rehearsal. "But San Francisco! One touch of that fragrant fog, to see and smell the sunlight in some street—the memories that brings back: my first tennis game on a hard court, a place at the corner of Van Ness and Lombard where they had these fabulous thick milkshakes, learning to drive on one of those Model T's with three pedals—I worked for a while with a pianist who lived right on one of the S-curves of Lombard, and when you've driven that you can drive anywhere—the Essex that blew a gasket on California somewhere between Powell and Stockton, my whole childhood, everything."

Stern had last worked with Kurt Sanderling when they had done the Brahms Concerto with the Leningrad Philharmonic thirty years ago. And it was in the Brahms that, four months shy of his seventeenth birthday, he made his official debut with Pierre Monteux and the San Francisco Symphony on 19 and 20 March 1937, the Orchestra's Silver Jubilee season. The "real but unofficial" debut had happened the year before with the Saint-Saëns B-minor Concerto under the direction of the Symphony's Assistant Conductor and Principal Cellist, Willem Van den Burg, with whom he had just enjoyed an unexpected reunion a few days before. "I was disappointed that Monteux wouldn't let me play the Sibelius," Stern remembers. "I didn't know any better." Did he recall the first time he heard the Brahms? A long, thoughtful silence yields the name of Kreisler, but tentatively. He shakes his head. "I don't know. Look it up and see who played it then." It was not Kreisler, who performed with the Symphony only once, in 1914, but it could have been Enescu, concertmaster Mishel Piastro, Nathan Milstein, Efrem Zimbalist, Heifetz, or the not quite fourteen-year-old Yehudi Menuhin.

San Francisco is where Isaac Stern grew up, but it was not his birthplace. That was a small Ukrainian town called Kremenetz. How did he come to be raised in San Francisco? "First of all, there was a revolution in Russia. That was the reason for getting out. We settled in San Francisco because my mother had relatives there. In Russia, my father had been trained to be an amateur— an amateur in painting, in music, in living. When he came to America he had to make a living, so he became a house painter. He died in 1945, of lead-poisoning." Estranged for a time, father and son were closer again toward the end: "He made folders and files for my music, kept track of my clippings. He lived long enough at least to see the possibilities of my life." Stern's mother, who sang and from whom he learned much in childhood, lived until 1981.

Where did the Sterns live? "All over the place. On 43rd Avenue, on California, on Buchanan near Mr. Blinder"—Naoum Blinder, the San Francisco Symphony's concertmaster and Stern's principal teacher. "In 1932 we moved to New York so that I could work with Louis Persinger"—former San Francisco Symphony concertmaster and teacher of Yehudi Menuhin. "We stayed for four months, but money and opportunity ran out and we came back." By then Stern had been studying violin for four years. "I began at the San Francisco Conservatory when I was eight. My very first teacher? Somebody. I'll get in trouble for not remembering. Then at the Conservatory, there was Ada Clement, Lilian Hodgehead, Nathan Abbas, Robert Pollack—Lord, these are names I haven't spoken in years. Ernest Bloch was Director of the Conservatory and conducted the orchestra, and I was his concertmaster before my feet could reach the floor." He laughs: "Everybody created my career; some really had a hand in it."

Stern continues to think of those who "really had a hand in it." "There was Miss Lutie D. Goldstein—it was always *Miss* Lutie D. Goldstein—who bought me my first fiddle, and Cantor Reuben Rinder, who made the *shittach* [did the match-making]. And Dr. Leo Eloasser, a brain surgeon, *so high*"—Stern levels his hand about four feet off the floor—"a most execrable violist and a remarkable man at whose house we used to play chamber music." At twelve, Isaac Stern was already somebody on the San Francisco musical scene. "Yes, all right, I was the talented kid on the block. I began at eight, when violinists are really already over the hill. Yes, my parents were surprised and they were delighted. They were not fulfilling a lack in their own lives by forcing me to become what they hadn't become. I learned music to be educated, not to become a fiddler. You weren't educated if you didn't play music."

Stern's return to San Francisco also marked the beginning of what he remembers as "the most seminal period" of his young years, those years from twelve to seventeen when he worked with Naoum Blinder, always referred to as "Mr. Blinder." Stern learned a lot of violin from Mr. Blinder, but what he learned about music more generally and about attitude, ethical stance, and commitment was no less important. The endless quartet parties with older musicians, most of them members of the Symphony, were an important part of that—"quartet upon quartet upon quartet, then an *enormous* meal, then another couple of quartets. *Hausmusik,* that's real living with music. That's why someone like Sanderling is so familiar to me, someone who comes out of that culture of living music, where music is essential. And how important it was to learn not just at lessons but in the doing. And these experienced musicians, with great love they didn't hesitate to give me hell." That was his real education. "I went to school for about a year. Then I got what they fancifully called tutors, people who had read a little more than I. When I was eleven I took the Stanford intelligence test. I tested out at sixteen. 'Go home,' they said."

He began going to hear a lot of music as well. The people who left the most powerful and lasting impression, time having sorted out so much, were Rachmaninoff, especially when he played Beethoven; Artur Schnabel; Bronislaw Huberman (whom Thomas Mann called "the ugly little sorcerer"— *der häßliche kleine Hexenmeister*), the great Polish violinist who went on to found what is now the Israel Philharmonic; "and of course Yehudi." Later there was Heifetz ("you really want to throw your fiddle away") and also Joseph Szigeti, whose performances of Bach and twentieth-century music made tremendous impact. The Symphony's conductor then was another great musician and memorable personality, Alfred Hertz, "bald as an egg and with a beard as dense as Rasputin's. He was the man with the hair in the wrong place. He was Jovian and jovial in one. He and [his wife] Lily were the artistic bosses in town, there was no question about that." Opera was important too. "Most of all I remember my first *Ring.* Bodanzky conducted, and we had Flagstad and Melchior and Lotte Lehmann in the same *Walküre,* and Friedrich Schorr, when you could still tell which note he was singing."

Not only did Stern log hours of chamber music each week, but he went to hear others play it as well. "I first heard all the Beethoven quartets with the

Budapest, and they played Bartók and other modern composers too. The members of the Quartet were younger than all the young quartets today, but mature! And those recordings stand up! Joseph Roisman"—the quartet's leader from 1929 until the group disbanded in 1967—"in those days had the best bow arm around. Heifetz used to come and watch him. It was from Roisman that I learned the essential thing, that you let the phrase determine the bowing and that you have to have the flexibility to do any bowing the phrase requires. Did you notice at the rehearsal that I got them to change some bowings in the first movement?" I had. Stern had done it wordlessly, with body language alone, and concertmaster Sidney Weiss and his section had picked it up without missing a beat. "That came right out of what I learned from watching Roisman."

Stern was sixteen when Pierre Monteux came to the San Francisco Symphony, and that began another crucial and wonderful chapter in his education. He went to Symphony rehearsals constantly. First he watched Mr. Blinder. "When he was leading, NOBODY sat like THIS!" Stern collapses into the back of his chair. "The conductor-concertmaster relationship is aid with respect in one direction, comradeship with respect in the other." Seeing Mr. Blinder and Monteux work together taught him this. "With Monteux the question was always 'What is it all about?' Why do you play, not *how*. Going to those rehearsals, I learned how to look. I learned how to know. Once, someone asked William Steinberg how he learned all that music, and he said—a thick layer of German accent suddenly covers Stern's comfortable voice—'I don't learn zem, I know zem.' Monteux was like that. He was imperturbable. There was no way you could shock him. He shocked me, though. When I first met him he asked me about girlfriends. I stuttered around and said I didn't have time. And he said, 'When I was your age I already had my sixth mistress.' You know, he'd started as a fiddler at the Folies-Bergères. I told him that was what I really called starting from the bottoms up. He liked that. I was supposed to have played the Brahms with him in London on the 4th of May 1964"— Monteux, at eighty-nine, was then in the third year of a twenty-five-year contract as Chief Conductor of the London Symphony. "It didn't happen, though, and he died that summer. Once I was together with Monteux and Casals, and I realized those two had 160 years of experience between them. Not just experience, but digested experience."

In 1937, Stern ventured to New York for his first recital there. "I didn't tear up the world. Chotzinoff, the *New York Post* critic, wrote, 'From the land of sunshine, orange juice, and Hollywood comes yet another one . . . ' In those days all the radio networks had their own orchestras, and Mutual offered me their concertmastership. I was seventeen. The day after my debut recital I spent five hours riding on the top of a double-decker bus, from Washington Square to Washington Heights and back again, up and down. I decided to stick with it, and the next year it went better." The strength for that decision came in part from Mr. Blinder. "What he left me and what I look for in others was that he kept me from doing the easy thing. He taught me how to teach myself, which should be the goal of every teacher, and he taught me how to listen, which is the beginning and end of all musicianship. Now how about some lunch?"

—M.S.

B. H. Haggin the Contrarian

For twelve years or so in my thirties and forties I was the music critic of the *Boston Globe*. From time to time someone would ask me what had led me to that position and why I had wanted to become a music critic. My answer usually began: "Well, there was this man called B. H. Haggin . . . " Haggin was a bewildering mix of the impossible and the admirable, and I cannot overstate what I learned from him and how important he was to me.

As a high school student in St. Louis, I lived with my mother for a year and a half or so in the house of a Miss Pickett—H. Lorine Pickett—who was a superlatively successful insurance underwriter and wonderfully feisty, energetic, and generous woman to whom I owe much. The capacious basement of her house, a big Midwestern box on a corner lot, embraced by a screened porch on two sides, was occupied in part by testimony to her New Deal political convictions, namely about fifteen years of back issues of *The Nation* and *The New Republic*, the latter still very far from making its swing to the right.

This was a treasure trove for me, a recent arrival in the United States, brought up to be sympathetic to left-wing causes and ideas, history loving, and eager to learn about my new country. I was discouraged from bringing the magazines upstairs because of the clouds of dust that moving them generated, and so I spent many hours in a corner of the basement. In the course of being instructed about the WPA, CCC, NRA (the National Recovery Act, not the rifle people), and Roosevelt's other new alphabet-soup government agencies, reading about the Spanish Civil War, and learning from James Agee about movies and Malcolm Cowley about literature, I noted that *The Nation* had a regular column on music—with occasional diversions into ballet—written by someone named B. H. Haggin. Once in a while there was also a Haggin column on jazz.

I had next to no context for reading Haggin. I knew almost none of the music he wrote about, and most of the performers whose work he discussed were only names to me, if that. I had just begun to explore books about music, and although I was an eager newspaper reader, I don't recall reading newspaper reviews of musical events. In sum, I was unaware at first how different Haggin was from others who wrote about music for magazines and newspapers. I was, however, drawn in by his firm-textured, clean writing, and even more by how sure he seemed to be of who he was, what he heard, and what he valued. At fifteen, I wouldn't have known how to express any of that. Mr. Hecker, my senior-year English teacher, constantly insisted on "specific reference" to bolster assertions we made in what we wrote, and something else that impressed me about Haggin was that clearly he too subscribed to the "specific reference" creed.

What most fascinated me about Haggin, at least to begin with, was that he wrote shocking things about famous musicians, those people my mother referred to as *"Respektspersonen"*—Koussevitzky ("italicizing distortion"), Bruno Walter ("flaccid"), Heifetz ("mincing, wailing little swells . . . sentimental and vulgar"), Horowitz ("the alternation of brio and affettuoso teasing that is the sum total of his playing"), Menuhin ("coarse and blowzy [tone] . . . finicky and chopped up [phrasing]"), and Serkin ("playing which when it isn't violent is nerveless and without force").[1] As he wrote in 1964 in the introduction to his compilation *Music Observed:* "I wasn't paid to genuflect before eminences or before the limited perceptions of the general public, but was paid, instead, to give the non-professional listeners who read me the benefit of my professional listener's sharper perceptions, by pointing out what those readers might otherwise not notice." For the benefit of readers such as the one who characterized his criticisms of Heifetz "snide and ill-mannered impertinence," he added: "If any of them couldn't hear what I pointed out or preferred to ignore it, this didn't mean I was wrong in hearing and reporting it." No less interesting was the fact that Haggin did not hesitate to give most of those performers generous credit when he heard something that touched him by its grace or color or some other quality he admired, although I can't recall an exception being made for Heifetz, ever. Here was an important early lesson that reviewing needed to deal with particularities, not generalities.

From time to time Haggin would refer to letters he received from younger readers, many of whom impressed him by how smart they were. Perhaps hoping

---

[1] Some of these quotations come from later years, but they are consistent with what I would have read in 1944–1945.

to impress him too, that gave me the courage after I had gone off to college to write to him about some of the concerts I had heard. That first letter and those that followed always got prompt and ample replies. I realize in retrospect that Haggin's letters often had something of the air of religious indoctrination about them; for example, after I had written about an exciting performance of Schubert's *Wanderer* Fantasy, he assured me that I too would in due time achieve disillusionment about Rudolf Serkin. When our chapel choir together with a chorus from what we then called a girls' college put on a performance of Beethoven's C-major Mass, then even less known than it is now and not yet recorded, I suggested he come down to Princeton to hear it. As he sat in the chapel for the dress rehearsal, I immediately recognized him from the photo—by Walker Evans, no less—on the dust jacket of one of his books: tall, slender, with black hair and penetrating eyes. On a brilliant Sunday morning with a flawless blue sky, he carried a furled black umbrella.

As I continued to read Haggin in *The Nation*, also in the *New York Herald-Tribune*, where for a while he had a column on music on the radio, there were more letters back and forth. Later, when I was settled in New York as a teacher and occasional writer of record reviews, my first wife and I would sometimes visit him. That involved taking the subway all the way up to 243rd Street, its northernmost station in Manhattan. There he would meet us and guide us the last few blocks to his apartment on Seaman Avenue. Gradually I got a picture of the austere life he lived. He told us he had the same dinner every night, an eight-ounce steak and half a package of frozen peas. His one indulgence was a preludial ounce of bourbon with an equal quantity of water but no ice, a drink I still call a Haggin. Once we persuaded him to come to dinner at our apartment. No sooner had he accepted the invitation than he sent a letter with a long list of foods he couldn't or wouldn't eat. We did well until dessert. Partly because this was a special occasion, partly to compensate for making him climb seventy-two steps to our sixth floor cold-water flat on Mulberry Street, my wife, who held Haggin in great regard, had made a delicious port wine jelly. This he eyed doubtfully for a few moments, then said: "Do you mind if I don't have any? It quivers."

Haggin spent summers in Camden, Maine, until it was spoiled for him by the filming of *Peyton Place* there. Every night dinner in Camden was lobster salad made and delivered to his doorstep by a neighbor. He owned an elderly Packard, which was kept on blocks in a garage in the Bronx and brought out only for the annual trip to Camden and back. In his apartment I saw iconic objects that occasionally made cameo appearances in his writings—a reproduction of a Cézanne still-life with apples and a framed note from Toscanini about the placement of the mutes in the Love Scene of Berlioz's *Roméo et Juliette*. His record reviews sometimes got highly specific about how things sounded on a particular pair of speakers or with a certain setting on his amplifier, and there indeed was the equipment I had read about so often. In fact at one point, when he was ready to graduate to some new speakers, I bought his old ones, and I admit it was a thrill for me to have them.

He played recordings for us, mostly unpublished Toscanini, who was as near to a cynosure and ideal as he had among performers. It was loud, and he told us that his upstairs neighbors, a German Jewish refugee couple, sometimes complained. He had not actually ever met those people, but once he got on the elevator to find them already on board. The wife looked meaningfully at her husband and said, "*Unser Feind*"—our enemy. Having enemies was somehow important to him. Haggin had a photographic-phonographic memory for dinner parties thirty years in the past, of who had sat next to whom and said what wrong-headed thing. He was full of stories about interesting people in the musical, literary, and artistic world he had known. Almost all those stories, though, ended with a tight-lipped "but we're no longer friendly." In later years, I too was on the "no longer friendly" list. The intensity of his passions and convictions was an essential part of what made Haggin a good critic and for me an immensely important one, but the dark side of those passions and convictions was that he was not good at even small disagreements and that in his personal life he was absolutely unforgiving of lapses from fealty. A story he enjoyed telling was of a dinner at the house of Ira Hirschmann, who used his fortune as founder and CEO of Bloomingdale's to establish the New Friends of Music, for years New York's most distinguished chamber music series. Hirschmann's wife, Hortense Monath, was a pianist who had studied with Artur Schnabel, most of whose playing Haggin loved immensely. The Hirschmanns enjoyed Haggin's outspokenness, but when once he ventured a critical opinion of Schnabel there was an instant reproof from the host: "Now you go too far." (That is still a household saying in my present life.)

In his musical opinions, Haggin could be quite flexible, though this was rarely acknowledged. He was famous for his often shocking dislikes, not only of some famous performers I mentioned earlier, but of much of Brahms and Wagner. At New Friends concerts he would flee to the lobby of Town Hall and sit in one of two majestic chairs, the other one occupied by the Brahms-hating Hermann Adler, a musicologist and record producer from Brahms's home town of Hamburg, and one of the more striking characters on the New York musical scene. Company was comfort to neither man, for they disliked each other as much as they did Brahms.

Haggin also thought of most twentieth-century music as "arid" or "hideous." In that category, though, he sometimes underwent a conversion, perhaps brought about by a particularly illuminating performance and sometimes because a Balanchine choreography allowed him to hear through his eyes, as it were, something that he had not caught through sound alone. Balanchine, whom he considered the twentieth century's greatest creative artist, brought him around to late Stravinsky and even to some Webern. Haggin actually enjoyed reporting that he had changed his mind or—this applied especially to performers—that he could not understand how he had written so pallidly about some long ago event such as his first hearing of Flagstad on a Metropolitan Opera broadcast or that it had taken him so long to understand what he called the "plastic continuity" and the greatness of Toscanini's performances and, conversely, to be put off by the distortions in those of Willem Mengelberg.

When Haggin wrote about Brahms and Wagner his devotion to specific reference kicked in, as it did not in his brusque dismissal of most modern music. With Brahms he even cited the exact beat in the exact measure of the slow movement of the F-major Cello Sonata where he felt that Brahms had stopped inventing and was just churning. Wagner has of course always been controversial, and disliking *The Nibelung's Ring* was and is not all that remarkable. But Brahms! To this day you can find people who say that George Bernard Shaw, not surprisingly one of Haggin's heroes, was a remarkable music critic *except* for the absurdity of his negative writing about Brahms. What bothered Haggin was when people called his dislike a prejudice, which self-evidently it was not.

For me, Haggin's heterodox views on Brahms and Wagner proved very productive. Partly because I was young and easily influenced, more importantly because I had already learned so much from Haggin about Mozart, Schubert, Berlioz, and others, I took his response to Brahms and Wagner seriously, actually to the point of trying to go with him on these issues. Mostly it just didn't work. But if I ended up in disagreement with him on these topics, my own relationship to those two composers became the richer for the thinking that Haggin had made me do. I had, so to speak, earned my love of Brahms and Wagner rather than simply accepted their greatness as a cultural given. Through the Wagner-Brahms experience I learned the importance of something Haggin often stressed in his own writing, the importance of believing the testimony of my ears rather than the declarations of authorities, of responding to acoustic and musical realities and not to the glamorous aura of a great reputation. It also encouraged me to move off on paths of my own. After all, the best teacher is the one who ultimately makes himself unnecessary.

That is the heart of a critic's job—to make readers think—and that Haggin could do. I always found it interesting that a significant part of the readership that took him seriously—and critically—was in the intellectual and literary community, where he was enormously respected. You can find a vivid account of that in *Poets in Their Youth*, the wonderful memoir of Eileen Simpson. She writes of the devotion to Haggin's writing of her own former husband, John Berryman, and that of others in that circle such as Dwight MacDonald, Irving Howe, Mark Van Doren, Randall Jarrell, and Stark Young. It was also not surprising that after he left *The Nation*, Haggin found a home at a somewhat esoteric literary quarterly, *The Hudson Review.* To the testimony of those writers I would add that of Virgil Thomson, not always praised by Haggin either as critic or composer, but who deemed Haggin's opinions "sound, as well as refreshingly non-canonical." Among still others I would mention James Levine; my wife, who studied with him at the Cleveland Institute of Music, tells me that Haggin was required reading for Levine's students.

In 1944, Haggin published a book titled *Music for the Man Who Enjoys "Hamlet,"* in which he discussed in some detail works he thought would provide an entryway into great music. His point of departure was a not entirely convincing portrayal of a man who responds to poetry but not to music, and whose wife has dragged him to hear a recital by Schnabel. At first he is frustrated because "the music seems to mean a lot to Schnabel, and I suppose it means something to all these other people; but it doesn't make sense to me." By the time Schnabel is into Beethoven's Opus 111, frustration has given way to anger at not being home after "a quiet dinner, [with] slippers, easy chair, and a much read copy of *Hamlet*," and he thinks: "I'll bet it doesn't mean any more to the others or to the old boy on the stage than it means to me. It *doesn't* make sense; and they're only pretending it does." The notion of people being conned or pretending is still voiced, particularly by people who like to throw the word "elitist" around. At any rate, from this donnée, Haggin goes on to show that Schubert's and Beethoven's sonatas are, like *Hamlet*, examples of "the employment, on large scale, of an artistic medium," conveying "insights of . . . mind and spirit," but through a different artistic medium. If Schubert's and Beethoven's insight and their play of fantasy "do not get through to your mind, it is because the *medium* is one to which, at the moment, you are not susceptible." In what follows, Haggin is an excellent, helpful guide.

But here—and this is an example of how maddening he could be—is an example of Haggin on Brahms from his *Listener's Musical Companion* (1956): "I recall a broadcast of a performance of the Piano Concerto No. 2 by Toscanini and the NBC Symphony with Horowitz as soloist. Sounds came through my radio that were evidence of attentive, purposeful activity by Brahms, Toscanini, Horowitz, the orchestra, the audience; but what also came through powerfully was the impression that this was the activity of people under a spell continuing to go through a long-established ritual that was without reality or meaning— performers and listeners going through the motions of esthetic response to a piece of music in which the composer went through the motions of esthetic creation. Anyone not under this spell, anyone able to listen freshly to the agitated statements of the piano that broke in on the quiet opening of the first movement, would, it seemed to me, perceive that they were the noisy motions of saying something portentous that really said absolutely nothing; and listening further he would discover that the entire movement was a succession of such attempts at now one such effect and now another." He goes on to cite Tchaikovsky, who criticizes in Brahms (in Haggin's summary) "the conscious aspiration to something for which there is no poetic impulse, the striving for something that must be unstriven for, the conscious attempt at Beethoven's profundity and power that results in a caricature of Beethoven" and, in Tchaikovsky's own words, "so many preparations and circumlocutions for something which ought to come and charm us at once."

Here Haggin is doing exactly what he condemns at the beginning of the *Hamlet* book where the poor man in the title assumes that everyone around him is under a spell and has been conned into mistaking pretend activity for real. And however wrong that is, it is also unanswerable: if I have come round to rejecting Haggin's and Tchaikovsky's assessment it only proves how powerful the spell is. Haggin is saying, "I hear it and therefore it *is* so." He actually liked quite a lot of Brahms, chiefly those works in which, and here he quoted the Australian critic W. J. Turner, he was not "going forth to war," was "entirely natural and self-forgetful" and "not obsessed by the tramp of Beethoven behind him." That is an understandable argument, and I would have to say of myself that of the Brahms symphonies, for example, I like the First least (and still think it an extraordinary work) and love the Third most.

In the *Hamlet* book, Haggin recommended recordings, citing exactly where on the 78-rpm disk something to which he wanted to draw particular attention would be found. "T-1: .1.5-, B-1.3+" meant side 1, just before 1½ inches from the rim, of Toscanini's recording of Mozart's G-minor Symphony, while B indicated the location of the same passage on the Beecham set. To help the reader, the book included a little white ruler to enable one to find these places. The measurements and the ruler caused great hilarity, but they were in fact useful, much as citations given in minutes and seconds are now useful in detailed reviews of CDs. (In fact this updated method appears in a later edition, which also got a new title, *Music for One Who Enjoys "Hamlet."*) In her memoir, Simpson touchingly describes John Berryman, ruler in hand, locating these musical gems. A certain penchant for pedantry also caused Haggin at one point in his career to classify composers' works as "incandescent," "great," "important works of lesser stature," and so on. Silly as that seems, his judgments were discriminating and made a lot of sense.

From Haggin I also learned something crucial about performance. His praise of the performers he admired and in some cases even revered—Toscanini, Schnabel, Bjoerling, to cite three very different ones—always related to what they did to the music itself. The same was true when he rejected a performance by, say, Heifetz or Horowitz. Tirelessly he pointed out that a performance is not a free-standing, independent object: it is a rendering *of* something and can only be judged in relation to that something, that symphony, sonata, aria, or whatever. This led him to make a crucial distinction, one difficult not only for lay listeners to grasp but also for some professionals and most students—namely, the distinction between the ability to play an instrument well, a skill Heifetz and Horowitz commanded to a superlative degree, and the ability to communicate the musical content of a composition, where they were not dependable. That distinction became a cornerstone of my own later activity as a music critic.

I admired Haggin's ability to face the truth that sometimes, as Horace told us long ago, sometimes Homer nods. Some truly great composers do too, notably Bach. Again, it was good to be reminded that the important thing was to deal, not with a great and revered generality called Bach, but with particular works, or even particular parts of those works. It is amusing to watch someone slowly and reluctantly, but ultimately with some relief, admit that here and there we find arias in the cantatas that are really boring or that the fugues in the sonatas for unaccompanied violin were excruciating even when Milstein played them. As a boy I learned from Haggin to face up to that truth even though expressing it invariably brought disapproval. And it has not affected my love for the many works I cherish and that I can't imagine not having in my life.

Something else Haggin did that was entirely unconventional was occasionally to write about other critics. It made him a kind of outlaw in the fraternity. For him, though, it was as natural and as important as writing about performers and composers. Critics were, after all, a highly visible part of the musical scene. He did not think much of most of them. The ones he valued—for their perceptions, their honesty, and their excellent style—were Berlioz most of all, Shaw, W. J. Henderson, who wrote for various New York papers between 1887 and 1924, and David Cairns, whose work he discovered when Cairns's collection *Responses* was published in 1973. He admired the virtuosity and grace of Virgil Thomson's style but was often put off by his spinning of theories that seemed to have little relation to musical realities. Clean writing was important to him. Not surprisingly he loathed the swollen prose of the *Times*'s Olin Downes and effusion like Jay Harrison's about *Amahl and the Night Visitors*: "Once again Mr. Menotti has demonstrated that the lyric stage is his destiny. It is a destiny that becomes him as golden robes do a prince." Haggin's own response was rather different: "I listened . . . with incredulous amazement—finding it difficult to believe I was really hearing those sugary, trashy tunes, that they could even have occurred to anyone operating as a serious composer today, that he could not have been too embarrassed by the mere thought of them to let anyone else hear them, and that other people could have considered them worth publishing to the world." But getting back to language, and this time not a critic's, discussing Bernstein's *Kaddish*, he observed that "the basic Norman Corwin style of vocal rhetoric is infused with a vulgarity of Bernstein's own, giving the words an awfulness that forbids quotation."

Haggin may have been unparalleled at excoriation, but he was also extraordinarily warm and emotional in appreciation. This comes across especially in the best of his dance writing. And I just reread his account of

Kirsten Flagstad's last concert in New York in 1955. He describes, as always hewing carefully to just what he heard,

> the shock, when she began to sing, of the loss in vocal beauty since the last time; then the amazement as the voice gained in luster of lower notes and power of higher ones, as it went with complete assurance wherever the phrase required it to go, and as it operated with complete flexibility in the inflections the phrasing required it to make. With all this, certainly, there was a loss since the last time: one noted that when the voice rose to a soft high note it produced that note carefully as a head tone; that climactic high notes, though astonishingly clear and powerful, were less powerful this time. Nevertheless it was true this time as last that even with what it had lost, the singing—the lustrous lower notes, the clear and powerful high ones, in the sustained phrases so exquisitely and touchingly inflected by musical feeling and taste—would have been considered remarkable if it had been done by a woman of thirty; and one heard it being done by a woman of sixty.
>
> That brings me to what there was to see. . . . There was an additional shock in the changes in her appearance: the graying blond hair now totally gray, the head and shoulders slightly hunched together, the face shadowed and impassive. All this as she stood waiting and listening; then, when the moment came for her to sing, one saw her face amazingly become animated, transfigured by what produced the beautiful phrases one heard. And this made the occasion moving in the way Toscanini's concerts had been in recent years, when one had seen the manifestations of increasing age and then the manifestations of continuing great musical powers.

As I look back on what I learned from Haggin and the ways in which he helped form me as a teacher and a writer, I am most grateful for the ways in which he opened up so much music to me when I was young and my taste and understanding were first being formed. And even though Haggin saying those unthinkable things about Brahms may come to mind first for many people, he loved a huge amount of music from Renaissance madrigals and motets onward. From Haggin I learned, as I would never in a million years have learned from the music columns of the *Times* or even the far better *Herald-Tribune* with the brilliant but mentally all-over-the-place Virgil Thomson, about the greatness of a lot of repertory not taken seriously in popular discourse on classical music in the 1940s and 1950s nor much heard in concert then—the Mozart piano concertos, the Schubert piano sonatas, or anything of Berlioz beyond the *Symphonie fantastique*. I have mentioned his intense feeling for Balanchine, which also brought about some of his most gripping writing, and this at a time when John Martin at the *Times* threw dead cats and dogs at Balanchine at every opportunity. Bernard Haggin may in many respects have been an eccentric crank, but the enlightening aspects of his work outweighed his strangenesses, and by far.

—M.S.

V.
AFFAIRS TO REMEMBER

Loving Memories of Movie Music

Had it not been for a movie, I might have had to wait another ten years before I knew how completely the sound of an orchestra can immobilize everything in your life but the present moment.

The movie was *The Seven Wonders of the World*, the third in that series of Cinerama epic travelogues made during the 1950s. Cinerama, if you don't recall, was the ultimate wide-screen process, and some film buffs maintain that it has not been equaled. This was the original moviegoing *experience*, one that promised to give viewers a genuine sense of reality. The Cinerama camera was loaded with three synchronized film magazines positioned side-by-side, in an arc. When the images captured by this trio were put together—cast by three synchronized projectors on a huge curved screen—the resulting panoramic montage duplicated the arc of human vision. Cinerama promised to put "you" in the middle of the action, and when the unwieldy camera was perched in a car on a Coney Island roller coaster or at the head of a rubber raft finding its way through the rapids of the Indus River, Cinerama delivered. A big part of the successful duping of the eye was the way Cinerama duped the ear. Seven channels of sound, fed through speakers distributed behind the screen and throughout the theater, created a sonic image as realistic as the picture.

All this might seem tame to us today, in a film world dominated by loud digital blockbusters and by IMAX. But to audiences in 1956, Cinerama was stunning. Part of its strategy to astound an audience was surprise. Things started out small and slow. As the lights went down we were made to sit through an introduction by Lowell Thomas, the narrator. The image on the screen seemed no larger than what you'd see in a home movie, and as Thomas, sitting at his desk, ticked off in his slightly manic delivery some trumped-up raisons d'être for the spectacle in which we were about to participate, the growing boredom threatened to annihilate any hope of entertainment, let alone the adventure we had been assured. And then suddenly the picture expanded to three times its "normal" size, we were hovering far above Iguaçú Falls, and a hundred-piece orchestra loaded with brass and percussion pounded out crescendo upon crescendo. My stomach rolled as the pitch of the aerial shot delineated the curve of the earth. But what really set my pores vibrating was the sound, bursting from an audio system so perfect it seemed the players were here, in this room. I had never experienced anything remotely like it, and I knew that this was how music was meant to sound.

Looking back, the effect was obviously cinematic, not what you'd call a true "musical" experience. For me, that came along roughly eight years after that day I heard the music over Iguaçú Falls, when I first encountered the scherzo and finale of the Beethoven Fifth and was suddenly thrust into a similar epiphany, the vision of my inner eye expanding to three times its normal size. I am speaking of Cinerama and Beethoven in the same breath because music for films can offer a key to how "serious" music gets to us. What we hear in the background when we're at the movies can tell us a lot about how to get the most from other music. For the notes in any film score are linked to what is happening on the celluloid as certainly as the notes of the Beethoven Fifth—or any of a thousand other concert works—stand for their own set of images and emotions.

Think of it. Might not Beethoven, given the chance, have written for films? With his profound sense of drama, his knowledge of how, like the best screenwriter or director, to build an audience's expectations and then fulfill or shatter them, he would have been a filmmaker's strongest ally. All his life he loved the theater. He would have been the first in line for a movie job. Motion pictures have been a seductive medium almost from the start, certainly long before anyone conceived of wide-screen, wide-sound extravaganzas. Arnold Schoenberg, of all people, wanted to write for films but never managed to accommodate himself to the way Hollywood worked. His 1930 *Music to Accompany a Film Scene* exemplifies his ambition. Stravinsky, too, was a motion picture hopeful, but he also had ideas about artistic control, and about music, that Hollywood didn't share. He was approached to score both *Jane Eyre* and *The Song of Bernadette*, and although the plans came to nothing, producers continued to fantasize about the classiness his name might lend to their efforts. As late as the mid-1960s he was considered for the Dino De Laurentiis epic *The Bible*. Perhaps the Symphony in Three Movements of 1946 tells us why

Stravinsky's movie aspirations never came to anything. It includes passages he claimed to have composed in response to documentary film and newsreel footage—music so aggressively personal that it would have overshadowed any images it intended "merely" to accompany.

You wonder whether movie music would be held in such contempt by the intelligentsia if more first-rate composers had written for films. Yet who can say that Ralph Vaughan Williams and Aaron Copland and Hugo Friedhofer and Erich Wolfgang Korngold are anything less than first-rate? We tend to forget that, at least in the golden days of Hollywood, very good composers were often at the command of those who didn't know much about music but who knew what they liked. In *No Minor Chords*, a memoir of his days in Hollywood, André Previn tells story after story about the struggles waged with otherwise intelligent and even brilliant individuals by those who wrote music for films. He recalls how Miklós Rósza, "during *Ben-Hur*, . . . was beside himself with impotent rage when the director, William Wyler, suggested that 'Silent Night, Holy Night' be played during the Nativity scene." Rósza won that fight. And in scoring that scene he managed both to preserve his own artistic integrity and to create music as memorable and moving as a hymn.

But this is not a guide to telling good film music from bad. We all know what bad movie music is: bombastic, sappy, overblown ersatz Rachmaninoff or Richard Strauss—though Korngold, for one, wrote some distinguished movie music whose cholesterol content is dangerously high. We should take to heart these generous words of one of the finest composers to have written for the movies, Bernard Herrmann, who said that he knew no "good composer who felt he was being degraded by writing for films." And Miklós Rózsa, looking back on his career in his 1982 memoir *Double Life*, asked himself, "[W]as I right to devote so much creative energy to the writing of film music? Did I betray my heritage?" He concluded he had not, "inasmuch as I never lost sight of my *real* profession: that of composer, not of music to order but simply of the music that was in me to write. . . . I have no time for any music which does not stimulate pleasure in life, and, even more importantly, *pride* in life." (In *A Heart at Fire's Center*, his 1991 biography of Bernard Herrmann, Steven Smith quotes Herrmann expressing a similar sentiment in virtually the same words.) Likewise, the musicians who play for soundtracks, whether the score calls for an ensemble of symphonic or chamber proportions, are among the best around, and they're drawn from major orchestras and conservatories. Previn has praised these men and women, who read through often complicated scores, often before the ink is dry. "These players were genuinely amazing. . . . The fact that the music might have been second-rate, or even tenth-rate, had no bearing on its degree of difficulty, but I never saw any of these instrumentalists come unglued."

While this isn't a checklist of things to listen and watch for, it might be a good idea to hear what some of film music's most eloquent practitioners have to say about it. In a 1972 interview with Ted Gilling in *Sight and Sound*, Bernard Herrmann laid out a virtual poetics of the genre:

> When a film is well made, the music's function is to fuse a piece of film so that it has an inevitable beginning and end. . . .
>
> Music essentially provides an unconscious series of anchors for the viewer. It isn't always apparent . . . but it serves its function. I think Cocteau said that a good film score should create the feeling that one is not aware whether the music is making the film go forward or whether the film is pushing the music forward. . . .
>
> I think that film music expresses what the actor can't show or tell.

Ralph Vaughan Williams, best known for nine symphonies that represent one of the twentieth century's great musical achievements, is another who relished his film work. (In fact his Seventh Symphony, the *Sinfonia antartica*, is a reworking of his score for *Scott of the Antarctic*.) "There are two ways of writing film music," he said. "One is that in which every action, word, gesture or incident is punctuated in sound. This . . . often leads to a mere scrappy succession of sounds of no musical value in itself. . . . The other method . . . is to ignore the details and to intensify the spirit of the whole situation by a continuous stream of music."

"Intensifying the spirit of the whole situation" is really what Herrmann is talking about, and it is also the essence of what the Russian director Sergei Eisenstein said about Prokofiev when the two of them collaborated on *Ivan the Terrible*. Prokofiev's music, said Eisenstein in his *Notes of a Film Director*, "presents a wonderful picture of the inner movement of the phenomenon and its dynamic structure, which embody the emotion and meaning of the event. . . . Prokofiev knows how to grasp the structural secret which conveys the broad meaning of the phenomenon."

This "grasp [of] the structural secret" is the mark of film music that does its job—that reinforces and projects a director's technique. Seen in this light, the blast of sound that accompanies the broad image of Iguaçú Falls lying below becomes not just a perfect wedding of sound and image but a union of sound and cinematic strategy, a means by which the filmmaker reaches his end, which in this case is (obviously) to overwhelm us. (Incidentally, I don't know who wrote the Iguaçú Falls music, but it was one of three composers who collaborated on the score for *Seven Wonders of the World*: David Raksin, perhaps best known for the theme from the Otto Preminger film *Laura*; Jerome Moross, a fine composer of concert music who in his score for William Wyler's *The Big Country* gave us music by which all other scores for Westerns are measured; and Emil Newman, who scored a string of minor films including *Pin Up Girl* and *Four*

Jills in a Jeep, who served as music director on *Guadalcanal Diary*, and whose brother Alfred went on to far greater fame as a film composer.)

Filmmakers and composers can also collaborate in more subtle ways to communicate with the audience. Alfred Hitchcock's *Vertigo*, as Steven Smith has pointed out in his Herrmann biography, is a film based on the French novel *D'Entre les Morts* (by Pierre Boileau and Thomas Narcejac), an updated version of the Tristan myth. Much of Herrmann's music for the film could almost be mistaken for Wagner's *Tristan* music, and Herrmann's strategy—withholding resolution virtually until the end—is similar to Wagner's in his opera. In the final seconds of *Vertigo*, Scottie Ferguson (James Stewart) looks down from the bell tower of the mission at San Juan Battista, an out-of-the-way village down the California coast from San Francisco. The terror of heights that has plagued Scottie since the film's opening is gone at last, and the film's conflict is resolved. Now the music, which for most of the past two hours has mirrored Scottie's ordeal in its search for ways to escape the minor mode, is suddenly free to rise into the major mode. (It has done so only twice previously, in *scènes d'amour*—I borrow that title from Herrmann himself—that end with the music shifting into major and the screen going dark: structural devices, but also metaphors for completion and the *petits morts* of love.)

Here is another example of how director and composer can join in conveying a point of view. In Elia Kazan's *On the Waterfront*, Terry Malloy (Marlon Brando) finds the body of his brother Charley (Rod Steiger), a mob operative who has been murdered for not following orders to kill Terry. Terry lifts Charley's corpse off a longshoreman's hook and onto his shoulders. For this grim scene, Leonard Bernstein conceived heartbreaking, tender music—music that, six minutes earlier, had first appeared in the "Contender" scene: "You was my brother, Charley," says Terry. "You shoulda looked out for me a little bit. . . . I coulda been a contender. I coulda been *somebody*, instead of a bum, which is what I am." Now Terry looks out for his slain brother in a scene accompanied by music that, in another context, might be construed as a lullaby—or perhaps in this context, too: just as, two hundred years earlier, Johann Sebastian Bach had created a sorrowful lullaby to the dead Christ at the end of the *Saint Matthew Passion*. The dirge for Charley in *On the Waterfront* is in stark contrast to the harsh dissonances to which we've become accustomed in Bernstein's score. This lovely music tells us that Terry has a side we have not yet seen. It also signals a turning point in the narrative.

Call all this what you will—"grasping the structural secret," "intensifying the spirit of the whole situation," "expressing what the actor can't show or tell." What it comes down to is the communication of ideas and emotions through sound. The most memorable film music, whether grand and epic (*Ben-Hur*, *Star Wars*) or intimate (*To Kill a Mockingbird*, *Our Town*), conveys the spirit of the moment and contributes to the overall impact. In other words, film music does exactly what we expect of concert music. It exists as a coherent entity that touches our hearts, and it can make us feel anything imaginable.

Movies made me fall in love with the sound of the orchestra, but there's more to this story. When we watch a film, we begin, after themes are introduced and recur a few times, to associate music with various characters and states of mind and places and situations. Usually we have no idea we're doing this. Part of our satisfaction at the end is created by the music that has been working on us. Music has become inextricably linked to the drama we've witnessed.

This sense of music *as* drama offers an enormously rich point of entry into the world of concert music. Personally, I have a debt of gratitude to repay men like Miklós Rósza and Alfred Newman. They provided much pleasure in their own right. They also led me to the music of their colleagues, Bach and Mozart and Tchaikovsky. For when we listen to the Dvořák Seventh, the Brahms Fourth, or the Bruckner Fifth *as dramas*, we need not concern ourselves with questions of key, harmony, development, or recapitulation any more than we would be consciously concerned with the technical aspects of lighting or camera position while watching *The Treasure of the Sierra Madre*.

What do I mean by listening to music as if it were a drama? Not attaching images to it in the manner of *Fantasia,* or correlating the sound with a succession of scenes as outlined by Richard Strauss and Mahler in those programs they sometimes provided for their music. What I mean is listening to what the music *says* in its own terms—hearing the patterns of loud and soft, sweet and bitter, slow and fast; recognizing tunes when they recur or come back in slightly different forms: louder or softer than when you heard them last, or slower, or played by one instrument instead of sixty instruments. Never again will any listener who discerns these patterns have to fear the revelation of an ignorance of sonata form. Music *speaks,* and it speaks as directly as any actor. But you have to be listening to hear what it has to say.

If you haven't done so already, try, the next time you're at a concert, giving an orchestra the kind of attention you give the screen when the trailers end and the lights go all the way down. Listen as though you were listening to dialogue—because you are. As though to miss a line now will lessen your comprehension of what may happen in five minutes—because it will. More often than you think, you will encounter music that speaks to you. Imagine that this is the score for some drama of particular import. Because it is. From it, you will take a memory of sound that will be yours forever, that will become part of you and accompany you as another drama unfolds: the one that means the most to you, the story of your life.

—L.R.

Vienna Trilogy:
Vignettes from the City of Music

I. Attitude on a Day in Old Vienna

I had my first taste of Vienna attitude in the summer of 1996, when my family and I spent a few days there visiting our friends Luna and Richard. Luna, who has become a proper Viennese lady, picked up her name when she was a hippie and felt a special kinship with the moon. Her birth name is Gertrud, but even today only Richard calls her that. They pass their winters in an old high-ceilinged apartment in Vienna's First District, near the Rathaus and University, a residence Richard found years ago and which is kept within their means by rent control. During the summer their home base is at the edge of the Vienna Woods, in Baden, a spa town where the Romans once diverted the hot springs into baths, where Constanze Mozart went to take the waters while Wolfgang was working on *The Magic Flute* and the Requiem, and where Beethoven composed parts of his Ninth Symphony. Midsummer temperatures in the resort are rarely as incapacitating as Vienna's, which is one of Baden's many attractions. So it was from here that we set out to explore the big city, boarding the blue tram called the Badener Bahn one morning for the hour-long ride that terminated near the busy intersection of Kärntnerstrasse and the Opern-Ring. When we disembarked, we found ourselves diagonally across from the Vienna State Opera, a grand temple of art that was bombed in World War II, restored to its original splendor, and today wears a cassock of Ringstrasse soot and the residue of pollutants unknown when it opened its doors in 1869.

Groups were gathering behind guides at the Opera House, ready to be led through its sacred corridors. When I asked at the ticket desk if an English-language tour were available, the cashier's eyes narrowed and she gave me a smile, tight-lipped and ambiguous. "*Ja*," she sneered. "*Especially* for you."

I hadn't expected to purchase attitude with the Schillings I handed over, in bills bearing the likeness of Dr. Freud. But I was a guest, so I simply returned the cashier's smile and picked up the tickets. No offense taken. As attitudes go, this woman's was mild. I had been warned about the Viennese, not only by Luna, who grew up near the Czech border of Austria, but even by Richard, who is Viennese himself. Yet I never reached a verdict. Having spent a total of three days of my life in Vienna, I did not grow intimate with the collective soul of its citizens. (Anyone who wishes to explore that subject is directed to *The Viennese* by Paul Hofmann, who approaches the issue with humor and the authority of a native.) And in Vienna, there is more than one kind of attitude to attract your focus. Because I was fortunate enough to encounter the city through friends, I could enter it as I would enter an embrace, never mind one surly cashier. I approached it, you could say, with the right attitude.

That attitude led to some discoveries. They were not unique. Even if you have never experienced Vienna yourself, you have undoubtedly heard it said that this city is an amazing place. That is a truth I repeat with no hesitation. Everywhere you look, Vienna meets your attitude with its own: with its commitment to grandeur, to beauty, and to elegance, a commitment that takes the form of public stance and spiritual position. It is an attitude expressed in the magnificence of the great Ringstrasse buildings, lavish monuments to aspiration, architecture that exudes unashamed emotionalism and sentiment. It is expressed in the formal restraint of the gardens that connect the Upper and Lower Belvedere palaces, in the lush geometries of the grounds around Schönbrunn, in the overwhelming presence of Saint Stephen's Cathedral, whose every stone seems to throb with hot energy, reinforcing the impression that this is some prototypical star cruiser about to lift off on a shot for heaven. And many of this attitude's most profound manifestations are in the reams of music conceived here, masterwork after masterwork—*conceived here*, as though the intersection of latitude and longitude in this corner of the earth had created an elemental force that shook music into being, a kind of Bermuda Triangle in reverse. Here, instead of vanishing down a bottomless tube of darkness, men and women regain a sense of priorities through the great life-giving forces of the harmonies that have taken shape and been born in this spot.

All this, in its most superficial form, makes it easy to mistake Vienna for a cultural theme park, a Straussland that caters to those in search of Sacher-Torte and a look at some of the houses once inhabited by Haydn and Beethoven. True, Vienna has its version—classier, of course—of the House of Wax and the Mystery Spot. This is the Mozart Concert, hawked throughout the center of town by characters who seem to have come from another age but who you soon discover are depressingly from our own. Dressed in powdered wigs and eighteenth-century breeches, they will give you a hard sell—in German, English, French, Spanish, or Italian—for a performance at the Musikverein, where for an outrageously expensive ticket you can have the privilege of hearing a pickup ensemble in period costume play excerpts from Mozart's most popular works.

Mozart Concerts and even the Ringstrasse buildings can make Vienna seem a great monument to the past, as fixed in time as the statue of Maria Theresa that stands in the plaza between the Museum of Art History and the Museum of Natural History, massive twin edifices that stare across at each other like mirror images of vanished empire. But when you see a billboard in front of the Art History Museum advertising an upcoming concert by Tina Turner at the Prater Stadium, you realize that here, as elsewhere, the minutes and hours and days and years continue to pass. Everywhere in Vienna, images remind you that time does not stand still. Here are some images I brought back with me: Schönbrunn, the country home of the Hapsburgs, is now surrounded by the city and accessible from a subway stop that bears its name. On a stage erected outside the palace entrance, an American jazz orchestra plays a brassy version of "Twist and Shout." At the Central Cemetery, where Vienna's great lie in rest, I ask a caretaker where Brahms's grave is, but I realize even as I phrase it that my question—*"Wo ist der Brahms?"*—must come across as though I'm talking about an acquaintance who might be waiting around the corner. No matter. The man responds in the same spirit, and I realize that this is perhaps the only place on earth where Johannes Brahms, d. 1897, can still in all seriousness be *der Brahms*. Yet when we reach his grave, right next to Johann Strauss, Jr.'s, and just opposite Beethoven's, we discover that not even this place is static, for a funeral procession is marching up a nearby walk, and the people gather before the priest to murmur prayers for their dead.

Outside the Hofburg Palace lies the Heldenplatz, a great open field where in 1938 Hitler gave his first address to the Viennese after the Anschluss. This evening another crowd is gathered here. From what I can make out, they have assembled for the opening of a conference on diversity in Austrian society. A poster is displayed prominently near the podium. It depicts photos of four brains. Three of these brains, equal in size, respectively bear the labels "European," "African," and "Asian." The fourth, which is tiny, is labeled "Racist." Though Vienna has been rebuilt to look as though the bombs of 1945 had never fallen, memory will not be deceived. The past, indeed, is a very mixed bag.

At the Upper Belvedere Palace, we find other pasts. Part of the Austrian Gallery is housed in this seventeenth-century building, and just now a retrospective on "Painting at the Turn of the Century" is on display. The Klimts and Kokoschkas evoke an era, and to be in their presence is suddenly to grasp Mahler and Schoenberg, to be reminded of the background from which they emerged: the astonishing intellectual cauldron that churned with the likes of Freud, Wittgenstein, Ernst Mach, Theodor Herzl, Alexander von Zemlinsky, Otto Wagner, Hugo von Hofmannsthal, Adolf Loos. Here, at the outside edge of Western Europe—Vienna lies farther east than Prague—this abundance of mind and emotion once hurtled forward at such speed that the weight of new insights far exceeded that of old spiritual and intellectual supports. The shaking of society's inner ground could have been measured on a seismic scale, and the energy released helped shape an attitude that carried civilization to the brink of World War I, the fault line that divided the world into Then and Now.

But there are attitudes and there are attitudes. If you hear a waltz in Vienna, it represents yet another stance, one poised to make the most of life as we find it—predating, coinciding with, and outlasting disaster. At a sidewalk cafe where we had had lunch, we now settle down for an evening snack—gently bucking tradition with an order not for strudel or Sacher-Torte, but for a veggie pizza. The redhaired waitress with whom I had chatted in both English and German is back at our table. We spoke English before, I remind her. "And did you want to do that again?" she asks, her voice suffused with the faintest hint of yet another kind of Vienna attitude. As night falls, we rush back to the Baden tram station at Opernplatz. The train, which runs only every hour, is preparing to pull out. I cannot get the ticket machine to accept my fifty-Schilling piece. The driver notices my desperation, gets out, and tries the machine himself, but his luck is no better than mine. He points to the waiting train car. "Get on," he tells us. "You're riding for free tonight." I am struck, as the tram finally makes its way out of the city and picks up speed under a gleaming moon, at how quiet the crowded car is. No one, it seems, would even think of playing a radio here. Times have not changed *that* much. But I wonder: If anyone did switch on some music, what would we hear? Would it be "The Blue Danube"? Or would it be Alanis Morrissette?

II. Back to the Future with Viennese Operetta

What is the sensibility we have come to call "Viennese," something as difficult to put into words as *Gemütlichkeit* is to render in English? It is a sense of cheerfulness, but also of wistfulness, that at its worst is sentimental but that at its best makes your throat lump up—immediately. Is this aura of nostalgia built into Viennese operetta? Or does it arise only from our own yearning for the idealized world these works represent as we look back and hear them a hundred years after they were born? Some of their bittersweet appeal comes from what we ourselves bring to them, but more is inherent, as when Alfred and Rosalinde in *Die Fledermaus* sing, "*Glücklich ist, wer vergisst was nicht zu ändern ist*"— "Happy is the person who forgets what can't be changed"—and of course "what can't be changed" is another way of saying "the past." This brand of worldly wisdom, which admits regrets but refuses to let them stop forward motion, is echoed by Richard Strauss's Marschallin in *Der Rosenkavalier*—an opera whose setting, plot, and reliance on dance rhythms reveal its heritage in the operetta tradition to which Strauss's namesake had contributed so brilliantly. "One must be light," the Marschallin sings, "light of heart and light of hand, to hold and take, hold and let go. . . . Life punishes those that are not so . . . and God has no mercy on them."

Sentiments such as these are especially suited to the New Year season and to that night of nights, New Year's Eve—a time to celebrate the old and the new, a time to look backward and forward, thankful for what we think of as a chance to begin again. And what could be more musically expressive of this simultaneous parting and greeting—and the pain in the gut created when our hearts are yanked in two directions at once—than the bittersweet sounds of the waltz, and the cheerfulness and heartbreak encompassed in the form that relies so heavily on the waltz, the operetta.

Operetta was a popular genre that blossomed for only a short time, from the middle of the nineteenth century until early in the twentieth, in Vienna—and in other places as well, though because Viennese operettas by Johann Strauss, Jr., and Franz Lehár scored international successes, we tend to think of operetta as an almost uniquely Viennese form. It came from France, and it was Jacques Offenbach who in 1864 suggested to Strauss Junior that he should take time out from composing waltzes and give operetta a shot. For operetta had a ready-made audience, and in the last half of the nineteenth century that audience ballooned. Between 1860 and 1890, Vienna's population grew by 259 percent. The new immigrants were hungry for fashionable entertainment that tasted great and was easy to digest—Lite Opera, Ninety-nine Percent Angst-Free.

Von Suppé had already produced what is considered the first Viennese operetta in 1860 with *Die Pensionat*, but Offenbach's French productions were still what drew crowds to the Theater an der Wien and the Carltheater. All that changed in 1871, when Strauss's *Indigo and the Forty Thieves* was produced. This set the style for Viennese operetta, with its emphasis on music built around dance forms, especially the waltz. Of the many operetta composers in Vienna between the 1870s and the 1890s, few are remembered today. Always there is Strauss, and of course von Suppé, but of someone like Hellmesberger—Joseph, Jr.—we hear only occasional numbers, in the United States at least. Lehár was responsible for the last great flowering of the Viennese operetta, and *The Merry Widow,* produced in 1905 and approaching an almost operatic integration of story and music—looking back to the Singspiel tradition of which *The Magic Flute* is a part—breathed life into the form even as it was expiring.

The Great War ended many things, and while it is impossible to establish cause and effect between that upheaval and the decline of operetta, the war made clear that the world as it was before August 1914 was now as uninhabitable as the moon. With the horrible knowledge of mortality and darkness brought home so indisputably, how could anyone take seriously plots of petty infidelities and mistaken identity, or military characters whose claim to distinction lay more in the cut of their uniforms and the luxuriance of their whiskers than in what they had done at the front? In *The Waltz Emperors: The Life and Times and Music of the Strauss Family*, Joseph Wechsberg quotes Paul Henry Lang, who said that the reasons Viennese operetta died out were part of its very essence: "senseless action, insipid content, insincere feelings, laboriously invented jokes." These may not be characteristics of the operettas we remember and love today, but if they describe the bulk of the genre, they explain why, by the 1920s and 1930s, though composers continued to write operettas— operettas full of charming moments—the form itself belonged to the past.

Fortunately, the best operettas have refused to go away. Strauss and Lehár will be with us always precisely because the sentiments their music touches— despite any inadequacies or inanities of plot and character—are sentiments that neither conflagration nor world calamity can erase completely, and we might even say that it is *because* of the bitter tragedies of the twentieth century and the beginning of the twenty-first that we look back with fondness on the simple sweetness of those light and tuneful Viennese dramas. In that world love triumphs, the good guys win, and the music is invigorating and beautiful. We know that is how it should be, and we want to believe that that is how it will be. Which is what makes this music so appropriate as an old year ends and a new year begins, as we look back at what we have left behind, for better or worse, and ahead to what, for better or worse, will come.

III. New Year's Eve, Vienna, 1900

None of them aspired to a dinner invitation at the Hofburg Palace. They understood that the guests at Franz Joseph's table—a table that seated twenty and more—were served, each in turn, after the Emperor of Austria and King of Hungary had been given his portion. He sat there, self-satisfied in his mutton-chops and medals. Claiming privilege of birth, he began eating as soon as the food was arranged on his plate. When he finished a course, it was a sign that you, the guest, were finished with it too, no matter if your place at the table meant you had not yet been served. The Emperor was not a big eater, but he was a fast one. Depending on where you had been seated, you could conceivably be a guest for a dinner you would never taste. Instead of eating, you could sit with your hands in your lap, admiring the shadows and patterns that the candlelight cast on the ivory walls. You could count the facets in the crystal serving tray that overflowed with grapes and apples and bananas at the table's center, fruit that would never be touched and that, when the guests had left, would be tossed into the trash with the rest of the uneaten meal while Vienna's poor huddled against the late-December cold, just a century after Louis XVI lost his head. You would leave hungry and sober. With luck, you would still have time to stop at a restaurant or *Lokal* for *Schweinsbraten* and sauerkraut.

Since they had never aspired to a dinner invitation at the Hofburg, they sat in their armchairs in this high-ceilinged room whose far corners were barely visible in the electric light, newly installed, that shone from the single chandelier. The room was in a large apartment in Vienna's First District, near the University and just off the Opera-quadrant of the Ringstrasse, a walk of no more than fifteen minutes from the Hofburg if you measured the distance in footsteps, though using other measures you might conclude that the space between the two places could not be covered in a lifetime. It was New Year's Eve, 1900. The guests at the Hofburg might still be unfed, but the trio gathered in this humbler room had full bellies and now they sipped plum brandy. Those Hofburg dinners were part of the collective past, just as the Emperor himself was, though he had been secure in his seat of hereditary power for five decades and seemed destined to live forever. That had not been the fate of his beautiful wife, who two years ago had been killed by an anarchist. Her life had symbolized old ways and an old world order. Sissi's assassin had used murder to restructure society. The men in this room had their own tools for dismantling the world and putting it back together again. They were Arnold Schoenberg, Gustav Mahler, and Sigmund Freud—the unmusical Dr. Freud, who might not have had much to do with the art of his distinguished contemporaries, though he certainly could relish the stimulation of their talk. They were, all of them, forces of the future in a city preparing to launch civilization into a new understanding of itself, for better or worse.

They were bent, as Carl Schorske has said, on "creating a new culture from an old," on "the excavation of the instinctual." Of course their gathering on that New Year's Eve is pure fantasy, but had they met that evening, what would the talk have been like? Schoenberg would go on to speak for all of them in his *Harmonielehre*, but he could as easily have spoken the words that night: "The organ of the Impressionist is a . . . seismograph which registers the quietest movement. . . . [The Impressionist] is drawn to the still, the scarcely audible, therefore mysterious. His curiosity is stimulated to taste what has never been tried." In their own ways, they were all Impressionists, each of them.

Yet on that night, looking ahead into empty space, at virgin time not yet ravished by incidents on the Marne, and at Auschwitz and Hiroshima and New York City, did they sense how much they would contribute to the vocabulary for understanding a new century? Surely they could not have known that here, in Vienna, in just fourteen years, the fate of the century would be outlined following Archduke Franz Ferdinand's assassination, when Austria's offended honor sparked a Great War that would be a rehearsal for an even greater conflict two decades later. Surely they were on the verge of more than even their vast imaginations could conceive.

They looked ahead. They had no use for Hofburg dinners. Yet they, who were standing at the edge of a new century just as we are, must have needed anchors, certainties that would stabilize their flight into unexplored terrain. In theory their goals might have been allied more closely with those of Vienna's Secession artists, but these three also knew the value of tradition. And if tradition took the form, at least once a year, of a Viennese waltz, they would have understood. The waltzes, like the seasons, keep returning. They remind us of certainties—not in a sentimental association with Vienna's Imperial past, which is the stability of rigor mortis, but because of what they say about our aspirations for beauty. The Strauss waltzes: if Freud simply tolerated them, surely Schoenberg and Mahler loved them, just as Brahms had loved *The Blue Danube*, loved it so much that he once confessed he wished he had written it himself. Those waltzes, like all great art, fulfill a craving for stability even as we search for the new, always hoping that our craving for the one will not scare us into abandoning our search for the other. Maybe Stanley Kubrick really *was* telling us something deeper than we imagined when he choreographed the graceful flight of his rocket ship in *2001* to *The Blue Danube*—music we're pretty sure will still exist years from now, as doubtful as its longevity (or ours) might have seemed in 1968, when Kubrick's film was released.

Strauss may represent the old culture, the life that continues steadily even on the far side of upheaval, as it did in 1918 and again in 1945. Freud and Mahler and Schoenberg could not have known it then, but the beloved waltzes of the Viennese, as much as that music might be identified with the old order, would outlast the old order by a century at least. And though none of them might have aspired to a dinner invitation at the Hofburg, they would have taken the opportunity to sit down for a beer with Johann Strauss, Jr., someone who would have taken pains to make sure his guests were attended to properly. Had that master still been alive on 1 January 1901, perhaps they would have gathered with him after the New Year's Day concert. They would have taken their seats around a table near the Musikverein and studied the sunlight of a new century, absorbing what it taught about continuity. Reassured, they would have raised their glasses. They would have thought of all they had left behind and of all they carried with them into the future. They would have toasted the known and the unknown. Then, ears full of waltzes and appetites keen, they would have wished each other a Happy New Year.

—L.R.

Music, True or False

I discovered concert music when I was sixteen, after watching a *Wonderful World of Disney* life of Beethoven, with the German actor Karl-Heinz Böhm portraying the composer. Beethoven's rage against his deafness, his struggle to write a kind of music that would be the ultimate obscene gesture to a Fate that had dealt him a lousy hand of cards—all this appealed to my adolescent sense of injustice and isolation and defiance. The *idea* of Beethoven-as-hero was appealing. To me he seemed a role model, with a disdain of manners and social convention that could match any teenager's, and with a moral and artistic superiority that set him apart and made him untouchable. Who would dare take on the composer of the Fifth Symphony for having a messy room? I discovered music, you see, through unmusical means. I saw it as a human being's stance in relation to his life, something to be worn as a label that listed the ingredients of the soul. I came to music by identifying its beauties and dramas with a kind of ethical position. That sounds severe and Germanic and pompous but, when you come to think of it, is really the only way to approach music if you approach music through Beethoven, who is not pompous at all. Music, and what it could say and where it could lead: all this was a discovery like one of the many discoveries that teenagers continue to make, believing that certain facts about life have lain in hiding for centuries. And I suppose those facts actually do remain hidden, awaiting detection just as a volume of Keats or a recording of Bach sits dormant until a reader or a listener comes along.

When I say that I was attracted to the *ethical* content of music, I'm distinguishing this from the technical content—from an awareness of harmony, meter, and any theoretical boundaries that composers take into account as they go about their work. I am talking about an idea rooted in the nineteenth century, when art was supposed to instruct and delight. I can sympathize with Stravinsky's insistence, years after he had written *The Rite of Spring*, that the music was intended not as a depiction of life in pagan Russia, but as a series of abstract sonic images. Sure, we can approach *The Rite of Spring* as something abstract—and we can approach the Beethoven Fifth from that point of view as well. In either case, the beauty of the formal structure will still appeal to something personal in the listener, because all of us hear the music in our own way. Am I just stating the obvious?

So I got hooked on Beethoven, and that led to harder stuff. I mean my tastes were expanding, and before I knew it I was immersed in the basic orchestral repertory. In an earlier time and place this might have taken more years than my patience or ability would have allowed. But by the late 1960s, the long-playing record was a fact of American life. The catalogue of Columbia Masterworks ("360 Sound") was dominated by Leonard Bernstein and the New York Philharmonic, Eugene Ormandy and the Philadelphia Orchestra, and George Szell and Cleveland. London Records ("Full Frequency Range Recording") gave us Ansermet and L'Orchestre de la Suisse Romande. On RCA ("Living Stereo"), we found Reiner and the Chicago Symphony, and Leinsdorf and Boston. On Angel and Deutsche Grammophon (no catchy nomenclature on *their* jackets to describe the sound of their vinyl) we encountered Klemperer and the Philharmonia (nothing wrong with your turntable—that first movement of the *Pastoral* Symphony *was* being played at half-speed) and Herbert von Karajan and the Berlin Philharmonic (deep-pile Beethoven, accompanied by liner notes in three languages, in a prose style that fed a sense of intellectual inadequacy among readers in the United States, the UK, France, and Germany). Among them, these artists duplicated just about every big symphonic work of the nineteenth century (the symphonies of Joachim Raff and Alexander von Zemlinsky would have to wait for the CD era for anything like name recognition). One of my great delights was spending time at Rose Records on Wabash Avenue, under the "L" tracks in the Chicago Loop. There, I flipped through the bins and avoided the salesmen, who all spoke in jaded tones and strange accents—possibly British, but probably not—and who were always irritated by the imperfectly phrased questions of a novice. I fantasized about owning Stokowski's recording of the Ives Fourth, and about Szell's box of Brahms symphonies. I was a geek.

My friend Peter was a geek, too—a science geek who was intrigued by high-tech sound, circa 1967. Today he would be called an audiophile. He built his own speakers and powered them with a tuner and amplifier in the days when most of us were still playing LPs and 45s on GE portables, the ones with the speakers you unsnapped from either side of the case and positioned around the room as far as the wires reached. Our parents, most of whom remembered playing platters as fragile as glass on crank-wound turntables, called these machines record players, and so did we. When I listened to Beethoven on my record player at home, I got a good idea of the sound's outline. When I played the same LP on Peter's system, I heard the music's soul. Actually, the sound he was able to conjure probably wasn't much better than what you get today from a boom-box you've picked up on sale at Circuit City, but in 1967 it was pretty wonderful. So as my collection expanded, I made a point regularly of taking my new records to Peter's, to hear what they really sounded like. I should tell you that, Peter's fascination with recorded sound notwithstanding, his idea of music was formed by just a few favorite albums. Three that I recall are Leinsdorf's Boston Symphony recording of the Mahler First; a collection called *One Stormy Night*, a precursor of "environmental music" by an ensemble identified as the Mystic Moods Orchestra, featuring string arrangements of "Misty" and "Girl from Ipanema" played against the background of falling rain; and *Holiday in New York*, a stereo demo disc disguised as an odd sonic travelogue, in which you heard things like a subway rumbling under the Manhattan streets and the gentle tap-tap, from left to right speaker and back, of a table tennis match at a local "Y." All this was a mixed bag, a bag whose contents were offered with such regularity that one album seemed to shift shape into another, and sometimes I still feel the urge to whack a Ping-Pong ball or check the sky for gathering clouds when I hear Mahler.

Peter's tastes stayed pretty close to home, yet he could enjoy an occasional experiment, and one day he brought home a recording of Karlheinz Stockhausen's *Gesang der Jünglinge*. He was more intrigued by that melange of electronically generated sounds than I was—because I approached music from the perspective of drama, beginning-middle-end, and I was clueless when I encountered anything that didn't fit that mold. For Peter, the sound was the thing, and though he always seemed to like hearing my latest acquisition, he was clearly more interested in the quality of reproduction than in the music itself.

One day, I visited Peter with my new recording of Bruckner's Eighth Symphony, Solti conducting the Vienna Philharmonic in London's latest *FFRR* sound. Parts of Bruckner's Eighth get about as loud as anything acoustic instruments can generate. Those of us who love this sort of thing characterize it as "sublime," and to us it signifies the heavens opening. It sounded magnificent on Peter's stereo equipment. If you know the Bruckner Eighth, you know that, by the time you reach the end, more than an hour from where you started, you feel you've been through a struggle for your life. In the final seconds, Bruckner (never one to miss beating a point into the ground) hammers away in a kind of religious ecstasy, having discovered how to tie up all the strands of his symphonic argument and bring it to an end, which (you guessed it) leaves us standing at heaven's gate. You are liberated and for a moment carried into another world. What you want when the music stops is a little space to gather your thoughts. But without pausing for breath as the stylus rose from the final groove of Side 4, Peter switched on his reel-to-reel tape recorder. "I want you to hear something I picked up off the radio yesterday," he told me.

A woman began singing Hank Williams's "Settin' the Woods on Fire." Her voice was clear and pure and as happy as a beauty queen's smile—none of the pepper and hot sauce of a country singer here. Her enunciation was perfect. This was the G-rated version of Hank's song. All the grit and sexiness of his original were gone, which meant that this wasn't Hank at all. It was Phony Hank. "Isn't that a great voice?" Peter asked, his enthusiasm on the rise. "What a sound!"

At this point Peter's mother, attracted by what was coming from the speakers, popped her head into his room. "I like that!" she announced. "Something *different!*" Then she looked at me, barely able to contain herself, and said something that seemed to give her great satisfaction. "It doesn't have to be *boom-boom* all the time!"

What? Oh: Bruckner. *Boom-boom.* Somehow I knew that it wasn't the sound level that was nagging her. We had cranked up the volume often, and often quite late, and not once had we heard an objection. For that matter, Phony Hank himself was blasting pretty loud. No. *Boom-boom* wasn't a question of *loud.* It was something else.

I dismissed Peter's mother's objection at the moment, but over the years her words have stayed with me and nagged me. Often I wonder: Does it or does it not have to be *boom-boom* all the time? Why would anyone prefer a sanitized version of Hank Williams to Bruckner? Why would anyone prefer a sanitized version of Hank Williams to Hank Williams? As I said, the year was 1967. It was a time of protests against the war in Vietnam. In Chicago, where we had been listening to Bruckner and now were listening to Phony Hank, Martin Luther King, Jr., had marched through white neighborhoods the summer before in support of open housing, and we had seen how quickly neighbors could turn into haters once you started talking racial integration. In another year, with King dead, the city's West Side up in smoke, and Mayor Daley issuing his infamous "shoot to kill" order, the atmosphere in Chicago was ugly, and Chicago's atmosphere was no different from the rest of the country's. Every day pitted the individual against the ruling powers, the independent against the machine. You didn't have to be a teenager to be angry, you just had to have a sense of social justice, like Beethoven's. In August 1968, when the Chicago Police Department demonstrated its unique version of crowd control in front of the world's TV cameras, most Americans believed that things could only get better, and they were wrong. Peter's mother trusted Mayor Daley and President Johnson, and she had once told me that anyone who chose to question his elected officials was best advised to go live in another country. America: Love it or leave it, she said, with the blunt eloquence of a bumper sticker. I think she sensed that Bruckner's sublime disregard of all this was an attitude that could poison the mind of impressionable youth. Bruckner might send you off in search of the ideal world he was referring to with all his *boom-boom*, but it was a search that was likely to land you in jail. Best to clean up "Settin' the Woods on Fire." Forget *boom-boom*.

For that matter, the real Hank Williams also comes with a pretty high quotient of *boom-boom*—not horns and trombones and timpani at full blast, but *Boom-boom*, with a capital B: the explosive and dangerous element Peter's mother detected in Bruckner and all the other concert music I schlepped over to pollute her son's mind. She sensed something there. She just didn't know what to call it. I don't really mean that as a criticism. None of us knows the proper name for *Boom-boom*. But none of us has seen the Almighty, either, for he wants no graven images of himself, and the word *Yahweh* was conceived because God's name is not to be uttered.

The choice we are given in art is really a choice between *Boom-boom* or Phony Hank. *Boom-boom* is serious, it deals with the issues, and it can be intimidating. It is not usually something that we understand perfectly on first acquaintance, which means that it has different layers, which is a code phrase for *complexity*, which, if you believe focus groups and Hollywood, is something Americans would rather avoid.

Those in the business of producing concerts of "serious" music are constantly on the lookout for new audiences, and a perennial theme is the need to recruit young listeners. These days, we tend to fear that shortened attention spans make concert music less appealing. Yet the average symphony or concerto is shorter than the average movie. For that matter, *an entire concert* generally lasts about two hours, not much longer than the average movie. The problem seems to be more one of language than length, though for a listener, the language of music has little to do with technical expertise, or the ability to read a score. Most of the works in the basic concert repertory were conceived to be enjoyed as dramas by an audience at least as attentive as the audience at a movie theater—and not necessarily an audience of specialists. Most works in the basic concert repertory are full of emotional peaks and valleys, gathering and dissipating tensions. To pay attention to these is to grasp musical narrative. To grasp this is to leap an important language barrier.

But what about complexity? Complexities in art grow out of the complexities we inherit at birth—the consequence of our ancestors having eaten the fruit in Eden. When you turn out the lights at night, those complexities come down to questions of life and death, of how to live most completely and most fully as a hedge against the inevitable, which is a simple question, with many answers. A question of life and death—it's what all good music is about, whether the music is Beethoven, Bruckner, Hank Williams, or Bruce Springsteen. The music you love is a stance in relation to life. It is on *Boom-boom*, in its various forms, that we can rely in the end. When our hearts are plummeting to the ground at supersonic speed, it is the interwoven fibers of the thing called *Boom-boom* that will be our safety net. Complexity means only that you're alive. Passion is better than indifference. A soul that comprehends Eros is closer to understanding its fellows than one that is emotionally celibate.

The world is bigger than Bruckner and Beethoven and Haydn and Stravinsky and Ives and Adams, but it is also bigger because of them. They are not the only ones with something to say about it, and even their commentaries are different. What they have in common is *Boom-boom*, the basic ingredient. Does it have to be *Boom-boom* all the time? Maybe the answer depends on what we mean by *all the time*. I would ask Peter's mother to clarify this, but in the years since she uttered her pronouncement we have lost contact, and I keep turning to Bruckner and Beethoven and their colleagues for the answer.

—L.R.

Why We Are Here

I t is now more than twenty years since I came across an article in the Sunday paper on how the rock generation of the 1960s and 1970s, approaching middle age, was turning into "the pop cultural establishment." It discussed such phenomena as Paul Simon's album *Hearts and Bones* and Linda Ronstadt's *What's New*, her recording of pre-rock standards such as "Someone to Watch over Me"—and that does seem to be something aging stars do, record songs that have aged better than they have. Of *Hearts and Bones*, the writer noted that it was "marketed as a pop record, but . . . in its sophistication is more like a collection of art songs." I bought *Hearts and Bones*, listened to it, and found it quite engaging but not a bit like *Winterreise* or *Winter Words*.

As Stravinsky once remarked in another context—and with no intent of denigration—it is a different fraternity. I intend no denigration either, but I do want to make a distinction. The music we are involved with in the concert hall, that music we have never managed to agree on a name for, neither "classical" nor "serious" serving quite convincingly, but the music responsible for bringing us by such diverse paths into concert halls and to read books like this one—in sum, Why We Are Here—this music has aspirations beyond those of *Hearts and Bones*.

At least this music is capable of such aspirations, and here I need to make a distinction within a distinction. We take some stuff too seriously, seated in rows and facing the front, attending, as though to "A Solemn Musick," to what Telemann or even Mozart intended as *Muzak*, for which there were names such as *Tafelmusik* and *cassazione*. It is also true that Mozart's *Muzak* includes moments that ravish the senses and pierce the heart—private addresses to the dinner guest who is undernourished by the pompous ass on the left and the airhead on the right, and who has started paying attention to the band. The language, the musical language, is capable of that, and there is a continuous spectrum from elegantly turned-out *musique de table* to *Figaro* or Beethoven's Opus 131 or the Mahler Ninth or wherever you choose to locate heaven.

Musical heaven, in any event, is attainable. It offers three sorts of pleasure or delight or nourishment—sensuous, intellectual, and emotional. The perception of sensuous pleasure in music requires no preparation, only clean ears. With experience your receptiveness will become broader, and with it your idea of pleasure. I think of Schoenberg, saying about a passage of deliciously idiosyncratic scoring in his Variations for Orchestra: "I hope that some day these sounds will be found beautiful." For that matter, I recall my own now long-ago dismay upon first hearing a countertenor or a harpsichord or a Baroque organ that didn't sound like a Cavaillé-Coll in a French cathedral.

The two other pleasures, the intellectual and the emotional, require, along with clean ears, preparation—or readiness—in that there is a language to understand, and also a set of conventions. The language is rich and complex. Musical discourse speaks to experience and, ideally, to a generously stocked and well-functioning memory. Obviously a musical event exists in the present, at the moment of its sounding, but it also has a past, a history. It comes from somewhere. Even if it stands at the beginning of a piece it comes from silence, and music can emerge from silence in different ways. Think of the Beethoven Fifth, then think of the *Pastoral*—and those differences matter. Each event also has a future, somewhere to go, even if only into silence and applause. In 1939, Thomas Mann once gave a lecture to students at Princeton about *The Magic Mountain*. He advised them to read it twice, "unless you were bored the first time." Mann went on to point out the musicality of the composition of his stupendous novel, declaring that was precisely the reason behind his "arrogant demand to read [it] twice. You can only fully take the measure of the complex of . . . relationships and enjoy it when you already know the themes and are in a position to interpret the allusions forwards as well as backwards." To remember a musical event is, so to speak, to put money in the bank, to make an investment in future pleasure.

Form, Walter Pater said, is the life history of an idea. The patterns made by these life-threads, by this play of backward and forward, of being here and in the past and in the future all at the same time, are in themselves fascinating, beautiful, and, to those sensible to their speech, moving. The mind—the ready mind—can find transcendence and be stirred to ecstasy as much as the body and the heart.

And the emotions? One road to the heart goes directly through the senses. We can be touched, stirred, moved by the beautiful tone of a voice or an instrument, by the insistence of one rhythm or the teasing suppleness of another, by the tension in a leap, by a stimulus as simple as the sound of a full orchestra at flood tide or by a barely audible hush. A rock musician I know—a colleague of one of my sons, a producer of rock recordings—attended his first symphony concert a few years ago. I recall his marveling not only at the richness of the percussion writing in Leonard Bernstein's *Halil* but also his thrilled astonishment at how much volume unamplified acoustic instruments could generate, how plain loud an orchestra could be.

Another road to the heart—not so easy a road—goes through the mind: the play of form, the unfolding of the life histories of the composer's ideas, that is not only lovely in itself but is also where the richest part of the expressive content of a piece resides. By "richest" I mean that which will longest yield new perceptions and where the familiar will longest stay verdant. We respond to the release of tension and suspense when we return to the home key and when we land in a recapitulation. And—if you have been paying attention— we can respond without having any intellectual concept of "tonic" or "recapitulation." I learned that more than half a century ago when I was a teaching assistant in an Introduction to Music course. One of my duties was to run sessions in which we played the recordings of that week's assignment and where I was available to answer questions. Always there were students who swore they couldn't follow what we were trying to tell them about sonata form; always, when the recapitulation of a Beethoven symphony movement arrived, those same students shifted in their chairs, visibly relaxed, and (remember, this was 1951) reached for a cigarette.

The sense of recognition, which depends on attention and memory, is essential to musical experience. The most subtle of the musician's resources, the one that challenges our most delicate attunement, is harmony, the sting— or the ache—of dissonance (to think in terms of detail) or the grandly farsighted strategy of a whole Beethoven quartet, a Bruckner symphony, or a Wagner opera. *Tristan und Isolde*, the very symbol for all that is recklessly emotional in art, depends for its effect on presenting a dissonance fifteen seconds into the piece and refusing to melt it into consonance until fifteen seconds from the end—something like five hours later. All that fever from an unresolved dominant seventh! And a work like *Tristan*, where the composer so carefully and so skillfully ties specific musical sounds to specific emotional jolts, also shows us how something in us vibrates to reminiscence, allusion, quotation.

I know that such talk can scare people and annoy them. But it's the *talk* that does it, the words—"dominant seventh," or even worse, "unresolved dominant seventh," "flat submediant," "Neapolitan sixth"—not the music itself. The words are useful: precise terms make conversation efficient and agreeable.

Imagine the nuisance of not being able to say "bunt" or "béchamel" or "backhand"! The term "flat submediant" may alarm you. But I know your heart is pierced when, in Elgar's *Enigma* Variations, the strings sneak an E-flat under that delicate bridge of a suspended G to begin that noble paean to friendship, the *Nimrod* Variation. But again I have to say, *only if you've been paying attention!* *Hamlet* speaks to you, or *King Lear*, in a way that Lamb's *Tales from Shakespeare* (the original Classics Comics) cannot, but you don't sit in the theater or in your living room counting to ten in your anxiety over the iambic pentameters or keeping track of just how many sibilants occur in

> There's hell, there's darkness, there's the sulphurous pit,
> Burning, scalding, stench, consumption. . . .

"*If* you've been paying attention," I said a moment ago. Great music is something for you to *do*, not just something for you to pay for and have done *to you* or *for you*. And so we come back to the issue on which I touched at the beginning. We are talking here about a human activity of high aspirations in the matter of touching people in their inmost regions. Each time I hear the Mahler Ninth, for example, I think what a frightening invasion of privacy it is. And it is an activity as rich in possibilities as it is ambitious in aspiration.

But again, this works only if we do our part. Music, this music, is a demanding partner in love. Those elements of musical experience that touch us most deeply, most lastingly, that can change our lives, are below the surface of experience. They are not meant for effortless access. Oh, and how many of our musical love affairs have begun in frustration and anger! How easy it is to say, "That's not what I call music!"

The violinist Rose Mary Harbison has written: "[Music] requires [from us] an intentional reaching out . . . a willingness to probe its rich intricacies, the capacity to be startled and dismayed, to have one's soul tormented a little, to come unadorned, emotionally fresh, to stand along with others and witness the hopes and the vision of the composer. And a truly great performer is one who is willing to reveal the hidden and difficult side of a piece."

Music has hidden and difficult sides and it offers rich intricacies for our delighted unraveling. Don't misunderstand me. I am not saying that music, or any form of art, should be a grim experience. In an article titled "The Degradation of Work and the Apotheosis of Art," Christopher Lasch cites one of my favorite history books, Johan Huizinga's *Homo Ludens*, a favorite in part because it is so ungrim. Huizinga writes: "The great archetypal activities of human society are all permeated with play from the start. . . . [Language, myth, and ritual], law and order, commerce and profit, craft and art, poetry, wisdom, and science [are all] rooted in the primeval soil of play." Lasch comments:

"The serious business of life, in other words, has always been colored by an attitude that . . . finds more satisfaction in gratuitous difficulty than in the achievement of a given objective with a minimum of effort. The play-spirit, if you will, values maximum effort for minimum results."

Compelling in all this is the intercutting of the serious and the playful. Goethe referred to his *Faust*—*chose sérieuse*, if ever there was—as "*diese sehr ernste Scherze*," these very serious jests. That we are capable of serious jests is one of the things that we, as human creatures, can be proud of. Lewis Thomas put it this way: "Computers will not take over the world, they cannot replace us, because they are not designed, as we are, for ambiguity." The designer who wired us for ambiguity blessed us at the same time with appetites both for complexity and simplicity, with a lust for solving problems, with delight in looking for the secret door, with the sense to realize, sometimes, that surfaces are only surfaces, with the joy of knowing that next time we hear the Mahler Ninth we shall hear and understand more and be moved that much more.

Once at a concert I found myself seated next to a lively and charming woman, a retired professor, and at some point during our chat she said, "Of course, the greatest living artist is X." Now X is indeed a first-rate musician and instrumentalist as well as a most beguiling performer. What bothered me was the idea that there should or could be such a creature at all as "the greatest living artist." It is typical of the distractions that the wizards of career management set in our path daily. It is a distraction from music itself, and it is a disservice in that it promotes the lie that a Beethoven concerto becomes worth our attention only when it is performed by a superstar. Those eternal cocktail party questions, "Which do you think is the greatest orchestra in the world?" or "Who do you think is the greatest conductor?" are fatiguing and discouraging, not just because I don't know the answer, not even because there can be no answer, but because of the confusion about values that lurks behind those questions. An outstandingly successful concert pianist remarked to me once that we were fast turning into a society where merely to be very good at something is regarded as a birth defect.

We are here because of music. That music is a profession and a business cannot be written out of the world order, but let us remember in the midst of the swirl that it is also the subject of a contract full of words like attention, listening, meditation, reflection, remembrance, wit, joy, torment, delight, heart, brain, spirit. Yes, the elevation of the spirit is the ultimate reward, the one that comes after we have learned to take that nourishment of the senses, the brain, and the heart, of which I spoke earlier. When I read the second volume of Elias Canetti's autobiography, *The Torch in My Ear*, I came across a thought that struck me hard. Canetti is speaking about painting, but what he says works for music too: "The reason pictures slumber for generations is that there is no one to see them with the experience that awakes them." There we have quite a challenge, but haven't we all had some searing moment of learning what may be given us, what we might become, when we do face up to that challenge? The reason we are here is, as Friedrich Nietzsche said so simply, that "without music, life would be a mistake."[1]

—M.S.

[1] I found the Nietzsche quotation in an obscure piece of writing, I think maybe an introduction to a book by someone else, by Thomas Mann. My essay was originally a talk at a function of the American Symphony Orchestra League in San Francisco in 1984, and I suspect that was the origin of the subsequent flood of T-shirts, coffee mugs, and so on, emblazoned with the German philosopher's excellent sentiment.

VI.
POSTLUDE

The Sounds *We* Make

An odd bit of theater took place at a recent concert here. Beethoven's *Emperor* Concerto was on the program, in a performance that had everything you would want by way of lyricism, intelligence, and crackling virtuosity. The way the first movement ends is unmistakably designed to elicit applause; at this concert, however, almost complete silence greeted those closing chords. "Almost," because there was in fact one single handclap, but the author of that sound, apparently feeling that he or she had done something wrong, immediately retreated from action. The pianist turned and nodded in the direction of the solitary clapper, but it was and remains unclear to me whether he was being courteous or sardonic. The audience, though, interpreted his action as a message that they probably should have applauded. They proceeded to do that, heartily, whereupon the pianist stood and responded with a full bow from the waist.

It was not that people hadn't enjoyed the performance. This pianist is well known to this audience and popular, he had drawn a full house, and the ovation at the end of the concerto was huge; rather, it seemed to me that too many members of this audience had been told too often that it is bad form to clap between movements. That notion is constantly reinforced by soloists and conductors who respond to applause between movements by presenting a posture of "I don't hear anything." I imagine that the smirking of orchestral musicians on those occasions has its effect too. This time, though, the solitary clapper was quite right, and I was happy that when the concert was repeated the following evening the crowd burst into applause at the end of the first movement. Audiences are unpredictable.

Beethoven would have been appalled by that silence at the first concert. When Brahms, surely no applause hound, played his D-minor Piano Concerto in Leipzig for the first time, he wrote in distress to his friend Joachim that not only was the work badly received at the end but that there was "no reaction at all to the first and second movements." Thirty-eight years later, when Brahms, then a dying man, went to a performance of his Fourth Symphony in Vienna—it was the last concert he was able to attend—each of the four movements was greeted by an ovation gladly acknowledged. At the premiere of Elgar's Symphony No. 1 in Manchester in 1908, the applause at the end of the first movement was such that the composer had to leave his box and take bows from the stage. Back in 1778, Mozart was thrilled when a particularly witty stroke of his in the finale of the *Paris* Symphony stirred the audience in the French capital to clap and cheer while the music was actually under way. Every time Haydn introduced one of his new symphonies in London in the 1790s the movements were not only all applauded, but many of them had to be repeated then and there. Coming back to the *Emperor,* the great nineteenth-century pianist Hans von Bülow reported that he regularly got a big hand at the end of the series of three cadenzas that open that work. When the thirteen-year-old Bronislaw Huberman performed the Brahms Violin Concerto in the composer's presence, he was deeply chagrined because the audience applauded at the end of the cadenza, blotting out part of the poetic coda. Brahms, far from being offended, simply consoled the boy, patting him on the shoulder and saying, "You shouldn't have played it so beautifully."

We seem to have forgotten all that. Applause in the "wrong" place is now a sin, like driving an SUV, eating red meat, and smoking cigars. What happened and what does it mean? In the last part of the nineteenth century people became interested in the question of what held a large, multi-movement work together as well as in the delights of its individual movements. One reason for this was fascination with the very long-range compositional strategies in the operas of Richard Wagner; another was the appearance of cyclic works in which themes from earlier movements or sections had crucial parts to play in later ones. Theorists and critics often cared more about such matters than the composers themselves. Mozart and Beethoven no doubt took pains to make the various movements of their pieces be well suited to one another, but neither composer hesitated on occasion to swap movements around. Mozart also had no qualms about playing three movements of a symphony at the beginning of a concert and ending the evening with the finale. Beethoven made what seem to us appalling suggestions about the re-ordering and omitting of movements of his *Hammerklavier* Sonata. At any rate the idea that the flow of an entire work was an essential part of its musical character and one that ought not to be interrupted began to take on more weight, and there is something to be said for that.

No less important is what happens at the ends of movements. In the *Emperor*, Beethoven builds a subtle harmonic bridge from the first movement to the second. The former E-flat keynote reappears as the first melody note of the Adagio, though now written as D-sharp in what sounds like very far-away B major. That is precious and wonderful, but is it really more important than the rhetoric of the dramatic gestures with which the Allegro ends? After all, getting excited by a soloist's artistry, virtuosity not excluded, is an essential part of the concerto experience, especially in a piece in which keyboard bravura is so central an element. Moreover, do we have to assume that fifteen seconds of applause necessarily blot out all memory of the E-flat harmonies with which the first movement so emphatically ends? Staying with the *Emperor*, we will come to that most magical place in it, that supremely happy-making moment when Beethoven leaps without pause from the meditative and poetic slow movement into the exuberant finale. He links movements in this manner in quite a few works, and many composers emulate him in this. This would seem to eliminate the applause problem. One exception occurs, surprisingly, in Mendelssohn, who is a bit maladroit in handling the bridge between the first two movements of his Violin Concerto, so that the quiet emergence of the Andante from the seemingly applause-bidding close of the Allegro is sometimes drowned in clapping. (Elsewhere in this book I tell a similar story about Weber's *Invitation to the Dance*.)

It can go the other way as well. Movements can arrive at their last notes and stop, but still be open-ended enough to need the first sounds of the next movement to complete or continue the musical thought. The stormy first movement of Beethoven's Opus 111, his last piano sonata, ends on a repressed C-major chord with the hands very far apart on the keyboard. The second movement begins with another quiet C-major chord, but with the hands now in mid-range, filling in the empty space in the preceding sonority. It would be horrible to interrupt that connection with applause. Another reason, one that probably speaks to listeners more immediately because it is directly connected to emotion and temper, is that ending in *pianissimo* is not by itself enough to defuse the turbulence of that first movement: it will take the whole of the second movement to accomplish that. In other words, the first movement, even though it ends, is not really finished. Similarly, in the *Appassionata* Sonata you can't stop at the end of the first movement for brow-mopping or applause or anything else: that last F-minor chord, even though the harmony hasn't shifted for six measures, is profoundly restless and the music has to move on into the Andante. In the *Waldstein* Sonata, on the other hand, you can, without harm to the music, fling your arms into the air on the first movement's last chords and even stand to take a bow if the audience responds to your invitation.

So OK, sometimes you mustn't, sometimes you may, sometimes you should. How do you know which is when? In the eighteenth century it was not a problem: you waited for your host or the highest-ranking nobleman present to applaud. If you clapped before His Highness you were being exceedingly impolite and you would not be invited to dinner again. The psychology of appealing to a single listener is very different from that of seeking to inflame an entire audience, and that is why Bach's *Brandenburg* Concertos don't end with extra temperature-raising chords but simply finish with the last note of the last phrase.

That, however, is not our situation today, and the incident I recounted at the beginning fascinated me as evidence of how uncertain we can be in our relationship to classical music and its performance. To clap after the first movement was bad form at one moment, but ten seconds later it was OK. Much of our concert life is determined by conventions about all sorts of matters—what performers wear, having the concertmaster at orchestral concerts make a solo entrance (or not), the tuning ritual, and what constitutes a normal amount of applause (very different conventions obtain for rock, jazz, classical music, opera, ballet, and regular theater). Today we expect the conductor to be recalled to the stage two or three times at the end of a concert, but not much more than a hundred years ago even a single recall was worth special notice in a newspaper review. In the last couple of decades, applause inflation has led to the standing ovation changing from a special and rare tribute to an obligatory event.

We also take it for granted that the conductor will ask the orchestra to rise and share in the applause; only half a century ago that was an uncommon and therefore a remarkable gesture. Right now, in fact, we are witnessing a convention in the process of change. When a conductor gets the orchestra up, the players have usually stood facing the podium just as they had done while seated and playing, and, I must add, most of them look as though all that noise out front cannot possibly have anything to do with them. In the last few years, though, some conductors have asked the musicians to face the audience, an innovation in which I believe Neeme Järvi in Detroit was the pioneer. Surprisingly, there is still some resistance to this, but when and where it is done the effect on the atmosphere is happy. Finally, and not least, even the very fact that we express pleasure—or just good manners—by clapping the palms of our hands together is a convention. At every concert there is someone for whom the experience is new and the ritual and convention unfamiliar and probably in part irrational or at least incomprehensible and confusing. How many times, for example, have I been asked about the concertmaster walk?

But let us think about what the music itself tells us. Loud, flashy, harmonically unambiguous endings are easy. They tell us: "Clap!" I would even go so far as to say that if the fever pitch seems to demand it, it would really be all right to start clapping right into the last long C that ends the Beethoven Fifth. That is very rare at concerts, but we routinely do it at the opera. That's what all those tonic chords at the end of a Verdi aria like *Sempre libera* are all about. German audiences tend to be very earnest about not disturbing the music, a good impulse, but it always feels funny to sit in solemn silence through those rabble-rousing noises that are really not meant to be listened to at all. Once in a while we experience the converse of this when a conductor starts the music right into the applause welcoming him to the stage. I still remember the hair-raising effect when the eighty-three-year-old Stokowski whipped into the *Flying Dutchman* Overture that way. That can be exciting, but it is a gimmick to be used sparingly.

It is the quiet endings that cause trouble. They leave us in a different kind of mood from the excited ones, perhaps dreamy (*Afternoon of a Faun*), transported to a faraway, private place (Beethoven Opus 111 or Mahler's *Song of the Earth*), unsettled (the Sibelius Fourth), or dark (Tchaikovsky's *Pathétique* or the Eighth Quartet of Shostakovich). A spell has been cast. Then what? Silence may be the ideal response. Applause rudely shifts the focus away from the music or wherever the music has taken us back to the performers, to a world of bows and smiles, embraces and bouquets. Just a few days ago I heard a profoundly moving performance of Elgar's *The Dream of Gerontius,* and I must say I both hated the applause that burst out after ten seconds of beautiful silence and that I joined in it. But even if we do recognize that silence is the right response we really don't know how to do that at a public concert. Habit (or convention) and the desire to express our gratitude to the performers interfere, and so does our need to release tension in ourselves.

At the very least, though, we need an interval of silence before the noise *we* make begins. More often than not, a conductor, pianist, violinist, or whatever can command silence at the end of a piece with body language and sheer force of personality; there is, however, no defense against the person who just has to demonstrate he owns the CD and knows when *Tapiola* is over. He will shout his "Bravo!" before the music has stopped resonating in the room ("he" because this seems to be a peculiarly male obnoxiousness). Some music needs to be cushioned by stillness, before and after: no less than sound, silence is an essential component of the musical experience. As the conductor David Zinman has put it: "Silence is the canvas on which the composer paints." Might it help to remind concertgoers that LISTEN is an anagram of SILENT? It is all a question of sensitivity, of tact, of experience, of the willingness to allow someone else to be in charge of the flow of events, and you can't legislate any of those things. Nothing, not even coughing, enrages musicians more than an audience's denial of that still moment in which to let the music sink in. What doesn't help is that we have become a society that abhors silence. Rock music does not know silence, and people brought up on it take every silence as a signal that the music is over. Silence is also frowned on in radio, and too often announcers leave no space between the end of a piece of music and the next words.

I mentioned coughing, and that is our other sonorous contribution to concerts. Applause can be iffy, but coughing is always bad. Less than one tenth of the coughing at concerts is caused by *bona fide* respiratory distress. For the rest, the pianist Claude Frank years ago put it to me very simply: "It means just one thing: they're not listening." Now the word "listen" has become devalued. People say they "listen" to classical music while studying or doing their taxes. That's not listening, that's hearing, overhearing, half-hearing. I know someone who calls some classical music "thinking music," meaning music that allows her to think about other, serious matters. Most coughing comes from inattention or out and out boredom. A Haydn symphony is as ingeniously plotted as a good crime novel, but the cougher, who would not read a book by Donna Leon or Henning Mankell with such inattention, is not following the story, else he would not turn his bronchial tubes inside out, *fortissimo,* at a hushed moment of greatest suspense. When it comes to gender, coughing is more of an equal opportunity pastime than premature clapping, but by and large it is the men who dominate. Something I have found interesting is that most coughing happens in the expensive seats, an observation that opens quite a few cans of worms regarding the sociology of our musical life.

I also find it remarkable that it does not occur to people, most of whom act with reasonable intelligence in other areas of their lives, that it is possible to cough other than *fortissimo.* But this, I have come to believe, is less an issue of intelligence than of morality. The loud, uninhibited cougher in a *pianissimo* passage or worse, in a silence, is inattentive, unmusical, and unmannerly. Most crucially and infuriatingly, he is arrogant—someone who takes it for granted that he is the most important person in the room, more important than Beethoven, than the musicians, than the rest of the audience. (I have not even touched on the plague of cell phones.) Coughing is a singularly touchy subject, and more than one conductor has told me that the nastiest mail they get is in response, not to playing music by Schoenberg or Wuorinen, but to their comments on audience noise. "Hey, this is America, we've paid good money, we're entitled. . . . " You wonder, though: how did these people ever find their way into a concert hall and get mixed up with Mozart and Mahler?

For a long time I took "it's simple, they're not listening" to be the end of the story, but I have come to think it's more complicated. Not long ago I attended a couple of performances of Britten's *War Requiem,* widely regarded as an important and meaningful work, and on these evenings sung and played as beautifully as I have ever heard it. Both performances, though, were blotted out by an unceasing tempest of coughing. I believe what happened there is that Wilfred Owen's poetry and those specific projections of it added up to something too eloquent, too urgent, too immediate for many in the audience, particularly at a time—April 2005—when much of the population was deeply troubled by this country's recent and current military history. The air was alive with acute discomfort, and the reaction was squirming, unrest, coughing. It doesn't have to be discomfort from that kind of a source either. A friend calls this the Embarrassment Theory of coughing. Few pages in the symphonic literature are in this sense more dangerous than the last five minutes—all *pianissimo* and less, and with many silences—of Mahler's Ninth Symphony. The emotional stakes are clearly so high, the tension so great, that some people simply cannot remain still. This is a story not of insufficient attention and engagement but of a need to escape frightening demands on one's emotional capacity.

The perfect audience does exist. When and where you will find it is unpredictable, like so much else about audiences. The subscription system, so necessary to the financial stability and health of performing arts organizations, not to forget the mental health of their administrators, can militate against getting the ideal audience into the hall. You get people who are there because it's Friday, not because they specifically wanted to hear the Bruckner Eighth. And what do they bring to concerts? Everything, I suppose: their whole life history and also what the parking lot attendant said at 7:45. At the *Gerontius* performance I mentioned, a single event in a fine church building, everything was just right. I don't know who that audience was. Some mixture, probably of oratorio buffs, Elgar lovers, devout Catholics, and that most important subset among concertgoers, the inquisitive, the people with open ears, open hearts, open minds. But then again, I heard Mahler's Sixth Symphony, not an easy listening experience, emotionally or in any other way, played for a totally concentrated and silent audience that was the same subscription audience that had obliterated the Britten *War Requiem* a couple of weeks before. Is it all just a part of chaos theory?

There is music such as Renaissance madrigals that is addressed primarily to those performing it, and there is private music, for example the late Beethoven quartets, for which one might ideally want to be an audience of one (or maybe two). But symphonies and operas and oratorios address crowds. The audience is, as it were, built into the piece. How embarrassing it is to experience the soapbox rhetoric of the Beethoven Ninth or a Bruckner or Mahler symphony all alone in your living room! Only yesterday someone said to me: "Books separate people, but music brings them together." When you do get the right audience it is a beautiful reminder of music's power to unite us.

—M.S.

I append a very short reading list:

Elias Canetti's fascinating study *Crowds and Power* (Continuum)

Lisel Mueller's poem *Brendel Playing Schubert* (in *Alive Together,* Louisiana State University Press)

Alfred Brendel's poem *Cologne* (in *One Finger Too Many,* English versions by the author with Richard Stokes, Faber and Faber), or in the original German as *Köln* (in *Fingerzeig,* Carl Hanser Verlag)